Women of Oklahoma,
1890–1920

Women of Oklahoma, 1890–1920

Linda Williams Reese

University of Oklahoma Press
Norman and London

Library of Congress Cataloging-in-Publication Data

Reese, Linda Williams, 1946–
Women of Oklahoma, 1890–1920 / Linda Williams Reese.
p.   cm.
Includes bibliographical references and index.
ISBN 0–8061–2955–7 (cloth : alk. paper)
ISBN 0–8061–2999–9 (paper)
1. Women pioneers—Oklahoma—History. 2. Women—Oklahoma—
History. 3. Minority women—Oklahoma—History. 4. Frontier and
pioneer life—Oklahoma. 5. Oklahoma—History. 6. Oklahoma—
Social conditions. I. Title.
F699.R44   1997
976.6'052—dc21   97–7549
CIP

Text design by Debora Hackworth.
Text is set in Century with Univers display.

The paper in this book meets the guidelines
for permanence and durability
of the Committee on Production Guidelines for Book Longevity
of the Council on Library Resources, Inc. ∞

1 2 3 4 5 6 7 8 9 10

To the memory of Arrell Morgan Gibson,
gentleman scholar

Contents

Illustrations

Illustrations xi

Maps

Preface

An examination of the settlement period and early statehood of Oklahoma and of the role of women in this process appealed to me, as a history graduate student, on both an emotional and an intellectual level. Some of my most treasured memories involve long summer evenings sitting in a rocking chair on the back porch with my grandmothers, listening to their stories of life in the early days of Oklahoma. One of my grandmothers, Naomi Davis Williams, was born in Oklahoma Territory in 1894. The other, Martha Grizzle Dodd, came with her family from Tennessee to Indian Territory shortly before statehood, riding in the back of a wagon.

Each of these women lived the history of the West as they raised their children and worked the land alongside their husbands. Their values shaped my parents' character and, ultimately, my own. When they

met death in advanced age, it was with courage and
acceptance. Yet, aside from family memories, they left
little historical record. I wanted to know more about
their relationships, ambitions, feelings, and world
views as young pioneer women.

At the beginning of the research, I was surprised
that so little investigation into Oklahoma women's
lives had been made, despite more than two decades of
emphasis within the profession on research in women's
and western history. The historical evidence in archival collections was abundant, but largely untapped.
Letters, diaries, autobiographies, poetry, newspaper
articles, and local histories contributed a wealth of
information. Census materials, manuscript collections,
oral-history interviews, and secondary works completed
the foundation for an exploration of women's lives and
experiences in Oklahoma. The nature of these sources
dictated an approach that focused on the intimate,
personal, specific concerns of individual lives within a
family context. The daily routines of work, family
adaptations, and relationships shaped by a new environment dominated the experiences of Oklahoma
women. A more personal approach allowed for the
omission of lengthy descriptions of homemaking chores
and the building of community institutions, which
have been documented by other historians, in favor of
a discussion of the multiple social interactions of these
women.

The challenge of the research lay in broadening the
perspective beyond white pioneering development in
order to consider factors of race, class, culture, region,
and era. Certainly black and Indian women had immi-
grated to this area early in the nineteenth century, and
some white women had joined them, as missionaries
and teachers. The opening of land to non-Indian settlement and development, however, created a collision of

interests. What emerged in bold relief were circles of
initiative among women of different backgrounds,
levels of economic security, and cultural orientation—
and shifting positions of power. The Oklahoma frontier
provided a single region in which Indian, black, and
white women and the ways that gender, ethnicity,
culture, and regional economy affected their choices
could be studied. It represented a virtual laboratory of
cross-cultural contacts among women during a time,
late in the nineteenth century, when national ideologies of race and gender seemed to exert powerful
influences. The Oklahoma frontier demanded that
women make an immediate and complex adjustment of
these ideologies to fit the conditions of life.

Oklahoma historian Angie Debo believed that in
Oklahoma the "dim facets of the American character
stand more clearly revealed. For in Oklahoma all the
experiences that went into the making of the nation
have been speeded up. Here all the American traits
have been intensified." Debo often wrote about the
clarifying light of history that settlers believed shone
on their everyday acts. One young schoolteacher remarked that her pioneering family moved to Oklahoma because they believed "something significant
was happening in this new America. If one did not
hurry and answer the call, one would miss out on
something very real and very momentous." This attitude may have accounted for the abundant primary
source material the women of this pioneering
generation left behind.[1]

This book represents an examination of the lives of
representative white, black, and Indian women, in
rural and urban settings, after the opening of Indian
Territory to non-Indian settlement. It focuses on the
intersection of race, gender, class, and culture in the
relationships among women in a rapidly changing

environment. An exploration of relationships among and between women of different races, and between women and men, provides insight into the daily negotiation of life in a multicultural setting. This volume must be seen only as a tentative, first effort at understanding complex processes and interactions; it investigates selected examples that reflect larger issues, and it makes no claim to the inclusion of all possible points of view. Future scholarly research will, no doubt, develop areas of conflict and accommodation that receive only scant suggestion here, such as the sizable Socialist Party in Oklahoma and female participation in its work; the role of women in black organizations in the larger, integrated Oklahoma cities; and Native American leadership in the direction of tribal affairs. The following chapters ask four principal questions of the historical evidence: Were gender considerations primary in women's adaptation to the Oklahoma frontier? To what extent did domestic ideology influence female interaction within and across racial lines? In what ways did women extend and circumscribe their own autonomy and test the limits of patriarchy? And finally, how did rising class expectations, based on land ownership, influence female behavior?

The essential experiences of women in Oklahoma centered less on their understanding of themselves as separate sexual beings with unique qualities than on their participation within the family unit. Work roles on the frontier were adaptable and interdependent, and they served to reshape gender ideologies into new configurations based on mutual respect. More than anything else, the attitudes and behavior of Oklahoma women indicated the extent of the erosion of a separate-sphere mentality and the breakdown of a rigidly patriarchal family structure. Women in Oklahoma discovered unity in their common striving toward middle-class status. This class position meant a great deal more than obtaining a measurable level of property. Middle-class status indicated a shared cluster of attitudes about life as it was and as it ought to be. Certainly economic security formed the base, but ideas about basic education, cleanliness, moral behavior, respectability, cultural accommodation, and social uplift also found common ground. Within the protected environment of all-black communities, black women worked toward middle-class life-styles as evidence of racial uplift. The extent to which Indian women adopted middle-class goals directly influenced their level of integration into mainstream white culture. Women's actions, whether submissive or aggressive, were directed toward securing at least the appearance of this class position for themselves, their families, and their communities. In this sense, the pioneering generation of Oklahoma women was a transitional one. They carried the rhetoric, if not the spirit, of domestic ideology to the frontier, tested it against a multicultural reality, and discarded it in favor of a progressive partnership on the land.

The personal and intellectual debts that I have accumulated in the course of this long project are many. My deepest appreciation goes to my husband, Bill, and my children, Jim, Susan, and Brian. Their love and faith sustain my life. My mother-in-law, Sarah Burton Reese, provided valuable encouragement and financial support that made the completion of this book possible.

I am grateful for the interest, patience, and professionalism of several academic mentors. This book began as a dissertation under the direction of William W. Savage, Jr. His scrupulous criticism and advice have guided its development. He and Robert L. Griswold insisted on a broader landscape of ideas than I would have envisioned alone, and this strengthened the research for this volume. Paul W. Glad, Norman L. Crockett, and Paul F. Sharp each, in many ways, contributed inspiration, encouragement, and direction along the way. Additional suggestions from Shirley Leckie, L. G. Moses, and Elliott West greatly enhanced the manuscript. I sincerely appreciate the skill and understanding of Jo Ann Reece, editor, University of Oklahoma Press. Any errors in fact or interpretation are due to my own inexperience. Special thanks go to Donald DeWitt and his excellent staff at the University of Oklahoma Western History Collections, where most of the research for this book took place.

Women of Oklahoma,
1890–1920

1

The Greatest Romance

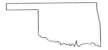

It took a lot to provoke anger in Elva Shartel Ferguson, owner of the *Watonga Republican* newspaper and widow of Territorial governor Thompson B. Ferguson. She had earned a reputation as one of the most important and well-known women in Oklahoma. During her long years in the state, she had survived the hardships of homesteading with young children, learned how to negotiate with Indians, managed a home in the crude circumstances of a frontier town, weathered the storms of politics in state-building, and lost a son during World War I. If anyone understood the story of Oklahoma, she believed she did, and novelist Edna Ferber's insult was too much. Ferguson sat down at her desk and penned a private response she titled, "The Truth About *Cimarron*." In this she wrote, "I hope someone with a pen more truthful than Miss Ferber's will someday write the human life story of

Oklahoma. Not seeking out the sensational events," she urged, "but building the story of a really great citizenship and state."[1]

The publication of Edna Ferber's romantic saga *Cimarron* in 1930 prompted Ferguson's angry reaction. *Cimarron* developed the story of Oklahoma statehood through the adventures of a female character named Sabra Cravat. Sabra's fictional life closely followed the contours of Elva Shartel Ferguson's life. Like Ferguson, Sabra Cravat left the established society of Kansas with her husband, Yancey, to build up a new country in the untamed Indian Territory. She raised a family and managed her husband's newspaper during his frequent absences, grimly helping convert a lawless frontier town into a respectable community. This taming of the frontier changed Sabra from a pampered southern belle to an autocratic woman of commanding presence. In the novel Yancey articulated the dreams of the new commonwealth, but he shirked the responsibilities of making the dreams a reality—that role fell to Sabra. In spite of her own racial prejudice, she capitalized on the Indian heritage of Cimarron, and she forced its mainstream white society to accept an Indian cultural presence by including her own Osage daughter-in-law in social functions of importance. At the end of *Cimarron*, Sabra emerged as the figure in control of the newspaper and the town, and as a power in the politics of the new state.[2]

In the foreword to her novel, Edna Ferber wrote that there was no single Sabra Cravat, but that her fictional character had been shaped by many interesting women who shared their memories of Oklahoma with her. Elva Ferguson truly resented this discourtesy; Ferber resided in the Ferguson home while researching the novel in Oklahoma. Ferguson insisted that the story of Sabra was modeled on her connection

Elva Shartel Ferguson, First Lady of Oklahoma, wife of Governor Thompson B. Ferguson, and copublisher of the *Watonga Republican* newspaper. Photo courtesy of the Archives & Manuscripts Division of the Oklahoma Historical Society.

to the *Watonga Republican*, even though Ferber failed to give her credit for the outline of the story or even to acknowledge her hospitality. Ferguson wrote that she approved of the novel as long as Ferber stayed within the pioneering story, where her interpretation was authentic, but she believed that Ferber distorted the record when she expanded the plot to include oil development and Indians. Ferguson expected the main characters to reflect the strength, courage, cooperation, and integrity that she believed defined the pioneering experience. In her own memoir, Ferguson suggested that the diverse personalities woven into the fabric of the history of the state created "the greatest romance of any time or place."[3]

To fulfill Elva Ferguson's request to write the "human life story" of Oklahoma and, especially, to consider women's contributions to the creation of the state, that story must be placed within the context of national and regional development. Oklahoma historian Angie Debo believed that all the contours of the American character and all the experience of national development could be observed in Oklahoma, but that the formation took place at a much faster pace. When she began her career, Debo drew upon the frontier writings of Frederick Jackson Turner and of her own mentor, Edward Everett Dale.

More than one hundred years have passed since the Superintendent of the Census made a brief statement in his 1890 report that announced the closing of a frontier line of settlement in America. Ironically, the same year marked the creation of the Territory of Oklahoma and the eventual opening of forty-five million acres of land to non-Indian agricultural development. In this twilight of the nineteenth century, Americans experienced for the last time the drama of national re-creation and renewal on a contiguous frontier. Wisconsin historian Frederick Jackson Turner took note of the obscure census report and prepared a paper suggesting his theory on the meaning of the frontier experience as it applied to the understanding of American history.

According to Turner, "The existence of an area of free land, its continuous recession, and the advance of

American settlement westward, explain American development." He believed that adaptation to the conditions of expansion shaped the distinctive American institutions and influenced the formation of the American character. "This perennial rebirth, this fluidity of American life, this expansion westward with its new opportunities, its continuous touch with the simplicity of primitive society, furnish the forces dominating the American character," he wrote. His composite American exhibited characteristics that were individualistic, democratic, nationalistic, practical, and mobile. Turner outlined a story of expansion carried out through the efforts of fishermen, trappers, traders, miners, soldiers, cattlemen, and farmers. He proposed in his essay the value of investigating these successive frontier waves and comparing the nature of each as a method for understanding and enriching the scope of American development and American society.[4]

Recent scholars, most notably Patricia Limerick, Richard White, William Cronon, and Donald Worster, have rejected Turner's understanding of the American experience and have proposed an alternative interpretation based on the idea of Euroamerican invasion and conquest. Turner's ideas, however, dominated historical writing throughout his lifetime. Between 1893 when Turner read his paper at the Chicago World's Fair and 1930, the frontier essay gained increasing notoriety and acceptance in scholarly circles and galvanized a generation of graduate students. One of the most glaring omissions of Turner's work, however, lay in his basic assumption that history resulted solely from the actions of men and that what was true of men's experiences applied to women as well. With few exceptions, this assumption pervaded historical writing until the late 1950s. David M. Potter published an essay in 1959 that used Turner's essay as the starting point for a discussion of the nature of the American character. Potter maintained: "What we say about the character of the American people should be said not in terms of half of the American population— even if it is the male half—but in terms of the character and totality of the people. . . . For the character of any nation is the composite of the character of its men and of its women."[5]

Esteemed Oklahoma historian Edward Everett Dale, a former student of Turner's, defined women's history within a family context. When he described the western pioneering experience, he portrayed a family tableau: A man journeyed forth with dreams of free land and opportunity, and his offspring scampered around the wagons eager for the adventure of the trip. For Dale, however, the woman in this scene represented a tragic figure. She smothered her tears in her apron as she packed a few treasures—a mantle clock, fragile earrings wrapped in lace, a special picture, carefully preserved flower seeds and plant roots—among the necessities. Then she bade farewell to friends and relatives, home, church, and established community to travel to a far-off country filled with danger and hardship. Dale continued this characterization in his discussion of homesteading: The move west gave men increased leisure time after the first busy months of getting the crop planted and the house built, and they took advantage of the new freedom to ride over to a neighbor's farm or into the nearest town for companionship. The sod-house mother continued her rounds of never-ending chores in lonely isolation.[6]

Dale's tragic figure conformed to an elaborate American literary and historical tradition that portrayed white frontier women as one of three familiar stereotypes. Sandra Myres, in her book, *Westering Women and the Frontier Experience, 1800–1915,*

Families camped together to await the 1889 Land Opening. Photo courtesy of the Western History Collections, University of Oklahoma Library.

extensively outlined these images. They included, first, the discouraged, physically ravaged drudge who wore out her body and soul with hard work; then, the brave pioneer mother who brought civilization to the West; and, finally, the hell-raising, woman-gone-bad. While the elements of deprivation, hard work, courage, and notoriety may certainly be found in the Oklahoma frontier experience, these stereotypes deny the complexity of women's lives, ignoring the conditions of a particular time and locale, racial and cultural preconceptions and interactions, and women's negotiation of changing class status. The opening of land in Oklahoma in 1889 and the homesteading experience that extended over the next seventeen years furnished the theater for the last pioneering experience in the contiguous United States. Oklahoma women came from a variety of backgrounds and brought with them a complex cultural baggage. Their relationships consisted of more than motherhood; they were sweethearts, wives, daughters, sisters, aunts, friends, neighbors, teachers, businesswomen, and midwives, and each of these associations provided a myriad of experiences and responsibilities. Looking beyond stereotypes enriches our understanding of women in the West and helps us establish their contributions to the frontier tradition. The diversity of the responses of Oklahoma women to frontier conditions demands a reevaluation of conventional assertions about the role of women in the West.[7]

With the advent of the social upheaval of the late 1960s and 1970s, long-unresolved tensions surrounding race, class, and gender inevitably led to questions about, discussions of, and challenges to traditional assumptions about the historical past. Women's history and ethnic history emerged as productive fields of study. In addition to scores of provocative essays, the last two decades of scholarship in women's history have produced major analytical studies of white women in the West and numerous collections of essays devoted to a multicultural approach. Julie Roy Jeffrey, in *Frontier Women, The Trans-Mississippi West, 1840–1880*, examined the documents left by two hundred westering women who traveled to the frontier during the time of heaviest western migration. Jeffrey enunciated the ideology directing women's lives as one of separate spheres. The development of a market economy and industrialization in America had changed both the place and the nature of work. As home manufacture gave way to factories and shops, the lives of men and women diverged. Men occupied a public, aggressive, materialistic world as compared to the private, passive, spiritual domain of the home. Women's function became that of caretaker of the home, repositor of moral virtues, and teacher of the nation's children. An ideology of domesticity emerged in the East among urban, middle-class white women that permeated national thought. This ideology centered on the supposed natural characteristics of women: purity, piety, submissiveness, and domesticity. As a feminist scholar, Jeffrey hoped to find in her study that westering women used the frontier to reject this restrictive stereotype. She discovered instead that the ideology "helped women hold on to their sexual identity and offered them hope of an ever-improving life." Faced with new demands and experiences, they clung to familiar ideals and worked toward the day when they might resurrect them again.[8]

The manner in which land was opened to non-Indian agricultural development in present-day Oklahoma created a unique frontier. There, homesteading failed to follow the traditional pattern of slow, cautious westward advance during which an area of land acquired first a regional culture and economy and then joined the culture and economy of the nation. Instead, the federal government threw open and then stitched together, like pieces of a quilt, the jagged parcels of land that had been confiscated from the resident Indian tribes. First came the two million acres of the Unassigned Lands that were opened through presidential proclamation in April 1889. Approximately fifty thousand expectant homesteaders, town promoters, and land speculators lined the borders awaiting the signal to rush onto the land and stake a claim to a town lot or a farm; within a few hours, the cities of Guthrie, Oklahoma City, Kingfisher, Norman, Stillwater, and El Reno were born. The Organic Act of 1890 created the territorial organization and added the western strip of No Man's Land (the present-day Oklahoma panhandle) to the Oklahoma territory. Additional sections of land were opened piecemeal through land runs as the Jerome Commission

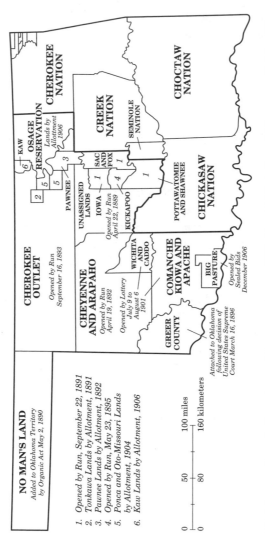

NO MAN'S LAND
Added to Oklahoma Territory
by Organic Act May 2, 1890

CHEROKEE OUTLET
Opened by Run
September 16, 1893

CHEROKEE NATION

KAW 6

OSAGE RESERVATION
Lands by Allotment 1906

3

2 5

5 PAWNEE

CREEK NATION

UNASSIGNED LANDS
Opened by Run
April 22, 1889

IOWA 1

SAC AND FOX 1

4

KICKAPOO

1

SEMINOLE NATION

CHEYENNE AND ARAPAHO
Opened by Run
April 19, 1892

WICHITA AND CADDO

Opened by Lottery
July 9 to
August 6
1901

COMANCHE KIOWA AND APACHE

BIG PASTURE

Opened by
Sealed Bids
December 1906

POTTAWATOMIE AND SHAWNEE

CHICKASAW NATION

CHOCTAW NATION

GREER COUNTY

Attached to Oklahoma
following decision of
United States Supreme
Court March 16, 1896

1. Opened by Run, September 22, 1891
2. Tonkawa Lands by Allotment, 1891
3. Pawnee Lands by Allotment, 1892
4. Opened by Run, May 23, 1895
5. Ponca and Oto-Missouri Lands
   by Allotment, 1904
6. Kaw Lands by Allotment, 1906

0   50   100 miles
0   80   160 kilometers

Oklahoma Land Openings. Map courtesy of W. David Baird and Danney Goble, *The Story of Oklahoma* (University of Oklahoma Press, 1994).

Four thousand wagons crossing the Salt Fork River on their way to make the 1889 Land Run. Photo courtesy of the Western History Collections, University of Oklahoma Library.

completed negotiations with the various tribes of western Indian Territory. Violence and disorder created by contested claims, fraud, and "sooners," who illegally entered the area and staked a claim before the official date, marred the success of the first openings. The largest land run, into six million acres of the Cherokee Outlet in 1893, convinced government officials that a better system of distribution was necessary. The last large areas of land, belonging to the Kiowa, Comanche, and Apache tribes, joined the territory through lottery and sealed auction bids. The United States Supreme Court added Greer County to the territory when it adjusted a Texas–Indian Territory boundary dispute. By the eve of statehood, only the lands belonging to the Five Nations stood apart— allotted and filled with non-Indian settlers, but not yet relinquished. As women travelled the wagon roads with their families into the Twin Territories (Indian Territory to the east, Oklahoma Territory to the west), their thoughts were occupied with what they had left behind and what lay ahead.[9]

Going to God's Country

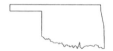

No one could deny the excitement of the late-nineteenth-century land runs. The assembled crowds contained gamblers of all descriptions—speculators, businessmen, farmers—and the poor. Among them was the young couple Elva and Thompson Ferguson, who were present at land openings in 1889, 1892, and 1893. The Fergusons first homesteaded a claim in the Unassigned Lands, but sold it quickly and returned to Kansas. They established a permanent residence in Watonga when the Cheyenne and Arapaho lands were opened in 1892. But when the Cherokee Outlet opened the following year, Elva drove a wagon in the run. At Pond Creek the Fergusons claimed a town lot that they later sold for ten dollars. In her memoirs Elva expressed the romantic vision of those long ago days. "I feel sorry for anyone who has never known the fascination of pioneering and starting at the beginning of things," she wrote. "I feel sorry for anyone who has never travelled in a covered wagon, stopping along the winding streams to make camp in God's beautiful outdoors."[1]

Women came alone and with their families to both Indian Territory and Oklahoma Territory. Some came as children accompanying their parents or as elderly participants, while others came as brides or as mothers of large families. Certainly a few may have come under duress, unwilling to live an initially rough, unsettled life. The surviving accounts indicate that most of the women had a desire to take advantage of an opportunity to get rich or, failing that, at least to secure a better quality of life than they had known. As one Missouri woman exclaimed, "We were going to God's Country. We were going to a new land and get rich. Then we could have a real home of our own." A woman could acquire both a 160-acre homestead and a town lot in her own right, if she was at least twenty-one years old and single. Female land seekers usually ranged in age from twenty-one years old to the late seventies, with the largest number in their twenties. Sending eligible women to stake a claim was an easy way to increase the size of the whole family's landholdings. Many of these women homesteaders either lived with relatives or chose claims that adjoined the farms of relatives. Black women participated in the first land runs as well; fourteen single black women staked claims in the initial 1889 Land Opening.[2]

The most notorious woman land rusher took part in four separate openings. Naunita R. H. Daisey, known in Oklahoma Territory as Annetta Daisey, arrived in 1889 to cover the land run as a newspaper correspondent and became so caught up in the excitement that she decided to stake a claim for herself. She jumped from the cowcatcher of the slow-moving train and tumbled across the prairie in her long skirts. Although bruised and shaken, she held down her claim in Oklahoma County despite a gun battle with a male contester who wounded her in the arm. In 1891 she rode a horse into the Iowa and Sac and Fox lands and secured a townsite lot in Chandler. Since she could not claim any more land for herself, she next participated as the leader of a company of women who were anxious to gain homesteads. When officials announced the opening of the Cheyenne and Arapaho lands in 1892, Daisey organized and led a group of eleven armed women into a ravine within the new lands. They intended to remain in hiding until after the official signal, then stake out claims that Daisey had previously helped them select. Daisey justified this "sooner" intrusion by telling reporters that they were only camped in the ravine for their own protection. Cavalry patrols failed to locate the women's camp, but they captured Daisey as she returned from a trip to El Reno for supplies and escorted her to the border. Daisey's next adventure involved the opening of the Cherokee Outlet, popularly called the Cherokee Strip, in 1893. Once again she led a group of female homesteaders, but this time they waited for the opening signal. Twenty-two of the thirty-six women succeeded in gaining land, and they set to work cooperatively building a home and planting crops. Daisey retired from her land-speculation activities after this, and by 1894, when she made proof on her original claim, she had married.[3]

Annetta Daisey's exploits no doubt made exciting news copy, but many other single women participated in the land openings for a variety of reasons. In the dry lands near Woodward, a former prostitute tried to hold her claim and make improvements all alone, despite sabotage by the "respectable" surrounding neighbors

First train into the Cherokee Strip Opening, 1893. Photo courtesy of the Western History Collections, University of Oklahoma Library.

who destroyed her fences and burned her pasture. For years she worked as a domestic helper for affluent town women, putting all of her earnings into the claim, and she eventually secured both the land and the towns-people's respect. In Wichita, Kansas, telephone operator Mattie Beal and her friend Florence Allen decided that it would be fun to take the train to El Reno and sign up for the Kiowa-Comanche-Apache land lottery. Among the 167,000 who registered for this land in 1901, 13,000 were women. The lottery made only 6,500 claims available, so Beal and Allen were shocked to find out that they held winning numbers. Beal's ticket was the second one drawn, entitling her to a choice Lawton townsite location. The first-place ticket holder, J. R. Woods, noted that three sides of Lawton were bounded by military and Indian agency land. He located his claim in a horizontal strip the entire length of the fourth side of town thereby cheating Beal out of a claim adjoining the townsite. Undaunted, Beal and her brother moved onto her land next to Woods and built a frame house. Beal cooked and sold food at her front door to the new residents of the area, and she claimed to have received 500 proposals of marriage from disappointed claim seekers.[4]

Charity Garner's father insisted that, since she was old enough, she should register for the lottery, and the family took a vacation from their homestead in Chandler to await the drawing. She also received a lucky number, and her father selected her claim for her. Charity expressed reluctance to leave Chandler: "When I thought about moving, I didn't know if I wanted to or not, but all my friends were so pleased for me and said I was such a lucky girl, that I finally became anxious to go." She married her neighbor on the adjoining claim, but he died after ten years, and she reared their five children alone on the half-section.[5]

Widows and divorcees also found the opportunity to own land in Oklahoma attractive. A destitute Kansas woman and her four children struggled to get to Kingfisher in time for the Cheyenne and Arapaho opening. She walked up to the border carrying her baby in her arms, but before the signal rang out, a woman bystander offered to hold the infant. Gratefully, the Kansas woman dashed across the line, among the horses, wagons, and buggies, and drove a stake into a claim. Other successful homesteaders helped her file the necessary papers and build a house.

Kate E. May's efforts to succeed in the Cherokee Strip symbolized the determination of female heads of households. May's husband, S. D. May, had participated in the first land run and had staked a claim near Oklahoma City. He also purchased two additional town lots. May died the day after the land run, and the family lost the homestead. Kate always believed that his death had resulted from an act of violence. She established a restaurant in Oklahoma City with the help of two daughters by May's previous marriage and her own six children. Both the restaurant and a second marriage failed in late 1892. Kate was pregnant again, and she devised a plan to make the run into the Strip and secure a claim near the proposed townsite of Perry, which was being publicized as the future boomtown of Oklahoma Territory. She mortgaged the two town lots to borrow the money to make the run, selected and trained a strong horse, and armed herself with a Smith & Wesson pistol.[6]

Four months after the birth of her seventh child, Kate May joined the race into the Strip and claimed what she believed would be an excellent site. The pistol proved handy when she found a "sooner" leisurely camped on her property. She fired at his camp equipment until she frightened him enough to make him move over to a nearby claim. Kate's brother joined the family on the new homestead, and he built her a fifteen-foot by fifteen-foot sod house. Kate, her brother, and the nine children worked on the claim, and she once again tried to operate a restaurant. A third, brief marriage also ended in divorce. Desperately, Kate and her children struggled to survive. The oldest boys, who were eleven and thirteen, sold snacks and newspapers to passengers at the Perry railroad station. The family made improvements on the land, but could not bring the required ten acres under cultivation. Still, Kate refused to break up the family. As her daughter later remarked, "It never occurred to mama to parcel the children out to relatives." The heavy work load left them all exhausted, and none of the children attended school at this time. The crops failed in 1894, and the restaurant rarely saw a profit. When a daughter developed tuberculosis and the rest of the family contracted typhoid fever, May knew that she had to relinquish the land. She turned the farm over to her third husband and his new wife, loaded the wagons, and returned to Oklahoma City. Although she failed in the Cherokee Strip, May made another homesteading attempt in the Kiowa-Comanche-Apache lands. She finally moved the family to the arid lands of New Mexico. Many women like May, who had been widowed in Oklahoma Territory, stayed on their husbands' claims and eventually received patents for the land.[7]

Young and old, affluent and poor, educated and illiterate—women packed their dreams as well as their possessions in the wagons headed to the Twin Territories. Some women saw the sunny, open lands of Oklahoma Territory as a place to renew their own health or that of family members. Addie Robertson's mother and father planned the move for a year preceding the trip. "Mama thought it rained too much at

Konowa [in Indian Territory]," Robertson remembered. "She was in ill health herself and thought the dampness wasn't healthy for us children." Addie's mother, Sadie Robertson, preserved and cured the food they would need for the trip and made four new feather beds. She also packed a small trunk of clothes that she wanted the children to wear at her funeral. "She knew her illness would never allow her to see western Oklahoma, but she made extra effort to see that her family would get there," Robertson wrote. Sadie died on the second day of the trip, and the family buried her in a nearby town. Robertson's father hired a woman to drive the buggy and cook for the five children, who were all under the age of nine, until they reached the homestead.[8]

Health concerns also entered into the decision a young Kansas couple made to homestead in the Cherokee Strip. Bertha and Dorsey Hutchins left Kansas in September 1897, following the death of their first child from a fever that had also left both of them weakened. Bertha's mother wrote to the grandparents in Indiana, "It is like taking ones very life almost to see her go off to live that way. . . . they are neither one strong—and they work too hard." Bertha and her mother kept up a frequent and lively correspondence for the next two years, as the couple developed their farm. Bertha's letters always expressed optimism, and she tried to calm her parents' worries about her health, outlining in detail what provisions they had and what they ate at meals. After only two months on the claim and while they were still living out of the wagon box, she wrote, "If you could see me now you would hardly know I was the same person who came away. . . . There are no hollows in my cheeks and I have plenty of color in my face. Living out doors a good deal agrees with me, I guess."[9]

But physical improvement failed to be the case for another young bride in Indian Territory. Nineteen-year-old Laura Bunch Sims's letters home outlined her happiness with her husband, but also expressed her deteriorating health and her homesickness for her family in Arkansas. She begged her mother for frequent letters and wrote, "If you was here I would be satisfied. . . . I think some times I don't know anybody much, and I get awful lonesome." She assured her mother that they had plenty to eat, except for dairy products, and dreams of milk and butter from home filled her letters. She also mentioned increasingly frequent illness from headaches and chills and wrote of taking pills that made her feel weak and disoriented. One of her husband's meddling aunts took these bouts as a sign of pregnancy, and Laura smugly informed her mother, "Aunt Pud though I was in a family way. She said she would make me some baby clothes. I told her I thanked her, but I didn't need them. . . . She has found out she didn't know as much as she thought." Aunt Pud continued to monitor Laura's health, however, and to aggravate her about it. Sadly, Laura confided to her mother, "She says I am a sickly woman, she says Will has got a sickly wife." In the next six years Laura Sims's health continued to decline, and she died at the age of twenty-five after the birth of her third child.[10]

Single women made the choice to move to present-day Oklahoma independently, but married women, according to law, precedent, and social dictates, followed the desires of their husbands. Most often the decision appeared to be made after careful family discussions. After all, pioneering new land required the cooperative efforts of all members of the family. Lucy Gage's parents called their adult daughter home to Wisconsin from a teaching career in Chicago to discuss the possibility of moving to Oklahoma Territory. She credited her mother with inspiring their excitement and confidence, as they studied published reports and publicity brochures. "We counselled together into the wee hours, taking no account of time," Gage remembered. It was her mother who finally ended the debate when she told her husband, "we have everything to gain and nothing to lose."[11]

Sometimes the family conferences failed to achieve the outcome the wife wanted, however. Sam Ross dropped out of medical school for financial reasons and assisted another doctor in Bonham, Texas, eventually marrying his employer's daughter, Maude. In 1897 Ross discussed with Maude the possibility of acquiring a certificate to practice medicine in Indian Territory. He believed that his Indian patients would be too ignorant to challenge his lack of credentials and the couple could save enough money for him to return to medical school. Maude argued against the plan, listing the dangers, the lack of civilization, and, finally, the social disadvantage for their young daughter. Maude believed she had succeeded in changing her husband's mind. Later that year, Ross convinced her that his widowed sister and mother, who were currently living in Indian Territory, wanted a visit from the family. After Maude and her daughter arrived, Ross broke the news to her: he had ordered all of their household possessions to be packed and moved to Indian Territory, where he intended the family to live. "He only smiled and *looked triumphant*," Maude later remarked, "as men usually do when they have *gained their point*." The couple remained in present-day Oklahoma for the rest of their lives.[12]

After the land openings, more families journeyed to present-day Oklahoma in search of good fortune. A single family rarely made the trip alone; most often groups of extended family and friends traveled together, and the closer they got to the borders of the Twin Territories, the larger the wagon trains became. Ruth Yelton, a sixteen-year-old Indiana girl, kept a diary of her family's two-month wagon trip to Oklahoma Territory in 1901. Surprisingly, the references to the amount of work required to keep a family of ten children on the road were few. Yelton's entries captured her fascination with the changing scenery. She interspersed notations of chores with ones of candy pulls, romps in the streams, weather reports, the kinds of crops and methods of cultivation, descriptions of the cities they passed through, and peculiarities about the people they met along the way. Yelton kept track of gypsy camps and of places where she saw black people. While in Illinois she exclaimed, "The women & girls all go barefoot & wear their hair short, & many of them smoke a pipe!" St. Louis, Missouri, terrified her because of all the traffic on the wagon bridge and because "The buildings were so high it was dark, & at first it was hard to breathe." She kept her head, however, and recorded the number of steamboats and ferry boats on the Mississippi River. The Yeltons began the trip with a neighbor and his son, but after two pleading letters from his wife, the neighbor turned back to Indiana. Even so, Yelton reported that in Kansas their caravan included nine wagons, seven dogs, eleven guns, ten women and girls, and twenty-four men and boys. Her diary ended with the family's arrival at the Cherokee Strip, where she concluded, "very glad & yet hating to end our great trip from Indiana to Oklahoma."[13]

The diaries of Anna Gillespie and Anna Wood presented more mature, but just as wonder-filled and optimistic, accounts of wagon travel to Oklahoma Territory. Gillespie was forty-eight years old and a mother of five when the family moved from Coxville, Nebraska, to Fay, Oklahoma Territory, in 1899. She and her family drove a herd of fifty horses along the seven-hundred-mile trail. In addition to providing for food and family care, Gillespie drove a wagon and shared herding duties at night. She expressed little regret at leaving Nebraska; four days into the trip she wrote, "I feel as if I had said goodbye to old Dawes County with the debts and discouragements, its hot winds, drouths, and hard times generally, and I intend to begin a new life." Like many Oklahoma Territory immigrants, Anna Wood, a Civil War widow, had experience pioneering new frontiers—in Wood's case, three times before her journey to Oklahoma Territory with her son and another family in 1893. Having moved from Vermont to Wisconsin to Kansas to Colorado and finally to Oklahoma, Wood was skilled in wagon travel. Her diary begins, "Well once more we are on the road bound for the promised land, viz., 'The Strip'." Her diary seems to indicate that it irritated her each time something broke or was misplaced, because she took great pride in her organization and packing, and it meant they would have to improvise.[14]

Both Gillespie's and Wood's traveling parties encountered strong winds and storms, but the women recorded these in an almost matter-of-fact manner. Gillespie even joked when a "embryo cyclone" blew the tent down that "it was an amusing sight to see the boys out in all kinds of costumes driving the stakes." When the same situation occurred two nights later, she recorded, "We were treated as usual to a negligee spectacle." Both women fell ill during the trip, and their ailments were no doubt complicated by the heat, fatigue, and mineral-laden water. But they feared less for their own ability to withstand conditions than for that of their animals, as each party lost mules and horses along the way to sickness. Indeed, both Annas observed evidence of dead animals and debris left by previous travelers. Anna Gillespie completely disapproved of one camping place because "the dirty shirts, old tin cans and other trash was not conducive to improve our appetites."[15]

Gillespie and Wood took for granted their right to enter into the decisions made along the way about the places to camp and the times to start and stop. When Joe Gillespie chose a disagreeable location, Anna confided to her diary, "I forsee that he will have to be sat down on, and I shall do the matter pretty effectually the next time he camps in a man's dooryard." She and Joe must have exchanged words, because the following day's entry mentioned that Joe had "one of his grumbling spells" and Anna intended to ride in a separate wagon until he had time to calm down. By nightfall Joe and Anna reconciled, and she wrote that all was serene again. Anna Wood found it a little more difficult to impose her wishes on her son. They failed to locate acceptable claims within a few days on the Strip, and her son decided that they should retreat to a friend's farm in Kansas until they had more information. Wood expressed her disapproval at leaving so soon, but she added, "Do not know whether it will be for the best or not but do not like to advise for fear that it may not turn out all right so will do whatever C.[larence] says."[16]

These late-nineteenth-century travelers enjoyed advantages unavailable to their predecessors; for most of the trip they rode through settled country in which they stopped at intervals and bought provisions, rested, and attended local events. Ruth Yelton's family toured the insane asylum at Nevada, Missouri, and went to hear Carry Nation give a temperance speech in Kansas. The travelers stopped at farms along the way to draw well water and to pasture their animals—most often free of charge except, occasionally, when the homesteader asked $1.00 for the privilege. Usually the farmer's wife sent new homesteaders on their way with fresh milk, butter, eggs, bread, and melons. Once established in Oklahoma Territory, these settlers reciprocated by sharing their hospitality when new home-seekers crossed their lands. One Cherokee Strip wife remembered, "Oh, how lonesome the vast areas looked. If you would sight some human being, riding horseback, or in a covered wagon, how we would watch and wonder about them and wish that by some chance they would come by."[17] Indeed, most travelers took it for granted that when they passed the fields of earlier homesteaders, they could take enough vegetables to feed their families. Many women mentioned this practice openly, using such terms as "rustle," "gypsy trick," and "snitch." Martha Smith, a mother of six, remembered how her wagon-train companions reacted when she took some heads of cabbage from a garden plot as they crossed Oklahoma Territory. Smith bought sweet potatoes, corn, and other vegetables, when they passed a farm house, to supplement the wild game her husband killed, but in stretches where no one lived close by, she scouted the area. "When we would stop for camp I would go out and hunt and find a vegetable patch," she wrote. "I tried to get some of them to go with me but they said that was stealing." When she returned with the cabbage, she shared it with the other families. They had been without fresh produce so long that they forgot their temporary opposition. At later camps, Smith refused to share her bounty unless some of the other women would go hunting with her. "Some of the bunch were very nice but some of them was so religious that I liked to tease them," she joked. "It was just Sunday religion and I did not pretend to be so good." Following this, even if she bought the vegetables, she hid the bag and pretended that she stole them just to irritate the more pious women.[18]

The roads were nonexistent or extremely rough, but since most newcomers made the trip with extended family and friends, all hands worked at fording the rivers and ascending the hills. Sometimes Indians assisted the wagon trains. Catherine Ward Allen remembered the leader of her family's wagon train negotiating with Ponca Indians for the use of their ferry to cross a river. The Indians received money and the assurance that no guns would be used against them. After the wagons crossed and the immigrants were camped on the other side, the Indians visited the train that night and listened to the settlers sing ballads and hymns from home.[19]

Confronted with fresh memories of the Custer battle, dime novels full of Indian stereotypes, and forebodings about the possibilities of Ghost Dance activity, most of the women settlers expressed fear in their initial encounters with the Plains Indians. These fears failed to incapacitate them, however, and in many cases taught them new negotiation skills. Sometimes one set of fears outweighed another. One girl, Nora Watson Cox, remembered her father "silently sitting with his back against the wagon wheel and that long, dangerous gun across his knees" as he guarded his family at night. Unknown to him, however, the girl's mother, who was more fearful of the gun than of the Indians, unloaded the weapon whenever she had the chance. In her memoir, *Going to God's Country*, Martha Smith gave this account of her first meeting with Indians: "The Osages would only grunt and look so mean we were most frighent [sic] to death. We were so afraid that they would try to take our litel girls for they would sneak up and peep in our wagons." The men stood guard with their shotguns every night. At one point the caravan ran out of water, and Smith's baby cried for hours from thirst. She spotted an Indian home in the distance, and her husband stopped the wagon. He stayed with the wagon and sent her, with a bucket, to ask for water. At first the Indian ignored her requests, even when she pantomimed drinking from the bucket and pointed to the well. Finally, she tossed him a piece of silver money, and he gave her a bucket of water.[20]

Smith explained that Indians appreciated kindness. She always acted friendly and offered them something they liked, but she refused to give them alcohol. They especially liked small change, and she kept a supply in her skirt pocket. She sewed the rest of the family's money into a pouch in the crown of her bonnet that she stored in the wagon. Other women in the wagon train hid money in their bustles or in tobacco sacks pinned to their undergarments. Smith claimed that she always got along with the Indians this way: "If you would allways give them a good hand shake or a smile it would be much better than to be cross or look like you were afraid or mad. I wasn't going to let them know that I was afraid. Some times I was just shakin but I would smile and just act like I knew them and had known them allways." She added that this method worked because if Indians knew a women was afraid, they would do things just to scare her. Other women found that, when confronted by a crowd of Indians, a good tactic was to offer food or some possession. One woman handed out apples to a camp of Kickapoos, and her daughter reported that they seemed very pleased but one of the elders had gone away angry when the woman refused to trade him her cat for part of his reservation.[21]

Whether they came from Iowa or Arkansas, had black or red or white skin, settled in Oklahoma

Territory or Indian Territory, these pioneer women faced the challenge of creating a home and forcing the land to yield them a livelihood. The magnitude of their labor alone justified the future erection of the Pioneer Woman Monument in Ponca City. The collected reminiscences of rural women concentrated on the successes they achieved, the honors they won, and the sunny days of strength and youth and optimism; few expressed any regrets. Yet, the historical record exposes pain, hardship, struggle, and failure as well as accomplishment. Among the most obvious examples challenging the progressive record were the destitute immigrants who wandered across the land barely keeping alive. Journalist Helen Candee applied the name "schooner population" to this group. She claimed that these people started out as hopeful families, but because of misfortune or lack of energy they drifted, "satisfied with life in the wagon," trailing assorted livestock. Many homesteading women shared what they could with the transients who camped from time to time near their door. Homesteader Mary Henderson recorded in her diary, "There was the hardest looking outfit camped in our pasture last night I ever saw." The group consisted of a middle-aged woman, an eleven-year-old boy, twelve-year-old girl, a grandmother, two pidgeons, and a cat. The travelers carried all of their possessions on their backs and in a baby carriage that was missing a wheel. Henderson gave them bread, milk, and sugar, and she reported, "I think they subsisted chiefly on what they begged." The family headed toward Kansas the next day.[22]

Maude Ross, as a doctor's wife, encountered families in even worse condition. A man in the family did not always guarantee appropriate support. On one occasion a wagon, carrying a man and his filthy, malnourished, desperately sick wife and children, slowly

pulled into the Ross yard. Dr. Ross located a shanty
nearby that would, at least, shelter the family, and
Maude and her sister-in-law took food, clothing, and
blankets to them. On the third visit to administer
medicine, Dr. Ross noticed that the man had made no
effort to clean up the shack or make his family comfortable. The doctor warned him that unless he took
action, the whole family might die. But the man
responded by asking, "What was the matter the women
folks didn't do what was needed to be done?" The doctor
advised him that Maude and his sister were needed at
home to tend to their own families.

Poverty marked the early days of settlement, especially after crop failures. The government distributed
aid, railroad companies provided free seed, and
engineers occasionally tossed out coal along the sides
of the tracks to provide fuel on the treeless plains.
These actions helped stabilize the landed, but the
schooner population reminded the settlers of the
gamble that they had undertaken.[23]

Homesteaders developed a complex structure of
barter in which women played a significant role. Many
women cooked and washed for single men and boarded
them in their temporary quarters in exchange for work
on their homes and land and the use of their machinery
and animals. Mary Henderson recorded in her diary a
wash day that included more than 150 garments. Henderson, like many others, kept the family financial-
account record in her diary. She scrupulously recorded
the items she and her husband bought to construct the
house ("500 brick $5.00, 600 lbs. sand .75 cts.") and the
prices she received for the garden produce she sold. The
egg, milk, and butter money she made from sales in the
nearby town belonged exclusively to her. But she
proudly confided that when she sent her oldest son into
town to sell the products for her, she allowed him a

share of the profits for his spending money. She took great pride in the extra dividend she earned for the family in this way. Her last entry for 1906 reported her total of nearly $300.00 in sales for the year.[24]

The first homes in the territories reflected both the limited funds of most newcomers and the shortage of building materials in some areas. In the wooded sections log cabins replaced caves as shelter. On the plains to the west, many settlers lived in tents or out of the wagon bed until they could construct either dugouts or sod houses, which were made from ten-inch by fifteen-inch bricks of earth cut out of the ground with a team and sod plow. Families with more money and those living closer to a rail station hauled in lumber for frame houses. The actions of a young Kansas couple, Bertha and Dorsey Hutchins, represented a typical pattern. Throughout September and October 1897, they debated about what kind of house to build as they camped out of the wagon box. Dorsey scooped out a trough three feet deep against a hillside, sloped it, and put boards across one end for temporary shelter. They planned for this shack to house the buggy once they built their home. At first they decided to build a frame house, but when they examined the quality and price of lumber available, they changed their minds. "We talked it over and concluded we had better build a sod house," Bertha wrote her mother. "We did not know what better to do, because we would be run so close to put so much into a house." The couple's best friends on the next quarter-section had just completed their two-room, twelve-by-twenty sod house for $48.00. The Hutchinses decided to follow their example and conserve their funds for taxes and supplies until they produced a crop.[25]

The women expressed their individuality and pride in the comfort and decor of these first crude dwellings.

Sod houses could be quite large and often had strutures built on as the family prospered. Photo courtesy of the Western History Collections, University of Oklahoma Library.

They constructed shelves and furniture out of packing boxes. They curtained off areas for privacy, planted flowers in pots, sewed bright window curtains, braided colorful rag rugs to cover the earthen floors or splintery wooden ones, and made decorative plaques from the dried gypsum that so tainted their water supplies. No article or scrap of fabric was so humble that it could not be put to some use. Present-day Oklahoma's relatively late settlement worked to the advantage of women to the extent that they enjoyed benefits of the Industrial Revolution and of extensive rail transportation that had been unavailable to earlier frontierswomen. If they did not bring stoves and sewing machines with them, most settlers acquired them quickly. Railroads made articles available that previously had been home manufactured and brought supplies that eased other homemaking chores. Concentrated lye, for instance, eliminated a step in soap production. Textiles, ready-made clothes, canned goods, and factory-made furniture arrived at the rail stations and were dispersed across the territories by way of small, general-merchandise stores set up at convenient homesteads. Some homemakers divided their time between running their homes and operating these rural stores. Some stores hired local widows and teenage girls to trim hats, display merchandise, and sell goods during peak times. Many homesteaders acquired necessities at the secondhand stores and closeout sales that proliferated in Oklahoma Territory, offering the possessions of original claimants who failed to survive the rough years.[26]

Homesteading women plastered or papered the interior walls of the sod houses in an effort to make them more cozy and clean. Try as they might, they could not prevent dust from sifting in, and dirt and insects became the bane of the frontier homemaker. Centipedes, fleas, spiders, and flies invaded the bedding and the floor coverings. Most homemakers kept rags dipped in kerosene tied around furniture legs and similar rags tied to their children's legs to ward off insects. After cleaning the bugs from her daughters' bed, Mary Henderson wrote, "I never saw them so bad in my life, sometimes they tempt me to leave this country." Body lice presented a problem that demanded immediate action. When men returned from work on railroad construction and grain harvests, they often brought an infestation home, and everything had to be boiled and scrubbed in lye soap to eliminate the source.[27]

Diagnosing lice trouble proved more complicated in female patients, and doctors sometimes preferred to call the problem "prairie itch." One youngster recalled a neighbor's visit to his home. The neighbor confidentially explained to his mother that she had seen the doctor for treatment of prairie itch, but she was still in

This woman completes her homemaking chores in her temporary tent home near Anadarko. Photo courtesy of the Western History Collections, University of Oklahoma Library.

agony—nothing seemed to help. When the boy's mother suggested that the neighbor had lice, the woman exploded with anger and began to scream in outrage at such an accusation. The boy's mother calmly asked the neighbor to open her clothing and to allow her to inspect the garments. If she found nothing, she would apologize. When the lice were located, a second explosion of anger erupted, this time directed at the incompetent doctor. The boy remembered that his mother calmed her friend's wrath by reminding her that if the doctor "had told you you were lousy, you'd a-talked to him just like you are talking to me and you wouldn't a-let him look to see if you was lousy." Boiling water and lye soap soon corrected the problem.[28]

Many of the women in the initial homesteading families lived on the claims with their children in order to satisfy residency requirements, while their

husbands worked away from home to acquire much-
needed cash. Once they built a house and got their
crops planted in the field, many men hired out their
labor and animals to haul freight, break sod, work on
railroad construction, or follow the harvest north.
During these absences, women assumed complete
responsibility for the farms. Female decisions under
these circumstances counted in all areas of family life
and productivity. In addition to work in the house, they
worked in the fields, adding their strength to the draft
animals when needed. They plowed, planted, weeded,
and harvested. As one family watched drought destroy
their wheat crop, the woman insisted, to her husband's
amusement, on planting black-eyed peas in the
scorched field. That winter the family survived by
consuming and bartering the peas, and thereafter her
husband and children respected her suggestions.[29]

Women directed the labor of their children in the
same way that their husbands supervised field hands,
and they also doctored and managed herds of livestock.
One woman recalled that to provide milk for her
children, she roped a wild cow (from a local cattleman's
herd) and drove it and its calf home. It took some
weeks, but she tamed the animal for milking, and it
provided the beginning for her own herd. Another
homesteader decided to save her cattle even if it meant
defying the instructions of her husband. The family
had discovered that a war veteran held a prior claim to
their land, but he had agreed to take their cattle in
payment instead of forcing them to move. In her
husband's absence, the woman drove the cattle into a
secluded canyon during a snowstorm to hide them. The
soldier went away empty-handed, but the woman kept
her secret until her husband returned with his wages.
Then they renegotiated a settlement that saved her
herd.[30]

The hard work of settlement and the loneliness of early homesteads exacted a heavy toll on some women. Seigniora Russell Laune's memories of homesteading near Woodward includes an account of the tragedy of a young mother of two who quietly took her own life one night in the midst of an extended heat wave. Laune employed a couple who also had a tragic story: Exhausted from the daily routine, the young wife asked her husband to take her to a carnival in the next town. He protested that he and the horses were too tired, and he refused. The woman explained to Laune: "I didn't do nothin' but slave all day, washing, ironing, scrubbing, cooking, hoeing in the garden, waiting on two kids, day after day. I never got to go nowhere, or see anybody. I was fed up with all the work and never having anything pretty, or doing anything but work." She told her husband that if he did not take her to the carnival, she planned to leave him and move back home with her parents.

She packed the buggy the next morning and left with the children, but far from her destination, a wind and ice storm stopped them. They were nearly frozen to death when her husband found them. After weeks in a hospital, they returned to their farm, but because of the severe frostbite they had suffered, the woman was missing the fingers from one hand and the daughter had one arm amputated. The bitterness between the couple compounded the seriousness of the injuries as each blamed the other for the tragedy. They soon moved away, leaving Laune's community, to try to start over yet again.[31]

Of course hard work and family responsibilities affected men as well. In her letters Bertha Hutchins discussed two families in her immediate area in which the husbands had periodic "crazy spells" and became abusive. One neighbor tried to deal with her husband's problems privately because she feared his anger and violence. After he committed suicide, she admitted to her friends that he had tried to kill her and the children several times. Another, Hutchins's close friend, confided her own predicament to Bertha: Her husband behaved strangely when he chewed tobacco, and she had begged him to quit. "Although he has not been dangerous either time, yet there is no telling when he might be," Bertha wrote to her mother. "Myrtle thinks and so do I that if he does not give it up altogether that he will go crazy for all time, and she told him if it happened a few more times she would not live with him." Women respected the marriage bonds, but they also saw divorce as a means of escape from intolerable circumstances.[32]

Legislation in Oklahoma Territory required only a ninety-day waiting period for divorce, and confusion existed as to district or probate court jurisdiction. Both of these factors made Oklahoma Territory an attractive place for nonresidents to obtain divorces, for land speculators to acquire land through marriage and then relieve themselves of marital responsibilities, and for lawyers to grow wealthy—a divorce action might cost anywhere from $250.00 to $3,000.00. Between 1890 and 1896, Oklahoma Territory gained a reputation as the leading divorce mill, outstripping the Dakotas. Attorneys advertised in major cities the ease and privacy of obtaining a divorce in Oklahoma Territory, and hotel and boardinghouse operators mailed circulars to leading newspapers. Divorce agents approached train passengers in an attempt to divert them either to Guthrie or to Oklahoma City, both cities competing for the trade. Congress changed the residency requirement to one year in 1896; but before the boom ended, one area newspaper compared the volume of divorce actions to land office business.[33]

Several homesteading women took advantage of the lax restrictions to separate themselves from difficult marriages. The consequences of delay became evident in a letter written to the advice columnist of *The Oklahoma Farmer-Stockman*. In the letter a homemaker described her circumstances and asked for help. She was a middle-aged mother of nine children who had fulfilled every duty as a wife and mother, shared in all outdoor and field work, and spent her family's money carefully. She was being victimized by her evil-tempered husband, and he threatened to throw her out if she objected to his abuse. The woman explained, "I have worked my children hard in the cotton patch and he has managed all the affairs, and it was just as though I wasn't in the deal for he never did seem to consider me in his business affairs and today we have no home." The female columnist responded that any woman who sacrificed her health and happiness in the name of duty made herself a slave and her husband a slave-driver. In such circumstances divorce represented an alternative.[34]

Isolation proved to be a short-lived condition in territorial Oklahoma. Because of the nature of the land openings, the subsequent turnover of claims, and the rail system that was in place prior to settlement, the area filled rapidly. From 1890 to 1910, population density per square mile increased from 3.7 persons in Oklahoma Territory to 23.9 persons statewide and remained predominantly rural. Rather than loneliness, at times it was the congestion, noise, and demands of living in close quarters that plagued the Oklahoma homemaker. Black homesteader Thomas Black, Sr., lived alone in a dugout on his claim until he married. He chose a city woman from Austin, Texas, as his bride. Not wanting her to suffer the inconvenience of the dugout, they moved in with his brother's family

This black family in the Creek Nation was joined by many others coming from the South to make a home in the newly opened lands. Photo courtesy of the Archives & Manuscripts Division of the Oklahoma Historical Society.

until he could build a suitable home. His bride later confessed that the lack of privacy made her miserable there. "I did not want his people to know I was unhappy," she told her daughter, "so each day I would slip out alone and go to the orchard behind their log cabin and cry my eyes out." The Blacks eventually moved into their own home, and their children were born. They prospered near the all-black community of Langston, Oklahoma, and unlike many black families they remained throughout the racially oppressive years of early statehood. They and their children strengthened and unified the black community in the state.[35]

Those families who survived homesteading put down deep roots that demanded their loyalty and that of the children they abundantly bore. They left a record of courage, sacrifice, thrift, determination, and hard

work. They also set an example of commitment to
marriage and to their children. Gender strife, abuse,
and divorce existed; but close, loving partnerships were
also formed by the hardships of frontier life. The letters
that Bertha and Dorsey Hutchins wrote to their
families in Kansas revealed a love, intimacy, and unity
that strengthened them both. When Dorsey chopped
cane, Bertha helped for awhile and then sat in the
shade, piecing a quilt and keeping him company.
Dorsey churned butter, washed dishes, and helped
Bertha with the much-hated task of laundry. They read
to each other in the evenings. Bertha's letters to her
mother contained descriptions of Dorsey's domestic
teasing, his compliments to her, and his kisses. Just
before her twenty-first birthday, Bertha gave birth to a
daughter, and Dorsey tenderly changed the bed
coverings, bathed Bertha, and cared for them both. The
new arrival somewhat assuaged the grief they had
suffered over the death of their first child before they
left Kansas. Dorsey kept up the family correspondence
until Bertha was strong enough to write again.[36]

Perhaps Bertha and Dorsey's mutual consideration
might be attributed to their youth, but it emerged in
the writings of older couples as well. Dr. Sam Ross may
have tricked Maude into moving to Indian Territory,
but she steadfastly assisted his medical practice for
years. Friends in Ada, Oklahoma, helped the couple
celebrate their golden wedding anniversary in 1936,
and Maude proudly wrote about the thirty-four college
students whom they had boarded in their home or had
sponsored during their education.[37]

Mary and Alpheus Henderson were in their mid-
thirties when they moved to Oklahoma Territory with
their six children. Her diary revealed three more births
between 1901 and 1906. Each time, "Alphie" wrote the
diary entries Mary dictated for about a week after the

births. The children performed most of the housework
at their mother's direction, but the diary references to
"Alphie" document their mutual respect and trust, and
their sharing of decisions and child-rearing worries
and joys. The concerns of a 1906 entry will seem
timeless to any parent. The oldest son had stayed out
late in town and driven the horses too hard coming
home. "Alphie is much vexed," Henderson wrote. "It
does seem that the children care for nothing these days
but having what they term *fun*. I try to work all the
time to get ahead in order to give our children the
opertunities that I was denied." While she confided
most of her fears and prayers in the diary, like many of
her contemporaries, the only suggestion of the
impending births came in references to backache and
fatigue. Then, in the privacy of her diary, she would
give in to her pain and discomfort. These entries rarely
appeared, among the notations of the astonishing
amounts of work she performed, until the two weeks
prior to the announcement of a birth.[38]

The babies of the Henderson family appeared to
arrive without complications, but frontier conditions
often endangered the lives of mothers and infants.
Poverty, malnutrition, overwork, and the inadequacy of
rural medicine contributed to maternal and neonatal
deaths. Elva Ferguson gave birth to five children, only
two of whom survived infancy. In one family a letter
exists that illustrates the compounded nature of such
tragedies. It also reveals the social constraints on
written disclosure of the intimate details surrounding
pregnancy and birth. A young woman identified as E.
wrote to her female cousin announcing the recent
death of their aunt after childbirth. The pregnant
woman had suffered a serious fall and had become ill.
"It was so soon after the death of Little Robert," E.
wrote, "They were afraid of a mis—— (remember I will

have to tell it all and you will, please, dare not show this letter to anyone.)" The woman grew worse, and her husband sent for relatives and doctors. She began to run a high fever, and the baby, born prematurely, died. The doctors diagnosed the problem as blood poisoning and bled her. She became unconscious, and the doctors believed "there was no hope but if they could bleed her from the other arm, they could at least bring her conscious. They tried it, but she would not bleed. There was nothing to do then but wait." After hours of convulsions the woman died, surrounded by her husband, sister, and hysterical older children. E. sent a dried flower to her cousin from their aunt's grave.[39]

Continual childbearing affected not only the pioneer women, but their daughters as well. In a survey of a dozen rural women of present-day Oklahoma who left autobiographies, the total recorded births numbered seventy-six. Only one of the women listed fewer than three births. A witty young schoolteacher's remark illustrated the situation: Responding to a question about her kinship to another member of the family, she quipped that they were distantly related; he was the oldest of eleven children, and she was the youngest. Of the twelve women examined in the survey, four openly discussed the deaths of at least one child, but none reported miscarriages. Husbands, midwives, and women neighbors assisted at births in the absence of doctors, and the older children provided the nursing care. Mary Henderson helped her friends through childbirth, and during one of her own confinements she wrote, "the children have been doing the work, also caring for the baby and me. . . . the girls said 40 people called yesterday."[40]

Oldest daughters served as their mothers' surrogates at these times. Six-year-old Chloe Holt stayed at home to help her mother after a difficult birth that left her ill for some time. Holt's father sent the younger two children to stay with relatives during the ordeal. Even after she had recovered, Chloe's mother depended on her for child-care help. Mrs. Holt gave birth to three more children, bringing the total to seven. Chloe refused to welcome the final pregnancy. When her mother questioned her sullen behavior, Chloe replied, "I'll do all I can to help with the work, but I don't see why you want to have another baby. I'm fifteen now and I'd like to have some fun, but with another baby coming along there won't be a chance. There's six of us now, and that's enough." Chloe's father died suddenly, within a year after the child's birth, and financial needs forced Chloe to seek a teaching position. She married quite late in life and had no children of her own.[41]

Oldest daughters frequently responded in one of two ways to their own history of responsibility in large families. Some, like Chloe Holt, pursued careers, but others ran away from home and married at an early age to escape the constant burdens. Martha Smith, mother of thirteen children, expressed surprise and dismay that both of her oldest daughters eloped when they were fifteen years old. The first one married before Smith completed childbearing. When the second daughter ran away, Smith remembered, "I was very badly hurt. . . . She was a perfect litel mother to care for the younger children. I could all ways leave all day and go out to work or anywhere and feel that the babys would be all right with her." These two girls at least found temporary surcease from the demands of their mother's childbearing cares before their own childbearing began.[42]

Rather than limiting their births, some women solved their domestic burdens in another way. One homesteader, after several births spaced over the usual two-year intervals, took action. "By gum, if I am going to be J. L.'s brood mare," she announced to her family, "I am going to claim a brood mare's privilege and not do any work around the house!" After that the family employed live-in domestic help who cooked, cleaned, and washed. This woman may not have depended on her own daughters, but domestic help consisted of some other less fortunate family's spare daughters. The usual wage paid to white women and Indian women for domestic help averaged between \$1.00 and \$1.50 per week and included all household responsibilities. Black domestic help sometimes received no wage at all; they either boarded with the family or received cast-off clothing and surplus foodstuffs as payment.[43]

Birth, family, marriage, work, death—each of these passages marked the lives of rural women on the Oklahoma frontier. Their experiences resembled a mosaic rather than a flat, one dimensional scene, because they related to the land, to men, to other women, and to members of disparate racial groups in a myriad of configurations. The circumstances of location, time, race, and economic status shaped their conduct—fearful and brave, weak and strong, selfish and compassionate, foolish and wise, deceitful and honest. They refused to bind their lives and their possibilities to a single notion of gender respectability; hungering as ardently for security, recognition, and success as any other generation of women, they put their hearts and hands to any work that enriched the quality and satisfaction of their lives. Pioneer women failed to see themselves either as victims or as heroic symbols. Rather, they understood the value of their lives, and they demanded and received consideration and respect. They recognized their handicaps, bargained for power, mourned their tragedies, and celebrated their triumphs. Most importantly, they built for a future they earnestly believed would be better. They carried the lessons of experience to the Oklahoma frontier, added the strength of their determination, and planted again the seeds of the American dream.

3

New Neighbors and Friends

Adjustment to the conditions of life in territorial Oklahoma during settlement required skill, courage, an open mind, and a sense of humor. Uprooted from stable local societies in which they enjoyed a protected status, middle-class white women encountered circumstances far different from any they had known before. Elva Ferguson never forgot her family's first Christmas in Watonga and the cold, gloomy atmosphere surrounding it. She remembered the place as a "strange town full of strange people . . . not calculated to cheer the homesick feeling of a woman with boys who had always lived in Kansas." The unexpected kindness of an elderly German baker saved the holiday from disaster. Speaking in broken English, he presented Ferguson with a basket of beautiful pastries as a surprise on Christmas morning. Years later she still recalled how this gesture renewed her spirits.[1]

The necessity of crossing boundaries and making connections with men and women from a variety of backgrounds became immediately obvious to women settling in the Twin Territories. Without these steps toward mutual recognition of interdependence, communities could not have survived. The strength and nature of the bonds women established—across lines of race, class, and culture—contributed to the satisfaction of their lives and to the creation of the distinct character of Oklahoma life.

Female relationships with Indians in territorial Oklahoma took on a multitude of configurations and depended on several factors. Most important among the conditions influencing white interaction with Indians were: the time of arrival (the settlers who arrived as part of the 1889 Land Run had less information, experience, and protection than later settlers); the number of Indians in close proximity (many homesteaders had no contact with Indian groups); and the characteristics of the Indian group (marked differences existed between the Five Nations and Plains tribes). The first homesteaders in old Oklahoma Territory encountered primarily the Cheyenne and Arapaho Indians near El Reno. Pioneer children enjoyed watching the processions of Indians from a safe distance. One girl remembered that she was very much afraid, but she hid behind a tree or a corner of the house to watch the Indians and their horses, wagons, and lean dogs pass by on the Chisholm Trail. Another gained an education watching Indian men, women, and children swimming in a nearby creek in their "mother-nature suits." Children also entered the game of exchange. The Meek children traded some watermelons to an Indian woman for her baby, and they were nearly home before the Indian father rode up to reclaim his child. They were doubly disappointed that they had to hand over the child when they found out the watermelons had already been devoured.[2]

Sometimes children's games got out of hand, however. On one occasion, while a group of Cheyenne and Arapaho women were camped along a road near a school, some older schoolboys started teasing them by throwing dirt clods at them. After a while the women retired to their wagons, and the boys milled around the school yard. Minutes later the women came running with their skirts tucked around their leather leggings. They were brandishing skinning knives and screeching high-pitched yells. One little girl froze in fear by the woodshed as they circled the school grounds. Not until the furies reached her could she see the laughing eyes of the leader, who patted her head and murmured "little one" and other soft endearments. After the speedy retreat of the boys, the Indian women returned to their wagons, the advantage won. The little girl remembered that her father spanked all of the children for their part in this episode.[3]

Real danger of violence existed for both the homesteaders and the Indians in times of heightened fear. In the winter of 1889, Edna Randolph Slaughter's family lived in the last house on the outskirts of Oklahoma City among the homes of other black families. One night a rider observed a big Indian campfire and rode into town warning the settlers to get prepared. Slaughter recalled that for two days men arrived at her home armed with guns and knives to await the attack. A United States marshall finally informed them that the Indian gathering was a wedding and not a war party. Rumor of an assault on a white woman in 1895 led a mob to shoot, stab, and beat the Indian suspect before army troops could extricate him. A jury later found him innocent, the victim of mistaken identity. Individual acts of prejudice in more recent times were recalled as well. One Cheyenne woman remembered that as a girl she had been thrown from the second-story window of a grade school because the teacher "just didn't like Indians."[4]

Depending on the location of a particular homestead and the temperament of the individual settlers, some new residents had few contacts with Indians. As one rural woman, who lived in an area that was both Creek and Comanche country, explained, "we had no truck with them to speak of; they let us alone and we let them alone." Plains tribes' ceremonials, pow-wows, and government ration distributions provided entertainment that compared in the settlers' minds to a traveling carnival. Such events brightened the long summer evenings and satisfied the curiosity of the "civilized" settlers.[5]

In September 1889, a group of young women friends and their male companions traveled by buggy from Oklahoma City to El Reno to watch the United States government issue beef to the Cheyenne and Arapaho Indians and to find out "if the gruesome reports were true." The crowd of spectators swelled in size as the hour approached. They watched in horrified fascination as the former warriors chased down the cattle, ripped open the carcasses, and drank some of the warm blood. Then the Indian women and children joined the celebration; they skinned and butchered the beef and ate the raw liver and entrails. In addition to the cattle, the Indians killed gophers that were hopping in all directions during the chase and tossed them into the wagon with the meat. The female narrator of this reminiscence observed, "On the whole the Indians were quiet and well behaved, ignoring with admirable dignity the curious stares of those whites who had come from near and far to shudder and to gape." For her part she felt that the event had been a

complete success until they prepared to leave and an
elderly Indian opened trade negotiations for one of the
attractive and elaborately dressed young women in her
party. The woman's escort saved her from total embarrassment by indicating an unapproachable price, and
the old warrior strode back to his family. Future beef
issues failed to offer this spectacular display, however,
because the government decided to distribute the meat
already processed in order to wean the Indians away
from the traditional patterns of the hunt.[6]

When the Kiowa, Comanche, and Apache lands
opened in 1901, new Lawton residents also flocked to
the camps to watch Indian rituals. Accompanied by a
woman missionary, schoolteacher Lucy Gage traveled
around the countryside in a buggy, stopping at the
grass Wichita villages and observing the ceremonial
dances. As part of the celebration Wichita men,
intoxicated with a drink called mescal, cut their limbs
and smeared the blood on their bodies into designs that
were highlighted with colored dyes. They danced until
they dropped from exhaustion. More sensitive than
most settlers, Gage wrote, "At times I felt we had no
right to be there. What looked to us so barbaric and so
gruesome, was to them a sacrificial ceremony, honoring
the harvest season." New homesteader Mary Henderson was too frightened to allow her six children to
attend an Indian dance when they arrived in November 1901. Within six months, however, she loaded her
family into the wagon and journeyed to Hobart to
attend a picnic. "We enjoyed the day very much," she
recorded in her diary. "Seeing so many Indians, in their
gaudy attire, was in itself quite a show." For some
women, then, relationships with Indians constituted
only a source of leisure-time amusement.[7]

Large numbers of Indians living in close proximity
to white settlers offered the opportunity for personal

relationships to develop. Indian-white intermarriage became exceedingly common in Oklahoma. By the 1910 federal census only one-third of the total Indian population in Oklahoma claimed to be full-blood. More Cherokees intermarried with white citizens than any other group of Indians in present-day Oklahoma. At statehood, nineteen thousand of the Cherokee population of approximately twenty-three thousand reported mixed-blood, and of these 83.6 percent listed more than half white blood. Enterprising white men found material advantages in marriages to Indian women, which gained them access to Indian natural resources and land. But, in spite of considerable social stigma, some white women also married Indian men, especially those of the Five Nations. More than one woman corresponded with the chief of the Cherokee Nation asking him to find her a suitable partner. From Illinois Susie Grey, a thirty-four-year-old widow with two children, wrote to the chief that although she did not know him personally, she was in love with his country. She asked that her letter be regarded as confidential, and she requested, "If you know of a good Indian who would like to marry a white Lady please give him my address and I will send my photo on receipt of a letter from him."[8]

Some independent-minded daughters defied their parents' wishes to marry Indian men. A rural Chandler couple begged their daughter not to date Indian men. She worked away from home as a domestic helper for several families near the Sac and Fox Agency. In 1893 the couple became frantic about reports of her latest interest, a Sac and Fox widower. Her mother informed her, "if you can't have a beau that is white for heavens sake don't have any and although we all want to see you don't come home at all if you have to come with an indian." Her father warned her that area settlers were gossiping, and he threatened: "Now mind. You are of age but not out of my reach by law yet. Come home or behave yourself." The young woman married the man of her choice in 1894, and reconciled to the decision, her parents wrote to her to bring their new son-in-law home to get acquainted.[9]

Occasionally, such reconciliations occurred only after the birth of a child. A Duncan woman refused to meet her new Chickasaw daughter-in-law, and when a baby arrived, she told relatives she did not want to hear about "that little papoose." In a few months friends and relatives concerned about the estrangement staged a charade to unite the family at a community picnic. They secretly switched another couple's baby with the woman's new grandchild. After the woman had rocked and cuddled and praised the baby all afternoon, they revealed their secret and teased her about not knowing her own grandchild. Following a day of soul-searching and embarrassment, the grandmother apologized and welcomed her new Indian relatives into the family.[10]

The particularly female activities of pioneering opened the way for close personal relationships among women of all races. Childbirth, child care, food preparation, laundry, sewing, nursing the sick, and preparing the dead for burial all had greater meaning for women than the acts themselves. In these moments, racial, language, and cultural barriers often disappeared. Initially, Indian women expressed just as much curiosity about white settlers as did those homesteaders who traveled miles to observe Indian ceremonials. Many a woman settler jumped in surprise to see an Indian man or woman peering through a window or door, or marching into a tent to handle foreign-looking articles and clothing. Schoolteacher Lucy Gage remembered the afternoon three Kiowa

Indian and white women and children gather to socialize in Anadarko, 1901. Photo courtesy of the Western History Collections, University of Oklahoma Library.

women visited her tent. They walked in and rifled through the women's dresses, all the while "jabbering Kiowa," and when they were "fully satisfied as to our cooking arrangements, our beds which they examined as to mattress and covering, they went as quietly on their way as they had come." Another Lawton woman looked up to see an Indian man and woman staring through the door as she began to comb her long, thick hair. The man spoke enough English to tell her that his wife thought her hair was so beautiful she wanted to touch it. Although she was terrified, she allowed the Indian woman to smooth her hair and lift the heavy braids, and she enjoyed the flattery of the "Indian ecstacies" in the unfamiliar language. Gestures such as these prepared the way for more meaningful exchanges between women settlers and Indian men and women.[11]

A new emigrant from Illinois to Lawton was certain that every time she heard a coyote howl it was the signal for an Indian massacre. "After I got acquainted with the Indians," she reported later, "I used to do things for them." She baked pies for her shaman neighbor's ritual medicine encampments. Whenever he left home for a few days, he tied red yarn around his chickens' legs and brought them over to her coop for protection. From time to time he also deposited sums of money with her to keep for him. He explained to her, "Comanche woman no savvy money, and white woman heavy savvy." Several homesteading women reported this practice. When they had to be away from home, Indian families frequently took their blankets and anything else of value to a trusted homesteading neighbor to keep in order to prevent the evidently widespread pilfering of their possessions.[12]

Indian women sometimes filled the hunger for female companionship on the isolated homestead. Twenty-two-year-old Isola Hover lived on leased land among the Creek Indians. One afternoon she looked up from hanging out the wash to see a Creek woman standing in the corner of her yard. The woman smiled at Hover and said in perfect English, "I came to see you. I thought you might be lonesome." Hover invited her in for a visit, and the two became close friends. After a time Hover asked why her friend never came up to the door and knocked. She told Hover that as a child she had heard such brutal stories from her grandparents about Indian removal that she was afraid of white people. Other Indian women visited Hover in the same way, although most of them spoke no English. They came to have coffee and a smoke or chew of tobacco or to help with the washing chores, and when they needed to borrow a certain supply, they brought an empty container to show what was needed. Hover remembered, "we managed to make ourselves understood surprisingly well." When Hover's baby was born all of her new friends came to hold and examine him and to bring him small gifts.[13]

Childbirth and child care often proved to be unifying experiences for women. Indian midwives occasionally attended the births of white children. A Cordell family grew quite attached to the Indian midwife who stayed three weeks after the birth to care for the family. As she prepared to leave the father paid her the amount agreed upon, and tearfully, the mother presented her with a gift—a red silk, lace petticoat. The midwife enlivened many a subsequent church service when she wore her new treasure outside her traditional dress. Maude Ross accompanied her doctor husband on his calls to deliver Indian babies, and she later wrote, "It was always understood my services were a free will offering."[14]

Margaret Fullerton's mother sent for her sister, Aunt Mina, in Iowa to come for the birth of a new

Fullerton baby on a farm near Lawton. When the child was two weeks old, the Fullertons' Comanche neighbors brought their aged grandmother to see the baby. Mrs. Fullerton served tea and cookies while the grandmother cuddled, unwrapped, and examined the infant and chattered in fascination at her blond, fuzzy curls. Aunt Mina fidgeted nervously in the background, but Margaret believed that this experience taught her "what we had told her all along. The Indians were our friends." Margaret and her brothers failed to understand the Indian woman's curiosity. They often played with the Comanche neighbor babies, and they thought the only difference lay in their own mother's embarrassing neglect to make a cradleboard for their little sister.[15]

Mrs. Fullerton and the Comanche women shared the work and the joys of child-rearing on the frontier. The Indian women taught her how to make the difficult task of washing in the hot summer more enjoyable: they showed her how to accomplish this work at the nearby stream by making three stone pools for soaking, washing, and rinsing. Meanwhile, the children stayed occupied swimming and fishing. At the end of the day they all enjoyed a fish fry. In return, Fullerton taught her neighbors how to use their government-issue sewing machines to sew rows and rows of bright-colored ribbons on their dresses. The women made such times day-long affairs in which the children played together and the women worked and visited.[16]

Margaret Fullerton believed that "It was really the children who were the binding factor in community integration." This seemed especially true in terms of relationships between black and white rural residents in the Twin Territories. Concern for children sometimes overrode longstanding racial antipathy and brought out the best examples of human cooperation.[17]

Among the successful participants in the 1893 Cherokee Strip run were Albert C. Davis and his wife, Georgia Ann. The Davis family was one of only a few black families who settled in what became Grant County. The Davises and their eight children built a half-dugout and farmed their land, surrounded by white neighbors, for twelve years. As statehood approached in 1905 and racial hostility became a political weapon of parties contending for power, the Davis family sold out and returned to Kansas. Fifty years later many of the old settlers recorded their memories of the homesteading experience. When their neighbors recalled the Davis family, they remembered three things. First, that Davis carried the mail along a sixty-four-mile route six days a week in an open buggy, never failing to get through in even the worst weather. This courage was made the more remarkable by the fact that a mob had hanged a black man at Pond Creek, one of the stops on the route. Second, the Davis family enriched the school and social events, church services, Christmas parties, and debates of the community. Most importantly, Arthur Baird vividly recalled the excitement of the time they worked together to save the life of a Davis child.[18]

Davis and the oldest son had gone to work the wheat harvest in Kansas, while Georgia Ann and the children held down the claim. One afternoon, fourteen-year-old Clarence Davis was bitten by a rattlesnake while he was herding cattle. The Davis girls ran to get their nearest neighbor, Baird, and he administered whiskey to the boy and sent for the doctor. When the doctor refused to come to a black homestead, the neighboring families gathered at the Davis home and decided to "sweat" the child. They brought quilts, blankets, pans, and jugs. They tied the child down in the sun, covered him with the quilts, and set tubs of boiling water on top of him. Clarence remained ill for some time, but he survived, and the homesteaders congratulated themselves on their cooperative effort. "Having a darky family in the neighborhood had its complications," Hattie Holladay remembered, "but there were several of the neighbors would break over the race prejudice and perform many kindly acts." She recalled a family that had welcomed Georgia Ann and her children at their table when the Davises ran out of food in Albert's absence and another occasion when some women baked a cake and surprised Georgia Ann with a party.[19]

Newlywed Lola Green illustrated the unspoken limits of private female relationships between black and white women. She and her husband bought their farm from a black couple, known as Uncle Jake and Aunt Bell, who continued to live in a cabin on the land. Green's parents had taught her to use the term "colored people," the word "nigger" being offensive and "Negro" too pretentious. She knew that neighbors hired blacks for farm work and kitchen help, but that they excluded them from any social gathering. Green found her new husband's attachment to Uncle Jake confusing. The two men sat for long periods chatting and whittling just as her husband did with other neighbors. "I tried my best to tone down Jim's friendliness with Uncle Jake," she wrote. Shortly after that Aunt Bell came to her door bringing fresh-baked bread, and "Before I realized it, I was sitting talking with her as freely as Jim did with her husband, forgetting all about her dark skin." For several years the two couples remained friends, but only within private boundaries. Green emphatically added to her memoirs that they continued their visits, but that unlike her relationships with their other neighbors, "Of course that doesn't mean that I ever called her and

Uncle Jake 'Mr. and Mrs. Anderson'!" Private friendships were accepted, but public courtesies were
denied.[20]

Humane, compassionate relationships and ugly,
violent actions existed side by side in the Twin
Territories. Margaret Rounds, the last of nine children
in a tenant-farming family, moved from farm to farm
up and down the Arkansas River bottomlands in the
Creek Nation. Often her white family constituted the
minority among homesteaders near all-black settlements such as Wybark. Rounds's mother nursed the
sick in this community, and when necessary she prepared the bodies for burial and lined the coffins with
white muslin. "Mother did anything for anybody that
she could," Rounds wrote. "It didn't matter to her if
they were good or bad, white or black, she was kind to
all." On one occasion after Rounds's mother nursed one
black child through a serious illness and prepared
another's coffin, the family was awakened in the
middle of the night when a relative of the child brought
in a freshly butchered side of beef to show his gratitude. Rounds's family refrained from asking any
questions about its ownership and accepted the gift
graciously. Rounds's memoirs reported more than
pleasant relationships, however. When the daughter of
a black neighbor shot and killed her own father,
Rounds remembered that "everyone just took the
attitude that it was just one less Negro, so nothing was
done about it." Rounds also described her own terror at
a violent black-white racial confrontation at Coweta
that left several people dead.[21]

Black children sensed the uneasy state of affairs
as well. Edna Randolph Slaughter, living on the outskirts of Oklahoma City, recounted, "I was afraid most
of the time, I don't know of what, possibly because my
mother cried so much." Pioneer women shared both

responsibility for courage against prejudice and blame for its ultimate result, as an incident in early-day Guthrie illustrated. A white woman charged a fifteen-year-old black boy with insulting her and had him locked in the jail. She then obtained a rope and spent the remainder of the day inciting a crowd to lynch the boy. The sheriff's wife, coming into town from their homestead, saw an angry mob gathering at the front of the jail. She devised a *Huckleberry Finn*-like charade to save the boy's life and, possibly, that of her husband. She blackened her own face and dressed the terrified boy in girls' clothing while her husband calmed the crowd. Then she and the boy exited through a rear door, both of them armed with pistols concealed in market baskets. She escorted the boy by train to Oklahoma City where she turned him over to the authorities. A jury later acquitted him of all charges.[22]

Between 1890 and 1920 the black population of Oklahoma hovered at only approximately 7 percent and was concentrated in five counties. As was the case with the Indian population, some white homesteading women rarely had any contact with blacks. One woman reported that she had read *Uncle Tom's Cabin* and had heard the most commonly used word for blacks, "nigger," but she had never seen a black person until she journeyed with her father to sell wheat. In a rather loud voice she asked her father, "Is that a nigger?" He scolded her and told her never to use that word again. "First place, it isn't right, second place they don't like it," he told her. After that she exercised care with her speech, but she seldom saw a black person until she grew up.[23]

The Davis children and other children of black settlers attended integrated sod-house schools at first, but distinctions existed in the way that these children were treated from the beginning. For example, white

Many of the first schools were integrated, as this Prairie Center School photograph indicates. Photo courtesy of the Western History Collections, University of Oklahoma Library.

children and black children drank from separate water buckets. Once a new teacher discovered an unpleasant practice: When the white children ran out of water, they used the other bucket and made the black children carry in more. The white youngsters had little concern about drinking after each other; they just wanted to get out of the work. "One of the first rules I put in force," the teacher stated, "was to see that the white children remained responsible for their own water." Near Kingfisher in Oklahoma Territory a girl remembered that her parents sent her to school at an earlier age than usual in order to fill up the schoolroom and crowd out the black children, so that a separate school would have to be built. Kingfisher operated segregated schools as early as 1892. Citizens in each county voted to determine whether there would be separate schools, which would require an additional tax for that purpose to be administered by county commissioners. In 1894 the Oklahoma territorial legislature passed an education segregation act mandating separate schools funded through a special property tax. Many counties ignored the laws and refused to support any education for blacks. As late as 1906, black parents in Pauls Valley were forced to sue the school board in district court to open a school for the forty children who had been refused admission to white schools. The segregation legislation and the subsequent poorer-quality education for blacks made interracial relationships among women, except in terms of a mistress/servant-level interaction, even less possible.[24]

Conflicting imperatives forced white women of the Twin Territories to examine interracial relationships. On the one hand, they expressed abiding confidence that they were building something new: The rest of the continental United States existed in complete form, but in their imaginations this virgin land offered the possibilities for making better choices, for creating an improved commonwealth. As an early settler expressed it, "We visioned then what a pleasant place would develop for those who would come along with the years to carry on our plans for good homes, good schools, and good churches." On the other hand, the population of the Five Nations had a strong southern legacy, and the majority of the white population emigrated from southern states. This heritage contributed a long-standing racial etiquette and still-vivid memories of the Civil War and Reconstruction. There was an increasing governmental apathy toward racial policy decisions after the Supreme Court case *Plessy* v. *Ferguson* established the legitimacy of a "separate but equal" doctrine. A growing national cultural stance, based on racial prejudice, added to the dilemma of interracial relations.[25]

Journalist Helen Candee's distorted description of territorial Oklahoma in *The Forum* in 1898 illustrated a pattern in national reporting. According to Candee, stranded blacks lived "literally on the crumbs which drop from the white man's table," but "water-melons to eat and cotton to pick are the two blessings which mitigate life's curse for the negro in Oklahoma." Two years later, Candee published a revised, glowing account of development on the Oklahoma frontier in the *Atlantic Monthly*, but she still found only black field hands—"the natural cotton-picker" with "short and optimistic views" that, according to Candee, limited their own productivity and harmed their white employers.[26]

What path might white women follow in a new land that would create a world of dignity and smooth the divisions already apparent in settlement? Unfortunately, in Oklahoma and Indian Territories that path constituted only temporary racial cosmetics and not substantive alteration. Women quibbled about the niceties of teaching their children a proper term to use for black people, but they also taught them racially derogatory expressions, songs, poems, and stories. For instance, one woman remembered her recitation as a child of a humorous speech about a black mother scolding her son for stealing a watermelon; the audience's laughter came when the mother reminded him to steal a ripe one next time. She performed this charade for groups of people on several occasions at her parents' request. Expressions of the times such as "there's a nigger in the woodpile" indicated that something was amiss in the situation. Brazil nuts were called "nigger toes," and slingshots were called "nigger shooters." White women limited social contacts with blacks, and when friendships arose, they believed they had to explain them away or hide them. Under no circumstances would they condone intermarriage. They hired black women to cook and scrub, and they paid them wages far lower than those paid to white women, then complained about their laziness. Finally, in the one arena in which Oklahoma and Indian Territory women could vote and hold office, school elections and school boards, they restricted opportunities for black education. In terms of black and white female relationships, outside of exceptional acts of courage and sorority, female actions in territorial Oklahoma mirrored those of their southern contemporaries.[27]

Aside from racial attitudes, the southern legacy in present-day Oklahoma also influenced the way white women related to each other. Margaret Fullerton described her northern-born mother's initiation into the predominantly southern society near Sterling in Oklahoma Territory. Mabell Fullerton "was enough different to be a minority and had to patiently work her way into being accepted," Margaret remembered.

Female friendships grew in shared tasks such as this sewing
bee in Mehan, c.1901. Photo courtesy of the Western History
Collections, University of Oklahoma Library.

Joining the Ladies' Aid Society offered the best
opportunity for rural women to meet, socialize, gossip,
exchange ideas, and do good works. They sometimes
held meetings at the homestead of new young couples,
and each woman contributed items such as baking
pans or pillowcases to help the young woman set up
housekeeping. They quilted, put up shelves, and wall-
papered the inside of the house, all the while enjoying
the company and the respite from their own routines.
Most of the time they met in the homes of the
members.[28]

Many of the women of the local Ladies' Aid Society
expressed apprehension about Mabell Fullerton. She
originated from Iowa, and she was a city woman with
a good education—that fact alone made her the object
of suspicion. P. G. Fullerton was not a real farmer. He
practiced law, and the Fullerton home was the finest in
the area, so the women thought Mabell might be
pretentious. Also, Margaret knew, "word had been

passed around that Mama was a northerner and had never learned to chew or spit. In fact, she didn't even smoke a pipe!" As the hour of the meeting approached, Fullerton noticed the women gathering in their wagons some distance from the house. One member parked her buggy at the top of the hill, waiting to see if anyone intended to stay. Finally, Fullerton went outside to invite them all into her home, and she found the Ladies' Aid Society engaged in a tobacco spitting contest, challenging each other to see who could shoot juice the highest over the wagon wheel. They intended to finish the chew before they went inside. This initial encounter proved that Fullerton was willing to accept their practices, and she became an active member of the group.[29]

Northern traditions and southern traditions in Oklahoma Territory required more fundamental accommodation as well. Margaret Fullerton remembered with the excitement of a child all the Fourth of July preparations in her family. Her mother fried doughnuts, the children wet down gunny sacks in a big tub of water and placed some over watermelons to cool them in the barn, and her father and grandfather rode into town to buy a load of fireworks. When they returned, they hung up the big American flag. The children started the noisy celebration early in the day and failed to notice for several hours that their neighbors' homes remained quiet. Margaret's father, P. G. Fullerton, went over to talk with them and was politely told that celebrating the Fourth of July was "strictly a Yankee idea." "This was a new interpretation of our holiday," Margaret recalled. The family talked the situation over and decided to make a second effort. Mabell Fullerton asked another northern family, who lived two miles away, to come over; and P. G. invited the Indian neighbors, who, Margaret stated, were "neutral as far as the Civil War was concerned. They had survived their own wars with the Americans and they always had lost."[30]

Margaret recalled that the grown-ups held a forum and explained to each other why the Civil War had been fought and why it was still important to sing "Dixie." They came to a compromise and agreed that the southern families would join the Fullerton celebration and the Fullertons would enjoy fireworks with the southerners on their celebration at Christmastime. P. G. Fullerton gave a patriotic speech, and the crowd alternately sang "Dixie" and "The Star-Spangled Banner." The booming fireworks lasted until late that night. "The Civil War was one step nearer to being finished," Margaret believed, and "At least a few more Indians knew that we were their friends." Actually, what had taken place was a cultural accommodation that incorporated southern sympathies. As Fullerton added, the practice of standing when "Dixie" was played was one that continued well into her high school years, and failure to show due honor carried a penalty.[31]

Territorial Oklahoma women of southern background brought with them the cultural mythology of the antebellum South, carefully nurtured memories of their antecedents, and a determination to preserve and dignify an image of themselves and their past. The daughter of a schoolteacher, Janice Holt grew up in Indian Territory. The family made yearly trips back to Charleston, Arkansas, in August to visit with family and to take part in the Confederate War Veterans reunion. The two-day affair opened with a parade of the veterans, marching smartly in their gray uniforms to the band's stirring rendition of "Dixie." Holt's grandfather carried the Confederate flag, and when it passed, the men removed their hats and the women wept. Holt sympathized, "They may have lost that war, and it broke their hearts to know they had lost it, but they were never truly defeated." She insisted that until the day he died, her grandfather believed that the southern states had a legal right to secede and form their own country. "I grew up saturated in that belief," Holt wrote, "and not until I was a mature woman did I quit quoting the Preamble to the Declaration of Independence as the basis of that belief." The reunion picnic, organized by the United Daughters of the Confederacy (UDC), followed the parade, and baseball games, speeches, and band music filled the afternoons and evenings.[32]

Holt's grandmother only discussed the fear, hunger, destruction, and shame of the war years in private moments. Holt understood that these memories summoned for her grandmother "a nightmare time of want and privation and the slow poison of defeat." With the passage of time Holt's grandmother could "talk about it all without bitterness, but it did something to her deep in her soul." She became penurious with money and provisions and kept scrupulous accounts of every penny in the family. She also demanded unquestioned family unity and mutual assistance in the face of tragedy. The memories of many southern women—of widowhood, families broken by death, and children left orphaned—created a strong impulse in them to extend the bonds of kinship and child-rearing.[33]

A familiar pattern emerged in another Oklahoma Territory pioneer's documentation of her family history: Laressa Cox wrote that her grandmother, a Civil War widow with three children, married a war-veteran widower with seven children and moved to Texas, where they developed a large farm. Their son brought home his infant daughter when his first wife died. Laressa, the girl reared by her grandmother and aunts, in turn took care of her father's seven children in Oklahoma Territory when his second wife died.[34]

All of the women in Janice Holt's family belonged to the Daughters of the Confederacy, which maintained an active membership in present-day Oklahoma. In 1906 Mrs. Serena Carter of Ardmore rallied the local chapter of the UDC to establish a home for indigent veterans, their wives, and widows. A temporary site was established at McAlester and existed until 1909, when the Oklahoma Division of the United Confederate Veterans and the UDC formed a private corporation and began soliciting funds to build a permanent home at Ardmore on a twenty-four-acre tract donated by Mrs. Lutie Hailey Walcott.[35]

During the campaign for donations, Ora Eddleman Reed wrote about the Oklahoma UDC for *Sturm's Magazine*. Reed, a part-Cherokee woman of exceptional ability, had written, edited, and published the unique *Twin Territories: The Indian Magazine* for six years (1898–1904), beginning when she was only eighteen years old. Reed, now married, continued to provide historical articles, interviews, and pieces of fiction for *Sturm's*. In 1910 she explained the character of the UDC:

> The women who are active in the work have come to Oklahoma from the old southern states, where loyalty to the cause for which the South suffered, bled and died, has never faltered, where heroic women stepped forth directly after the war and picked up the thread of broken fortunes, made new homes in places left desolate by cruel war, buoyed the helpless, and by womanly strength and courage have done a noble part in the upbuilding of the South.

Now they engaged in projects like the Confederate Veterans' Home to create a more equitable attitude

The Cherokee Teachers Institute drew participants from a large area, 1890. Photo courtesy of the Western History Collections, University of Oklahoma Library.

toward the South and its institutions. At all UDC state and national meetings, the stars and bars flew side by side with the stars and stripes, both beloved by the "true womanhood" of the organization.[36]

When construction on the veterans' home halted due to a shortage of funds, Governor Lee Cruce agreed to complete the facility on the condition that the corporation transfer the deed to the state of Oklahoma. In 1911 the UDC state chapters completely furnished the rooms, and the home opened to eighty-five residents. The UDC chapters continued to support the home and its occupants and provided teas and special parties for the veterans' entertainment. As late as 1955, twelve Confederate widows remained, in addition to veterans from subsequent American wars.

A southern mind-set also influenced education for women in Oklahoma. Anne Wade O'Neill of Chickasha contacted a number of the new state legislators to convince them to establish a separate women's preparatory school in addition to the coeducational institutions of the state. They responded in 1908 by creating the Oklahoma Industrial Institute and College for Girls. Cattleman J. B. Sparks donated land near Chickasha that had been his Chickasaw daughter's allotment. Sparks had sent his daughter away to a prestigious women's college in Missouri, and she had died there in 1904. In her memory, he wanted to provide an institution to educate young Oklahoma women close to home. The legislators modeled the school after the Mississippi State College for Women and opened it to white female Oklahoma citizens between the ages of twelve and thirty-five who possessed a good moral character and passed a basic skills examination. The aims of the school were to provide a literary education and an industrial education. Officials wanted to educate the future homemakers of the country with skills to provide "not only economy, comfort and convenience but harmony, culture, and refinement." The school motto read, "Not for livelihood but for life."[37]

The institution struggled to survive the funding handicaps of its first few years, operating out of local churches until 1911 when the school moved into its new main building. Another early hindrance to growth resulted from the name: in some states "industrial institute" implied a correctional facility. In 1912, after a few uninformed county judges sentenced some incorrigible girls to the college, school administrators decided to change the name to the Oklahoma College for Women. At this time they also refined the curriculum to develop an academic degree and a technical degree in addition to the four-year preparatory program. The college prospered and improved under the direction of President G. W. Austin and received accreditation in 1919. It remained an institution devoted exclusively to women until 1965.[38]

In addition to their material possessions, homesteading women carried the cultural freight of their former environments with them to the Twin Territories. The divided heritage of North and South met in the West and demanded accommodation. Women's responses took many shapes, and they formed partnerships for survival that transcended barriers of race, class, and culture. However, they placed limitations on the extent of those relationships, according to complex standards of acceptable behavior that they defined themselves. Individual friendships might vary in nature, but mainstream responsiveness to non-whites depended on a combination of cultural factors.

4

Educating the Cherokee Elite

Elva Ferguson's pioneer narrative represents exclusively the western half of what would become the state of Oklahoma: short grass country of wheat, cattle, and independent sod-house homesteaders. She recognized, however, that "a state is but a gathering together of communities," the whole was created by "the combined efforts of all its citizens." Eastward, the inhabitants of Indian Territory contributed a different heritage to this partnership on the land.[1]

The state of Oklahoma came into existence through the political unification of Oklahoma Territory and Indian Territory in 1907. That union also solemnized the most powerful and enduring metaphor of the state and its people, an image of cowboys and Indians. Disregarding the actual statehood proceedings, contemporary journalists promoted the creation of the two archetypes: Mr. Oklahoma Territory, in boots and broad-brimmed hat, proved himself an acceptable suitor by virtue of the hard work it had taken to convert the rolling, semiarid lands into wheat fields and substantial stock farms. Miss Indian Territory, clad in buckskin, brought to the union her dowry of fertile soil, mineral wealth, and forests. The constitution of the new state had cleared the way for this interracial marriage by providing in Article Twenty-three that the term "white race" applied to all persons except those of African descent. The children of this union could thereby grow up with the rights and privileges of the citizens of all other states. On November 16, 1907, President Theodore Roosevelt signed the proclamation declaring Oklahoma a state.[2]

At 10:00 A.M. on the steps of Carnegie Library in Guthrie, Oklahoma, the first governor, Charles N. Haskell, took the oath of office and a mock wedding ceremony commenced. Contrary to innumerable school pageants that subsequently reenacted this drama, Mr. Oklahoma Territory left his boots and cowboy hat at home and Miss Indian Territory certainly refused to wear feathers and buckskin. As historian Murial Wright wrote, Indian Territory citizens "were sensitive to the idea that they were uncultured, living in a backwoods region." They wanted the rest of the United States to appreciate what they considered a long history of culture, refinement, and prosperity. Oklahoma City businessman C. G. Jones represented Oklahoma Territory and married in formal, striped trousers and black suit coat. The bride, Anna Trainor Bennett, of Muskogee, wore a stylish, floor-length lavender satin dress, a large picture hat, and gloves. She carried a single mauve chrysanthemum. Mrs. Bennett was of Cherokee descent and was known for her beauty and charm. Cherokee schoolgirls sang the "Star-Spangled Banner" and traditional wedding selections, and Reverend W. H. Dodson, pastor of the First Baptist Church of Guthrie, performed the ceremony.[3]

In this scenario, the mock marriage of the cowboy to the Indian "princess" represented a blend of American myth and historical reality. White men often intermarried with Indian women in Oklahoma and thereby secured tribal rights to land and natural resources. Western-history scholars have given considerable attention to the importance of the cowboy to Oklahoma culture, to the American West as a whole, and even to the American identity. The perseverance of an imaginary Indian princess, however, requires closer examination. Since colonial days a dual image of Indian women existed in American culture: on one side was the beautiful Pocahontas, the Powhatan chief's daughter who, according to legend, saved John Smith's life and helped feed the starving colonists at Jamestown, and on the other side were the ugly, vicious drudges of the captivity narratives and the early novels. Image and reality confronted each other regularly in the person of the Indian woman. The arrival of the mythic Cherokee princess on statehood day resulted from years of cultivation of the image of an Indian princess by missionaries, teachers, and government employees—many of them women. The symbol of a Cherokee "bride" also attempted to establish the primacy in the national public mind of the acculturated Five Tribes (the so-called Five "Civilized" Tribes) over the Plains Indian cultures. The diversity of the approximately sixty-seven Indian groups in Oklahoma after the Civil War makes an analysis of the lives of Indian women nearly impossible, but an examination of selected experiences of Cherokee and Kiowa women and of the white female agents of acculturation living among them provides a revealing contrast.

Turn-of-the-century Wild West shows toured America impressing white audiences with trick riding, fancy shooting, and pageantry. The high point of the program, a reenactment of the death of General George Custer and his troops at the Little Big Horn, portrayed Indians as screaming, blood-thirsty feathered savages. Reformers insisted, however, that Indians were educated, elegant, artistic, refined, and prosperous—or capable of becoming so. Somewhere between the two extremes, Indian women struggled to define their own lives in a rapidly changing world. Cherokee and Kiowa women responded to a differing range of alternatives that had been thrust upon them by government officials and by white agents of acculturation. The extent to which they embraced expected patterns of behavior determined their acceptability within white culture. However, in psychological and material ways both groups insisted on preserving a sense of their tribal identity within the new cultural model.[4]

The Cherokees, originally mountain people of the upper Ohio River area, had been pushed south by their Iroquois enemies to the present Tennessee-Carolinas-Georgia region by the time of European contact. Approximately twenty thousand Cherokees lived in villages composed of clay dwellings surrounding a centrally located town house. The women cultivated corn, beans, and potatoes and produced pottery and baskets. Household responsibilities provided the major duties of women, but they held a relatively high status in village life. Land inheritance and kinship were matrilineal, and women originally participated in council meetings and elections and, sometimes, in warfare. The men cleared the fields, hunted, and trapped, selling furs and pelts to the traders. Leisure-time activities might include dances, ball games, and gambling using painted beans. One historian described the Cherokees as "well-built," "medium to tall in height," and noted for their beautiful women. By the middle of the eighteenth century the tribe engaged extensively in international trade, to the point of dependency on trader supplies of guns, knives, utensils, cloth, and vermillion.[5]

The production of cloth proved to be an opening wedge to acculturation. The Cherokees appreciated elegant dress, and the women initially began to cultivate cotton and to request instruction in the use of spinning wheels, cards, and looms that were offered by the American government. Cherokee men resisted agriculture at first, telling agent Return J. Meigs that as the "favorites of the great Spirit" they were not intended to "live the laborious lives of whites." Meigs continued to dispense farming implements, however, and he simultaneously encouraged the marriage of Cherokee women to neighboring non-Indian men. The intermarriage of the Cherokees—with Irish, German, English, Welsh, and Scottish families—produced a mixed-blood elite who acquired slaves and developed extensive plantations, stock farms, and businesses.[6]

The first thirty years of the nineteenth century brought both the zenith of the Cherokees in the East and the beginning of a long, futile struggle to retain tribal sovereignty. Sequoyah (George Guess) perfected the eighty-five-character syllabary of the Cherokee language, and reading and writing spread through the tribe. In 1827, a convention of tribal delegates adopted a code of laws, a constitution, and a government composed of legislative, executive, and judicial departments. The first Indian newspaper in America, the *Cherokee Phoenix* (printed in both English and Cherokee), appeared a year later. The American Board of Commissioners of Foreign Missions sent missionaries to establish schools and churches, to convert the

Cherokees to Christianity, and also to inculcate in them the values of capitalism and republicanism. The American Board schools concentrated their efforts on the children of the tribal elite, especially the young women. "It is of great consequence to have the females of the principal families well instructed," one board member counseled, and "In this way only will education become popular and fashionable." Missionaries taught the young women to read and to write English, to recite Bible verses, and to work arithmetic problems. They held out to the young women the promise of prosperous marriages to substantial young men if they acquired education, refinement, and modesty. The training also required that they be able to spin, weave, quilt, manage a tidy household, and do fancy stitchery.[7]

In spite of these many advances toward an Anglicized way of life, the pressure of American settlers for Cherokee land that had begun with the first treaty in 1785 now reached overwhelming proportions. At New Echota, Georgia, in 1835, factions of the Cherokee Nation signed a treaty in which they agreed to removal to Indian Territory. Some groups fled to the isolated mountain retreats to hide and remained there, forming what is known today as the Eastern Cherokees. Another faction, under the leadership of Principal Chief John Ross, attempted to fight removal through the courts (*The Cherokee Nation* v. *Georgia*) and to delay the ratification and execution of the removal treaty. General Winfield Scott supervised the forced removal of the Cherokees over the eight-hundred-mile march to Indian Territory in the fall and winter of 1838–39. This travail became known as the "Trail of Tears."[8] Deaths resulting from hardship, disease, and starvation have never been accurately calculated, but a recent population study indicates

that the majority of the Cherokees reached Indian
Territory only to die in great numbers there. The
Cherokee population may have declined by as much as
30 percent until stability was reached in the 1850s.
After this, intermarriage with non-Indians and
adoption from other Indian groups contributed to the
growth in numbers to a recorded population of approximately 22,000 in 1890. By 1910, the federal census
listed a Cherokee population of 29,610, only approximately 6,000 of whom claimed full blood.[9]

The Cherokee immigrants initially concentrated
their settlements in the eastern wooded valleys of the
land allocated to them in the northeastern corner of
Indian Territory, not venturing beyond the area
bounded by the Grand and Arkansas Rivers. Some of
the more resistant members again retreated to isolated
areas, clinging to a traditional way of life. At Tahlequah the disparate factions of the tribe reunited,
formed a new government, and began to build anew the
accustomed southern small farm and business
economy or, in some cases, the slave-owning, plantation
production system. Presbyterian, Moravian, Baptist,
and Methodist-Episcopal missionaries established or
strengthened mission stations and schools. The most
prominent among them were Park Hill, under the
direction of Samuel Austin and Ann Orr Worcester,
which was located near Tahlequah, and Dwight
Mission, which had been in operation since 1820 in
Arkansas and had moved to a Sallisaw Creek location
in 1829.[10]

The Cherokee Nation established a public school
system in 1841 that grew to eighteen schools within
two years, providing a common-school education in
both English and Cherokee. Sons and daughters of the
elite continued their higher education at eastern
schools such as Princeton, Yale, Dartmouth, and

Mount Holyoke Seminary. In addition, numerous
Cherokee girls attended Miss Sophia Sawyer's School
for Girls in Fayetteville, Arkansas. Delia A. Vann
represented the ideal model of a successful Cherokee
woman. Delia was the daughter of Joseph "Rich Joe"
Vann, a wealthy plantation owner in Georgia. After
Georgia officials seized his home, Vann emigrated west
and duplicated his Georgia home near Webbers Falls,
Indian Territory. He owned several hundred slaves, the
fastest racehorse in the territory, a mercantile
business, ferry service, and steamboat. Delia first
attended tribal schools, then Sawyer's School for Girls,
and she completed her education at Mount Holyoke
Seminary. In 1856 she married Oliver Hazard Perry
Brewer, who achieved the rank of lieutenant colonel in
the Confederate Army during the Civil War, served as
superintendent of education for the Cherokee Nation,
and became a justice on the Supreme Court of the
Cherokee Nation. Delia's youngest son, Oliver Hazard
Perry Brewer, Jr., became chairman of the Cherokee
National Board of Education, a delegate to the Oklahoma State Constitutional Convention, and later a
state district judge. Delia Vann and numerous other
young Cherokee women became internal agents of
acculturation, and their success illustrated the
primary factors in an important equation: proper
education plus fortuitous marriage equalled Ameri-
canized offspring—a pattern that was repeated
consistently in the Cherokee Nation.[11]

By 1846, Cherokee agent Pierce M. Butler had
reason to boast of the progress of the Cherokee people
in Indian Territory. In a report to the superintendent
of the Western Territory, Major William Armstrong,
Butler discussed the advancement of the Cherokee
farms and praised the contributions of the women:
"They are fond of spinning and weaving and manifest

great ingenuity in the manufacture of domestic cloth,"
he wrote. "The material is well manufactured, and in
the selection, variety, and arrangement of colors, they
exhibit great taste and skill." Subject to the decision of
a committee of leading Cherokee women, Butler had
awarded silver cups as prizes in a competition a year
earlier for the best examples of homespun cloth,
coverlets, belts, and socks. This competition led to the
organization of the Agricultural Society of the
Cherokee Nation. Promoting the advancement of agriculture, domestic manufacture, and livestock production, the members met annually in Tahlequah to
exhibit their workmanship, hear programs, exchange
information, and receive their awards. In his report,
Butler also included praise for the Cherokee printing
press and for the strength of the temperance movement, citing these developments as positive stimuli to
Cherokee progress.[12]

Butler also reported an improved attitude toward
tribal women that greatly impressed him. He commented that among Cherokees a woman was no longer
regarded "as a slave—as personal property—but as a
friend and companion." Evidence of this could be seen
in the "now high and exalted estimate of female
character, disclosed by the countenance and encouragement given to her cultivation, and the many
opportunities afforded her of improvement." Butler
believed that this new respect for women influenced
the general improvement in manners, dress, and
conduct of all the Cherokees. These observations
reflected Butler's approval of the Cherokees' adoption
of Euroamerican cultural standards of dress and
gender roles and his failure to understand or to
appreciate the valued position of women in traditional
Cherokee culture. Contrary to Butler's observation,
Cherokee women had never been considered slaves or

personal property by their own people. He continued his report with special mention of a Tahlequah school and its Cherokee teacher, Miss Mary Hoyt, who had "few if any superiors" in "acquirement, lady-like deportment and capacity for government." The *Cherokee Advocate* also publicized the opening of a female seminary in connection with the Baptist Mission (near present-day Westville, Oklahoma), advertising that it would rival opportunities at eastern schools. Miss Sarah Hale Hibbard supervised the school. Its purpose, as noted in the *Advocate*, was to provide for "the improvement, subsequent usefulness, and ultimate happiness of the young ladies of the Cherokee Nation."[13]

Not long after this, the Cherokee government made provisions for its young people to obtain a high-school education within Indian Territory. In 1847 the Cherokee Council used the dividends from investments in stocks, which had been purchased with money obtained from the sale of lands to the United States government, to establish a male seminary one and a half miles southwest of Tahlequah, the Cherokee capitol. They also provided for a female seminary three miles southeast of Tahlequah at Park Hill. Both buildings, constructed of local brick, were three stories high, 185 feet long, and 109 feet wide; they were the most impressive buildings in Indian Territory. The Cherokee National Male Seminary opened on May 6, 1851, and the Female Seminary opened the following day. Cherokee officials intended both schools to set a standard of excellence in education—education for the advancement of Cherokees in white culture, not for the retention of Cherokee tribal ways. At the request of Cherokee government officials, Mary Chapin, principal of Mount Holyoke Seminary in South Hadley, Massachusetts, drew up the curriculum for the Female

Seminary and Ellen Whitmore, a Mount Holyoke graduate, assumed the duties of principal teacher. Sarah Worcester, daughter of Samuel Austin and Ann Orr Worcester and also a Mount Holyoke student, assisted Whitmore. Mount Holyoke provided teachers for the seminary throughout the pre–Civil War period. The first class of twenty-five students met admission standards requiring proficiency in reading, English, arithmetic, grammar, and geography. Worcester, having grown up with the Cherokees, knew their level of acculturation, but upon her arrival Whitmore fell victim to a prank in which some of the girls dressed up in paint and feathers to look like Plains Indians and frighten their principal. Whitmore admitted that they were quite successful in carrying out this "farce."[14]

Both full-blood and mixed-blood students attended the seminaries. They paid no tuition, but a $5.00 per month fee for housing, meals, books, supplies, and laundry was required for the boarding students. Some pupils attended free of charge, subsidized by the Cherokee government, and others found work nearby to pay the fees. The demanding course of study at the female seminary included Latin, algebra, botany, geography, grammar, arithmetic, and vocal music. Not all of the girls chose to remain through four years of the strict boarding-school regimen. Whitmore regretted that during her second term, "two of my loveliest girls" had not returned and a third, a fifteen-year-old, had gotten married. Still, the first two graduating classes in 1855 and 1856 included twelve and fourteen members respectively with last names that read like the Who's Who of the Cherokee Nation: Adair, Bushyhead, Vann, Ross, McNair, Hicks, and Scrimsher.[15]

The friendships formed during these school years, the experiences shared, and the reinforcement of non-Indian cultural values shaped the lives of Cherokee women for generations. Hannah Worcester, who was a daughter of the missionary Worcesters, described the yearly ceremony on May 7 that celebrated the opening of the Female Seminary. As the Fort Gibson military band played, the students, wearing lovely pastel dresses, sang and marched to a bower of vines and flowers where they placed a crown of roses on the head of their May queen. After the ceremony and speeches, "gentlemen and ladies in pairs, promenaded round and round to the music of the band." More than a half century after the opening of the school, the Tuesday Club of Bartlesville reenacted the same kind of pageant in honor of the seventy-fifth birthday of Narcissa Owen, who was the Cherokee mother of Oklahoma's senator Robert Owen and a former seminary music teacher. The thirty members of the club, many of whom were not Cherokees, gathered at Owen's Oklahoma home, rode around the farm in a hay wagon, sang songs, and heard speeches. Rain prevented the wrapping of the May pole and the dance, but they placed the crown of roses on Owen, naming her May queen. Owen's Cherokee kinswoman Mrs. Sidney Bell presented her with a cut-glass vase that symbolized Owen's productive life, the "sparkle and brilliancy" of her intellect, and the "purity" of her days.[16]

These rituals of friendship and symbols of shared identity bound Cherokee women to each other and became acceptable bonds of communion among women who shared a similar social status, if not the tribal heritage, of the Cherokees. The mutual ties were so common and so strong that Kate Pearson Burwell, writing in *Sturm's Statehood Magazine* about the Indian Territory Federation of Women's Clubs, boasted that territorial Oklahoma women set an example for the nation. "That there was a vivid sprinkling of Indian blood, in the veins of some of the brightest

members, argued well for the dignity of ancestral Lo,"
she stated. "The territory womanhood can give their
sisters of other states some valuable suggestions as to
what progressive and aggressive enlightenment
means, in a new country."[17]

From the beginning the young students attending
the Female Seminary believed they were destined for
superior status—if not all May queens, then at least all
rosebuds. The students published a magazine they
titled *The Cherokee Rose Buds* that was printed in
Cherokee and English and devoted to "the Good, the
Beautiful and the True." Significantly, some of the
articles appeared under the bylines of the students'
English names (Fannie, Ada, Flora, and Bessie), but
some authors signed with Cherokee names such as Ka-
Ya-Kun-stah, Wa-Li, and Wah-Yoo-Kah, probably inten-
tionally denoting their Cherokee identification. The
idealism of youth marked the original poetry and
articles submitted by the students, and recognition of
their special mission as the elite of the nation permeated the pages. One poem described the school and
its students as

> our garden fair,
> And we, the flowers planted there.
> Like roses bright we hope to grow,
> And o'er our home such beauty throw,
> In future years—that all may see,
> Loveliest of lands,—the Cherokee.

Another student description in straight-forward prose
stated simply that "Everything around denotes taste,
refinement, and progress of civilization among our
people: well may they vie with the long enlightened
inhabitants of the east." As graduation approached in
1856, Lucinda M. Ross wrote in a poem for her cousin
Victoria Hicks that described the close relationships:

Many friends we've here found,
Within these favored walls
And sad will be the sound,
When we say farewell, to all.
But may we in friendship, dwell united,
and our lives be love

Ross belonged to the last class that was to graduate until after the Civil War. Financial problems closed the school in 1856, and the dislocation, economic chaos, and destruction caused by the war prevented its reopening until 1871.[18]

During the interim, in the years between the school's closing and those immediately following the war, Cherokee women continued to develop networks that strengthened a southern-lady identity, flavored with a Mount Holyoke educational tradition. Many attended school at Cane Hill Female Seminary (forty miles east of Tahlequah near Evansville, Arkansas) and Amanda Buchanan's school in Van Buren, Arkansas. Others found teaching opportunities at schools such as these and then joined the faculty of the Cherokee Female Seminary when it reopened. Narcissa Owen, widowed and desperate for money to support herself and her two sons after the war, taught music first at Sawyer's School, then at the Cherokee Female Seminary. Intergenerational continuity also promoted a sense of Cherokee particularity in educational and social opportunities for young women. Delia Vann Brewer attended the Seminary, Sawyer's School, and Mount Holyoke. Her daughter, Mary Brewer, later taught at the Cherokee Female Seminary.[19]

Cane Hill Female Seminary opened in 1834 as an adjunct of the all-male Cane Hill College. The curriculum and standards followed the Mount Holyoke model, and the first principal, Laura Graham, had graduated from Mount Holyoke. The school operated, however, in an environment shaped by southern immigration, attitudes, and sympathies. During the Civil War, a lieutenant in the Second Cherokee Confederate Regiment wrote home to his sister in Indian Territory about the fighting in Arkansas and the reception of his troop's encampment at Cane Hill: "The people in Cane Hill are the strongest southern people I ever saw," he wrote, "with the exception of a few families who are union." Cherokee sisters Mary America Scrimsher (the mother of Will Rogers) and Alabama Elizabeth Scrimsher attended both Cane Hill and the Cherokee Female Seminary. Eliza Jane Ross, niece of Principal Chief John Ross, attended Cane Hill Seminary and taught at various periods at the Cherokee Female Seminary. An 1880 graduate, Nannie Daniel Fite, remembered Ross as "especially loved by all old Seminary girls as a sweet gentle woman."[20]

Amanda Buchanan, born in Cane Hill, went first to Oxford Ladies Seminary in Mississippi and then to Mount Holyoke, where she was graduated in 1854. Buchanan returned to Cane Hill to teach at the Seminary and later opened her own school in Van Buren, Arkansas. Ann Florence Wilson, another Cane Hill resident, was graduated from LaGrange Female College in Jackson, Tennessee. She joined Buchanan's faculty in Van Buren, and there she instructed a number of Cherokee girls, among them Ella Coodey Robinson, who was a grandniece of Principal Chief John Ross. Wilson then taught at the Tahlequah public school, and later, in 1875, she accepted the position of principal teacher of the Cherokee National Female Seminary. Here she exerted a profound influence on the lives of hundreds of Cherokee girls for the next twenty-six years. The educational, geographic, and

Ann Florence Wilson, principal of the
Cherokee National Female Seminary,
1875–1901. Photo courtesy of the
Archives & Manuscript Division of the
Oklahoma Historical Society.

generational connections among these women fostered
a sense of special identity and loyal sisterhood that
combined the high aspirations of a New England
schoolgirl and the social graces of a southern lady with
a fidelity to their Cherokee inheritance.[21]

Ann Florence Wilson administered the Cherokee
National Female Seminary from 1875 until 1901.
Indeed, students attending the school during these
years considered Wilson the embodiment of seminary

spirit. Following the example she had seen established at Cane Hill, employed under Amanda Buchanan's supervision and practiced by precedents of the Cherokee Seminary, Wilson carried out the Mount Holyoke plan to the letter. Wilson and her staff defined the standard model of acculturation for Cherokee women. She personally directed the curriculum, school activities, and daily lives of the students with iron-handed consistency, even when her personal sympathy urged her to be lenient. After one disciplinary episode, Wilson confided to a coteacher, "I hate to be so severe with her. I can see her side of it, but we have these rules and I must enforce them." She made an awe-inspiring figure patrolling the halls of the building in her starched black, tailored dress trimmed in white at the collar and cuffs, with her hair severely parted and impeccably combed into a bun. Occasionally, students caught her smiling and talking to herself as she swept down the halls. "The thoughtless ones laughed, the more thoughtful ones wondered if she were not living in a world of her own," two students remembered. In any case, when they thought of her in later years they admitted that they certainly had been afraid of her.[22]

The post–Civil War curriculum included mathematics (arithmetic, algebra, and geometry), science (physiology, zoology, and chemistry), English (grammar, composition, rhetoric, and literature), general history, Latin, philosophy, vocal music, and Bible lessons. Wilson's favorite courses seemed to be "mental" arithmetic and history with an emphasis on government and politics. She directed the students in verbal drills on math facts and then tested them by having them individually solve problems for the rest of the class without figuring on paper. She urged seminary teachers to conduct discussions of current events in the classes, and she often attended political rallies in

Tahlequah. During the interval of 1887–89 when the original seminary building burned and had to be rebuilt, this time in Tahlequah, Wilson attended the advanced English course at the Oswego Normal School in New York. After returning to the seminary, Wilson supervised the weekly spelling matches and memory competitions of literary pieces and Bible verses, and the students participated eagerly in these events hoping to win an approving nod or perhaps a small gift for an exemplary performance.[23]

Music education grew in importance as the seminary developed. From the beginning, Sarah Worcester taught singing, social graces, and "meticulous refinements thought essential to good breeding," and seminary girls were often in demand for charity concerts, church performances, and public gatherings. Although Wilson had no musical ability, she encouraged every seminary girl to participate in some way in musical exhibitions, and she would listen for hours as the students played the piano. Cherokee pride in their school increased with the knowledge that nearly all of the seminary students could play the piano and the organ. The students learned the music fashionable for the parlor of any Victorian young lady; thrilling runs and powerful chords rang out across the grounds as the girls practiced concert polkas, marches, and waltzes. Missionaries, army officers, and early Cherokee emigrants had hauled musical instruments overland by wagon to Indian Territory. Narcissa Owen received a massive, elegantly carved Stieff piano as a wedding gift from her husband, Colonel Robert Latham Owen. After his death, she gave lessons on it to support her family, and she moved this piano to the Female Seminary when she joined the faculty in 1880. Miraculously, it was one of the few things to survive the fire in 1887. By 1906 the seminary boasted of a six-level graded program of music study, emphasizing harmony, theory, and playing from memory. Students practiced selections from Beethoven, Chopin, and Liszt on new practice pianos and gave frequent recitals, as the school catalog reported, "to accustom them to public performance and enable them to acquire self-possession."[24]

Florence Wilson represented an ever-present model of discipline in aspects of student lives that were entirely separate from academic studies. She monitored their health, personally administering a daily dose of sulphur and molasses and, sometimes, caster oil to each girl. She also conducted the daily required afternoon walk of one to three miles for good general health. The girls lined up in a column of twos dressed in their blue serge suit-dresses, ties, and mortarboard caps. Sometimes they paraded through town, but in the spring, jaunts to nearby McSpadden Mill or Ivy Spring for glorious bouquets of wild flowers proved more common. Wilson also inspected the girls for good personal-hygiene habits, checking for clean fingernails, tidy hair, and mended clothing. School rules required students to bathe regularly and to use disinfectants. Wilson led the attack against ubiquitous head lice and checked rooms regularly for order and cleanliness.[25]

Wilson showed special interest in the development of the full-blood Cherokees. The girls roomed together on the top floor of the building, separate from the mixed-blood students, and, as one student remembered, "kept very much to themselves." They often experienced desperate homesickness, frustration at the finishing-school seminary environment, and difficulty with education exclusively taught in English. They also faced the prejudice and ridicule of their more acculturated mixed-blood kinswomen. Wilson

Students at the Cherokee National Female Seminary, c. 1892. Photo courtesy of the Archives & Manuscript Division of the Oklahoma Historical Society.

sometimes aided the poorer students financially and rewarded persistent effort with small gifts, and she occasionally gave failing students another chance at exams. These acts of kindness brought Wilson a widening circle of respect and loyalty. Full-blood mothers dressed their new babies in finery and brought them to the seminary to show to Wilson, and some of them named their daughters after her. A full-blood student, Mollie Comingdeer, alerted Wilson to the tragic fire that destroyed the building in 1887. In appreciation of her interest and sympathy, one full-blood girl gave Wilson the ultimate compliment: "Miss Wilson no white woman—she Cherokee."[26]

The seminary operated on a rigid daily schedule and a strict code of behavior. The morning bell rang at 5:30 A.M.; breakfast and morning chores followed. Wilson opened the required chapel services with the Lord's Prayer. Classes lasted until the noon meal and resumed again at 1:00 P.M., continuing until 4:00 P.M. Afternoon exercise, the evening meal, and a study hour rounded out the day, and all lights went out at approximately 9:00 P.M. This schedule varied only slightly from the post–Civil War period until the seminary closed in 1908. Rules governed every aspect of the daily routine. Leaving the campus without a chaperone and having any contact with the opposite sex, especially Male Seminary students, were prohibited. The behavior code forbade carrying weapons, using liquor, playing cards, and gambling. In addition, any "intentional disrespect or disobedience to any teacher or officer of the Seminary" carried the penalty of suspension.[27]

Principal Wilson scrupulously administered the demerit system for violations of these rules. Other punishments might include spanking, standing in a corner, or expulsion. Most students acquired demerits

sparingly, only for minor infractions such as whisper-
ing, tardiness, or staying up after curfew, because too
many demerits prevented them from participating in
chaperoned trips into town and other activities with
Male Seminary students. Wilson seemed especially
alert to late night gatherings in the girls' rooms.
Decades after their seminary days, former students
shared stories about Wilson catching them in clan-
destine meetings. One night several girls got together
to cook wild onions and eggs, a favorite Cherokee dish,
over a small oil stove. Wilson caught them, confiscated
the food, and fined them each five demerits. On
another occasion, Wilson suspected a spend-the-night
party in progress. When the guilty girl emerged from
hiding under the bed, "Miss Wilson spanked her jaws
and ordered her to her room." The girls lost all
privileges and were put on probation for a month.[28]

The most serious offense, however, was a meeting
with a member of the opposite sex. Sometimes the
Male Seminary students sneaked over in groups to
serenade the girls. Wilson permitted the girls to toss
flowers down to the boys, but not to talk with them.
When Wilson occasionally allowed some of the older
girls to stroll outside the grounds, she admonished
them, "Now if you see a man or boy run home." Any
supposed male relative who visited the seminary had
to be cleared through the principal first. Wilson's
studious adherence to a Victorian standard of morality
and conduct, her insistence on academic excellence,
and her dedication to the creation of her vision of the
accomplished woman provided the role model for
acculturation of the Cherokee elite. Former student
Lillian Alexander Wyly credited Wilson with putting
"conviction and discipline and stability in their lives."
Two other students wrote that Wilson's leadership
resulted in "two generations of women who saw the

responsibilities of life and accepted them, who had a code of conduct and lived up to it."[29]

The new building, completed in 1889 with Cherokee Strip Live Stock Association lease funds, added modern conveniences and greatly expanded space to accommodate two hundred students. The curriculum broadened in keeping with national trends emphasizing domestic science to include instruction in "the art of handling the broom and in the science of the dust cloth." In addition to daily maintenance duties, the students received direction in such chores as cooking, mending, and cleaning that were essential to a well-regulated home. They prepared exhibitions of hand and machine sewing, embroidery, and plain and fancy knitting. The agricultural course gave them experience in gardening. "The value of this department can not be overestimated," declared D. Frank Redd, supervisor of Cherokee schools, "since practically all are from the country with at least one 'allotment' in her own name." Before they graduated these Cherokee girls could conjugate a Latin verb, play a Beethoven composition, make a stylish dress, bake bread, and arrange an elegant table setting.[30]

Primary and preparatory departments drew in the talented younger girls of the Cherokee Nation and prepared them for the rigorous high school program. These departments in turn needed experienced teachers, and after 1890, seminary graduates regularly filled the teaching positions. Students took pride in the fact that the women of their nation shared equal status with the teachers recruited from Cornell and Vassar. Former students, turned teachers, aggressively pursued plans to develop the complete woman. Rachel Caroline (Callie) Eaton and Sarah Jane (Bluie) Adair organized a chapter of the Young Women's Christian Association at the seminary in 1896 with the object of

Members of the Junior Class of the Cherokee National Female Seminary, 1898. Photo courtesy of the Western History Collections, University of Oklahoma Library.

the "development of Christian character in the school."
The organization conducted morning prayer services
and Sunday afternoon devotionals. Literary societies
proliferated—Philomathean, Minervian, Hypathian,
Germanae, and others. Each appealed to a particular
age level and had its own officers, colors, and motto.
The seminary catalog summarized the intent and
value of these organizations: They aimed "to give the
girls training in parliamentary usage, to develop
literary, musical and dramatic talent, and to enable
them to acquire the grace and dignity necessary to a
pleasing appearance before the public." Seminary
graduates also filled teaching positions in public
schools across the Cherokee Nation. In D. Frank Redd's
report made shortly before statehood to the Department of the Interior, the names of seminary graduates
who were now teaching appeared in every district.[31]

Wilson left the seminary in disappointment in
1901 after President William McKinley vetoed a bill
passed by the Cherokee National Council appointing
Wilson principal for life. Although Wilson could only
see this as a rebuke of her performance, the veto
actually reflected the federal government's efforts to
complete the dissolution of Indian tribal authority.
Wilson taught again briefly in the Cherokee public
schools, but she died within two years. Management of
the school passed into the hands of midwesterners Etta
J. Rider of Iowa and M. Eleanor Allen from Indiana,
both of whom prepared for the impending transfer of
the school into the governmental agencies of the new
state of Oklahoma. Wilson's procedures, however,
remained intact until the end. In 1909 the Oklahoma
state legislature created the Northeastern State
Normal School at the seminary location. In recognition
of the advanced course of study and the quality of
instruction, the state granted sixty-two hours of college

credit to the graduates of the Cherokee National Female and Male Seminaries. A decade later the school became a four-year institution, and the name changed to Northeastern State College. Homecoming at the college continued to be celebrated on May 7 in honor of the original seminary opening, and the stately brick structure remains in use more than one hundred years after its construction.

The nature of seminary life, the modern facilities, and the emphasis on upper-class non-Indian culture rather than traditional Cherokee culture fostered intimate, reciprocal, long-standing friendships among non-Indian teachers and their Cherokee pupils. One non-Indian instructor who moved to Kansas wrote back to a favorite student in 1894, "I do not think I will ever meet any girls I will love as dearly as I do the little girls who belonged to me at the Sem." Ida Wetzel Tinnin expressed the mutual affection. Tinnin, a member of the last seminary graduating class in 1908, cherished her memories of her ten years on the campus. Fifty years later she remembered Florence Wilson and other seminary teachers with pride as individuals who "set the high standard of scholarship and established acceptable patterns of social behavior." Tinnin noted that Wilson surrounded herself with teachers who shared the same philosophy of life and who prepared their students to create good homes, rear good families, and "find a place of service in their community, state and nation."[32]

Lives of service seemed the ultimate goal as seminary graduates took up positions of prestige, social distinction, and community leadership. The traditional avenue to prominence through advantageous marriage remained open. Not surprisingly, graduates of the Cherokee Male Seminary sought wives with the same advantages they had known and found them at the

Narcissa Owen, teacher at the Cherokee National Female Seminary and mother of one of Oklahoma's first senators, Robert L. Owen. Photo courtesy of the Western History Collections, University of Oklahoma Library.

Female Seminary. Joel B. Mayes, Chief Justice of the Supreme Court of the Cherokee Nation and twice-elected principal chief, chose a seminary graduate each of the three times he married. Many of the women remained unmarried, however, and continued careers in education. Although they adopted the dress, manners, religion, and behavior patterns of the non-Indian culture, they never relinquished their identification

with their Cherokee heritage and loyalty to their
seminary experience. They cherished their lines of
Cherokee descent and clan membership as well as that
of their white forebears, and they cultivated the
understanding of their tribal history as a part of the
American experience. As Narcissa Owen wrote in
1908, "I have always felt a pride in my father's people,
the Cherokees—in their mental capability, in their
natural nobility, in their great courage and resolution,
in their native generosity and integrity, and in their
patriotism."[33]

Members of the Alumnae Association of the
Cherokee Female Seminary dedicated themselves to
the promotion of education and to the revival of the
pleasant associations that had developed around the
seminary life, and they met yearly to renew those early
friendships. The seminary seemed to verify their
Cherokee particularity among all other women. As one
1905 senior expressed it, the seminary was their alma
mater, "their dear old second Mother," who had cared
for them in the "sweet years of their girlhood." She
ended a long tribute with this prayer:

> That, as future years roll onward
> blotting out our race of people,
> She may stand here always ready
> Glad to welcome Indian children
> And to keep alive tradition—
> Monument to all the greatness
> Of this proudest Indian Nation.[34]

Eliza Bushyhead Alberty (class of 1856), president
of the alumni association in 1906, maintained the
closest contact with the school throughout her life and
presented a typical example of this commitment. After
graduation, Alberty taught in the public schools for
two years, then married. Three years after her first

husband's death, she married Bluford West Alberty,
and together they served as stewards of the Cherokee
Male Seminary. At the Male Seminary she acquired
the appellation "Aunt Eliza" by which she was known
for the rest of her life. The stewards purchased all
seminary supplies and collected payment of all student
bills. Aunt Eliza often kept a boy enrolled in school by
waiting until harvest time for payment or by finding
some way for him to earn the money to cover the fees.
Her only child died in infancy, but Alberty reared and
educated several nieces and nephews and adopted a
full-blood Cherokee baby girl. This propensity to take
in homeless or orphaned children occurred repeatedly
among Cherokee women.[35]

For a time the Albertys operated the Cherokee
Insane Hospital, but in 1885, they bought the National
Hotel in Tahlequah and began to maintain it as a
family-style inn. The hotel functioned as the gathering
place for celebrated visitors to Indian Territory, including politicians, generals, and distinguished writers.
Aunt Eliza, widowed again in 1889, continued to
manage the hotel alone until her death in 1919. She
always reserved certain rooms in the hotel for special
friends, and frequently she invited a seminary girl to
spend the weekend as her guest there. In this way she
could keep up with seminary happenings and offer
support and encouragement to the homesick schoolgirls. She actively lobbied for the state to purchase the
seminary facilities and continue operating it as
Northeastern State College, and Governor Charles
Haskell presented her with the pen he used to sign the
bill into law. Alberty, along with Callie Eaton, also
promoted the organization of the Sequoyah Historical
Society to preserve Cherokee history and cultural
relics. "Don't let it get quiet and still," she urged Eaton
in a 1908 letter, "but keep it in the minds of all."

Fittingly, close friend Nannie Daniel Fite (class of 1880), delivered Alberty's eulogy, summing up her life as one of "usefulness—a life of long self-sacrifice, and ministering to her people. As a woman she belonged to the old regime; kind, sympathetic, quiet and unassuming, yet commanding and dignified. She was the widest known and best loved woman in Oklahoma."[36]

The names abound of numerous other Cherokee women honored for their accomplishments. The following examples serve to illustrate the diversity and widespread impact of their leadership in the early statehood period of Oklahoma. A descendent of Nancy Ward, who was the last Cherokee Beloved Woman (woman chief), Rachel Caroline (Callie) Eaton graduated from the Female Seminary in 1887 and continued her education in Missouri. She received her M.A. and Ph.D. degrees from the University of Chicago. She taught at the Female Seminary and at several schools across the United States and later served as Rogers County superintendent of schools. Her interest in Cherokee history led to the publication in 1910 of a study of Principal Chief John Ross that she entitled *John Ross and the Cherokee Indians*. She joined the Tulsa Indian Women's Club and worked in the Order of the Eastern Star. In 1936 the state of Oklahoma honored her as one of its outstanding women.[37]

Ellen Howard Miller, known as the "Bird Woman of Oklahoma," pursued diverse civic, cultural, and conservation interests. She directed the campaign to designate a bridge under construction across the Caney River as the "Memorial Bridge," in honor of area World War I veterans. She then raised the funds to landscape the site and erect tablets at the bridge listing the names of Washington County servicemen. Miller organized the Washington County Indian Association and the Indian Women's Club of Bartlesville, using these organizations to publicize Indian welfare issues. Conservation of wildlife served as the dominant interest of her life. Miller held office as the Chairman of the Committee on Birds, Flowers, and Wildlife for the Oklahoma Federation of Women's Clubs and successively for the National Federation of Women's Clubs for several years. She studied ornithology at the University of Oklahoma and lectured and published extensively on the construction of bird sanctuaries. Her farm, south of Bartlesville, became the nucleus of the two-thousand-acre Ellen Howard Miller Game Preserve. The *Bartlesville Daily Enterprise* commented in 1944 that Miller's name "was synonymous with character and service to mankind and to the wildlife."[38]

Carlotta Archer, a granddaughter of Joseph Vann, graduated from the Cherokee National Female Seminary in 1883 and made a reputation early as an accomplished musician. At the age of fifteen she received a medal designating her the best musician under twenty-one years of age in the Five Tribes. She taught music for eleven years at the Female Seminary. According to one student, she exerted such a marked influence on her pupils that sixty years later they could still play pieces from memory that Archer had taught them. She served on the Cherokee Nation Board of Education, the only woman to hold this office, and after statehood she continued as Mayes County superintendent of education for nineteen years. She ended her career with twenty years of service in the federal Indian Office at Muskogee.[39]

Finally, Anna Trainor Matheson, described by historian Carolyn Foreman as "a devoted wife and homemaker," achieved recognition as Miss Indian Territory in Statehood Day ceremonies in 1907. She was also selected to be a member of the Betsy Ross Association and to prepare a star for the new United

States flag to be flown in Philadelphia after Oklahoma statehood. Matheson, at that time the wife of Five Tribes agent Leo Bennett, outlived four husbands and reared a sister, a brother, the son of a cousin, and three orphaned children of Bennett's previous marriage in addition to her own three children. Celebrated for her impressive beauty, Matheson's friends described her as a woman who "met life with a smile in spite of troubles that would have overcome most persons." Certainly, not all Cherokee women attained the prominence of these five, but their lives illustrate the success of the seminary experience in promoting talent, ambition, and commitment to social service.[40]

The legacy of the Cherokee Female Seminary represented much more than an architecturally interesting building, scattered catalogs of courses and rules, and photographs of young ladies in Victorian dress. The Cherokee Female Seminary provided the matrix for a unique cultural synergism that appealed to the citizens of territorial Oklahoma as a worthy representation of themselves. Seminary graduates personified ideals such as honor, beauty, intelligence, wealth, and refinement. These women served as living models of assimilation, the standard to which all other women in the territory, Indian or non-Indian, compared themselves, and as the caretakers of Oklahoma's cultural image of the Indian princess.

5

Christianity for the Kiowas

For women of Elva Ferguson's social position, establishing friendships with graduates of the Cherokee
Seminaries posed little problem. Finding a context of
mutual understanding with members of Plains Indian
culture proved a far harder task. Similar to most of her
contemporaries, Ferguson modified many of her attitudes about Plains Indians after a series of experiences
with them as individuals. Initial fear gave way to
curiosity, gratitude for assistance, and cautious acceptance. Shortly after arriving in Watonga, Ferguson was
terrified by the appearance of a Cheyenne warrior in
traditional dress inside her kitchen. Her husband
responded to her screams and tears with assurances
that the visit was just a friendly courtesy call.

Over time, the Cheyenne proved himself a loyal
family friend. He became especially attached to
Ferguson's youngest son, Trad, and grieved openly

when he died serving in World War I. On one occasion,
his Indian protection proved valuable. Ferguson had
taken the young boys on a long trip alone when her
horse went lame, stranding her at the edge of a
Cheyenne encampment. This same warrior remained
at her side all night and accompanied them home the
next day. Ferguson remembered him in her memoirs as
"one of our best Indian friends." Yet he remains
anonymous, because on both occasions that she wrote
about him, she failed to identify him by name. He is
remembered only as a Cheyenne warrior. Partnerships
among vastly different cultures required patience,
compassion, and flexibility.[1]

Perhaps no other group of Indian women offered as
great a contrast to the example of the Cherokees as
those of the Kiowa tribe located in the southwestern
quadrant of Indian Territory. By the 1870s the
Cherokee culture that whites had encountered at first
contact had modified through the slow and steady
process of acculturation with Christianity, capitalism,
and republicanism. Traditional Kiowa culture, however, faced military harassment and suffered complete
disarray. They accepted confinement on the Kiowa,
Comanche, and Apache Reservation. However, the
insistence of this tiny tribe, now scarcely more than
one thousand members strong, on retaining the
remnants of a nomadic Plains way of life and a distinct
tribal identity thwarted the best efforts of Indian
agents, missionaries, and schoolteachers to turn them
into good yeoman farmers. Kiowa women, characterized by some non-Indian scholars as little more than
slaves, resisted the confining role of the farmer's wife
that was assigned to them. Forced to accept a new
material culture, they clung to the familiar, private
social and family dynamics that gave meaning to their
individual lives. Ultimately, some syncretic changes

occurred through non-Indian female interventions in just these private areas of life. Citizens of the territory of Oklahoma knew, however, that no matter how often they publicized the accomplishments of the Cherokee lady, farther away on Saddle Mountain her Kiowa counterpart resisted efforts to change her way of life.[2]

The Kiowa, known in their ancient language as *Kwu-da* or "coming out people," had never been a very large tribe. Their creation myth explained that they had emerged into the world one by one through a hollow log until a woman, her body swollen in pregnancy, got stuck in the log and prevented any others from coming out. Physically, they tended to be dark-skinned, short, stocky, and broad-chested. Oral history placed their original location in the mountains of western Montana, but a dispute between two chiefs caused a separation of the tribe. One group retreated to the northwest, and the other moved out onto the northern plains. The *Gaigwu*, or southern group, made a peaceful alliance with the Crow Indians and adopted the religious worship of the *Tai-me*, or Sun Dance medicine, and several other Crow traits. Most importantly, the Kiowa acquisition of horses revolutionized their way of life: The horse made the Kiowa mobile, independent, wealthy, and masters of their environment. According to historian Mildred Mayhall, the horse caused an evolution of the historic Plains culture by providing a broad new complex of material and psychological ideas. Of the eleven typical Plains tribes, Mayhall believed that the Kiowas had more horses per person than any other tribe and exhibited most notably the character traits of bravery, predatoriness, and audacity. Plains culture diffused rapidly from north to south.[3]

From about 1740 to 1835 the Kiowa and their Comanche neighbors dominated the southern plains from the headwaters of the Arkansas River to northern Mexico. Small bands, composed mostly of brothers and their wives and children under the leadership of a band chief, traversed the plains living exclusively in relation to their main food source, the buffalo. They raided Mexican *placitas* and other Indian camps stealing silver, blankets, and horses. They took captives whom they either retained as slaves or adopted into the tribe. Each year the bands met in early summer to renew their religious commitment to the *Tai-me* and the medicine bundles known as the Ten Grandmothers and to celebrate the Sun Dance. At these meetings political divisions could be reunited, marriages arranged, horses traded, and "give-aways" (distributions of gifts) that leavened the wealth of the tribe could be consummated.

Most non-Indian authorities agreed that the women in this hunting, warrior society held very low status. One form of punishment a Kiowa man might inflict on an adulterous or difficult wife involved "throwing her away," that is, abandoning her on the Plains and in some cases arranging for her mass rape by other warriors. He could beat her or physically maim her, most commonly by cutting off her nose. Gruesome as these punishments were, a Kiowa wife did not have to remain married to an abusive man. She could obtain a divorce, usually with her brother's consent, by moving her possessions back into her parent's home. N. Scott Momaday, in his eloquent journey into the Kiowa past, *The Way To Rainy Mountain*, wrote that the Kiowa calendar history provided ample proof that "the lives of women were hard, whether they were 'bad women' or not." However, even excluding the treatment of dishonored women, the position of Kiowa women in traditional culture needs reassessment. Non-Indian observers in the

military or in fur-trading operations, such as John
Treat Irving and Edwin T. Denig, reported unflattering
descriptions of most Plains Indian women. They
viewed Indian women in contrast to middle-class
American women in an age of industrialization and
consumerism. An examination of their status within
their own culture reveals that Kiowa women fulfilled
valuable economic and social roles that maintained
stability in an erratic existence and grew in importance as the United States government rigorously
circumscribed Kiowa mobility.[4]

Kiowa women owned virtually all of the family's
material possessions with the exception of the horse
herds. They determined the location of the camps in
relation to the availability of adequate water and
forage. The cedar tipi poles of their family's lodge were
given to them by their mothers when they married.
They laboriously worked and tanned the twenty to
thirty buffalo hides necessary for the tipi, bartering for
extra hides and exchanging goods or labor with other
women for help in the curing, cutting, and sewing. They
made and ornamented the family clothing with embroidery, paint, quills, and beadwork. They constructed
the willow-reed beds and prepared the hides for bed-
covers. They owned the cooking pots and the leather
parfleches that they decorated with geometric designs.
They dried the meat, gathered and preserved the fruits
and berries, and prepared pemmican. They cooked and
divided the portions of all food.[5]

Kiowa women also held positions of responsibility
during raids and on buffalo hunts. They tended the
horses—the tribe's source of wealth—or supervised
children and slaves in this work. They also safeguarded
their warrior's shield, weapons, and war ponies with
their individualized "medicine" signs. In addition, they
skinned and butchered the buffalo at the site of the kill

Good Eye (Kiowa), mother of Jim Apeahtone, building a summer arbor. Photo courtesy of the Western History Collections, University of Oklahoma Library.

and brought home the products on their own ponies. Kiowa men hunted, but after the kill, the production of food, clothing, and shelter remained in the Kiowa woman's jurisdiction.[6]

Kiowa women provided the initial education of the young children, differentiating from the beginning male and female roles within their culture. They taught the children their first lessons in tribal history, the Kiowa language, and religion. Although not as numerous or diverse as the male societies, women had their own sororial associations. Older women belonged to a dancing society known as Calf Old Women or a secret, and reportedly terrifying, religious society of Bear Women. The closest associations seemed to exist between children and their grandparents, who gave them their names. Kiowas designated a certain child within the family as a favorite child, or *ade*, and this child received preferential treatment. Girls as well as boys gained this distinction.[7]

The degraded, servile, drudge-like status ascribed to Plains Indian women has received too much emphasis. Kiowa women failed to achieve the notoriety and honor associated with a successful hunt or a lucrative raid, but they gained band recognition through skill with the knife and the awl. Women sometimes earned a higher rank within the stratified Kiowa society through demonstrations of talent in crafts or sports. They remained excluded from the inner religious ceremonies of the Sun Dance, but they protected their own warrior's sacred medicine. They accumulated little personal wealth, but they owned everything that sustained family life. They never held tribal political positions, but by virtue of their control of food appropriations, they influenced the status of their husbands within the band by exhibiting the highly prized attributes of generosity and hospitality. They also had some influence on decisionmaking. While a very few refused to observe the established female role and accumulated wealth through their own actions, most women occupied a social position inferior to that of men. This position could be augmented, however, through expertise at valued skills and in private family intercessions available to Kiowa women. In these ways, they could realize some sense of empowerment. Within the tribal community, Kiowa women functioned as a vital component of survival.[8]

The Treaty of Medicine Lodge in 1867 forced the leading Kiowa chiefs to accept confinement, in association with the Comanche and Apache tribes, to reservation land near the Wichita mountains. Loathe to give up their freedom and rights to a much broader hunting territory, the Kiowas continued to raid and to harass wagon trains and settlers. Army units chased them, government officials bargained with them, and Quaker agents cajoled the Kiowas to stay on the reservation and stop their raiding. Outbreaks continued until after the Battle of Adobe Walls in 1874, when Kiowa resistance fell apart under relentless military and economic siege. White hunters systematically obliterated the buffalo herds. As the bands surrendered at Fort Sill, the army stripped them of their weapons, arrested the chiefs, and confiscated their horses, which were then sold or destroyed. The cooperative chief Kickingbird selected twenty-six band leaders who, along with forty-four Comanche, Cheyenne, and Arapaho chiefs, were sent to prison at Fort Marion in Saint Augustine, Florida.[9]

Scattered families, starving and demoralized, faced the ruin of their once-free existence. Lacking any resources—horses, guns, leaders, or buffalo—with which to continue the fight, they relied only on their own recalcitrance as they confronted the "white man's road." The Kiowas insisted on living lives centered on the concept of *what is* rather than *what will be*. They continued to live in tipis and brush arbors, storing the useless farm equipment that they had been given in the government-built houses. Lacking buffalo to hunt, Kiowa warriors staged mock chases of army-issued beef cattle. Kiowa women used canvas for tipis and army blankets and calico in place of hides to make traditional loose-fitting garments. They held the last Sun Dance in 1887 by purchasing a buffalo for sacrifice in the ceremony from rancher Charles Goodnight. When they tried to hold the dance in 1890, no buffalo could be found. In its place, they threw an old buffalo robe over the sacred pole, but soldiers from Fort Sill stopped the dance, and the celebrants dispersed. The loss of the Sun Dance devastated the spirit of the Kiowa people, and this attack on their religion, coupled with immobility and impoverishment, severely altered the continuation of a traditional, unified Kiowa culture. Individual bands attempted to find a way to reconcile a Kiowa identity with the reality of an imposed non-Indian culture and existence.[10]

The prospect of Kiowa assimilation into mainstream American culture appeared impossible, according to those closest to the Kiowas. They were scrutinized and compared unfavorably to other Native American groups with long histories of Euroamerican proximity and relationships. Criticisms came from every quarter. Anthropologist James Mooney, who studied the Kiowas during the 1890s, regretfully found them deficient in admirable qualities of character. "They have the savage virtue of bravery, as they have abundantly proven," he observed, "but as a people they have less honor, gratitude and general reliability than perhaps any other tribe on the plains." Comanche parents argued that they did not want to send their children to school with the Kiowa children, because the Kiowas had poor morals. Non-Indian neighbors in the town of Chickasha made no effort to hide their contempt as they demanded that the government drive out the "pests" and "scabs."[11]

Agent Charles E. Adams also found the Indians under his care sadly behind in all of the factors that indicated acculturated behavior. In his report to the Commissioner of Indian Affairs in 1891, Adams included the 1,151 Kiowa with the 1,624 Comanche, 325 Apache, and 1,066 members of various smaller tribes in his jurisdiction. Of the total 4,166, only 12 percent had wholly or partially adopted white dress. Indians occupied 197 of the government-built houses; the rest continued to live in tipis. Less than 10 percent could use enough English for conversation and just a slightly higher number could read. Adams expressed hope that the training the children received in mission and government schools would lead to acculturation. He added, however, "Until radical changes are effected in manner of dress and life there must necessarily be but little improvement from year to year in the general sanitary condition of these people."[12]

Reservation administration during this period reeked of incompetence, corruption, fraud, and failure. Cattlemen, peddlers, miners, gamblers, and whiskey merchants invaded the reservation, duping the less-knowledgeable Indians. Annuity payments and rations arrived unpredictably and, often, late. Unscrupulous traders bartered spoiled and inferior goods for high prices. Politically influenced appointments, nepotism, and low salaries plagued the institutions that were responsible for acculturation by providing employment for individuals who were unfit or unsuited for the work. In the opinion of historian William T. Hagan, these appointments included "instructors in agriculture

Girls at the Kiowa Indian School, Anadarko, 1891. Photo courtesy of the Western History Collections, University of Oklahoma Library.

who had never farmed, clerks who couldn't write, and teachers too dissolute or incompetent to hold positions in other schools." The Kiowa School at Anadarko proved an especially poor example: between 1885 and 1889 four men served as superintendent at the school, and each left after dismissal for serious offenses. Other personnel exhibited low morale and undesirable performance until reservation appointments came under Civil Service control in 1891.[13]

Kiowa parents complained bitterly to the agent about abusive treatment of their children, and they frequently withdrew them from school. The complaints reflected realistic concerns, as illustrated by the following episode: James Louis Avant accepted the job of school disciplinarian at the Kiowa School in 1890. He and his wife, Mattie, had previously aided Methodist missionary J. J. Methvin in setting up a mission school in Anadarko. Mattie became matron at the school, and James was rewarded with the position of farmer-in-charge of the school's 160 acres of land and stock. According to Avant, the Kiowa School had lost three disciplinarians within days of their appointments because they could not cope with the antagonistic behavior displayed by the Indian children. Avant observed a Kiowa youth ride into the school yard and strike the superintendent with a quirt. Avant believed that the students "had no respect for the school or anyone connected with it." He accepted the job, with a raise in pay, and pledged to then-superintendent G. P. Gregory that he would insure order.[14] Shortly after his arrival, Avant encountered three boys on the stairs as he made his nightly rounds. Avant slugged the first boy and knocked him unconscious, and the other two boys fled to their beds. Avant never explained to the superintendent or agent how he was able to handle the young man so easily, but years later when he recounted the incident, he bragged that "it was with a good pair of [brass] knucks." Avant washed the blood off the boy and took him to the dormitory room. He then went down to the harness room and cut a strip of leather the width of his hand. Returning to the sleeping room, he told the three boys to roll over, and one at a time he thrashed them hard enough that "all three had to stand up for breakfast next morning." This kind of corporal punishment violated Kiowa child-rearing practices that relied on ridicule as a stronger form of behavioral control. To abuse a child who had been taught to withstand pain as a symbol of his strength of body and spirit defeated the purpose of that training and of the corporal punishment. Unfortunately, many teachers such as Avant deemed this form of punishment necessary to the acculturating regimen.[15]

Whippings at the school led to an incident in 1891 that precipitated Superintendent Gregory's dismissal and reinforced the aversion of Kiowa parents to sending their children to school. With the help of Ioleta Hunt MacElhaney as interpreter, Spear Woman [pseudonym] related the story of that incident to Alice Marriott in 1935–36: Walter Burns and Bear's Head resented the confinement at the Kiowa School, and they frequently stole food from the cook's pantry. They also devised disruptive pranks, such as turning the cows loose into the garden, for which the boys were punished. Spring seemed the hardest time for the Kiowa youths because they knew their families were camped nearby, and because it was the season of greatest activity and movement. The two boys took some food and ran away. Ned Hamilton, a younger boy, joined them in their retreat. Superintendent Gregory sent a Kiowa named Wood Fire to look for them, but before the day ended, sleet and a snowstorm struck, driving Wood Fire to a nearby camp and preventing any further search. When the storm abated four days later, they could find no trace of the boys.

Spear Woman accompanied her husband to pick up their own son at the school later that spring, and the family found what was left of the boys, the pile of rags and bones, on top of an exposed bluff. "This was what sending boys to school did," Spear Woman believed. "It made them so restless they ran away, and it took away the knowledge of how to care for themselves, so that they froze to death on top of a hill." A contingency of Kiowa warriors threatened the school. Agent Charles Adams's removal of Gregory and his recruitment of a new faculty eased the situation. In explaining the incident, Adams wrote that he had expected the occurrence to precipitate "most serious results," but he was pleased with the Kiowa's "growing spirit of self control" and their "desire to stand by lawful authority. I find reasoning more effectual and threatening less necessary as the months go by."[16]

Female students appeared more outwardly malleable in most ways, but they too suffered desperate homesickness and fear of the strange environment. One Comanche girl remembered her roommates crying in their beds. "I try to encourage them," she related, "but my heart was always busting." Myrtle Paudlety Ware went to the Rainy Mountain School at age five when her mother died. She thought it would be a place where she could play with other children. She told an interviewer many years later, "That's all I was thinking about. Play with the children, you know, and I didn't even sit down to try to learn." Ware quickly found out that she had to work part of the day in the kitchen, dining room, sewing room, and laundry facilities, in addition to a half day of basic academic study.[17]

The students performed these duties with equipment that was in poor repair and in small, dilapidated buildings. Superintendent Frank A. Thackrey complained about the laundry facilities at the Riverside School at Anadarko in 1900. Since the monotony and hard work inspired little enthusiasm, Thackrey found it necessary "arbitrarily to detail them to this department in order to get the necessary laundry work done." Thackrey believed the work too physically exhausting under the conditions then present for his students, whose average age was ten years old. With understatement he reported, "After a pupil has rubbed hard on a washboard over hot suds for a half day he or she is not in the proper condition to enter the classroom and apply the mind to thinking and study as it should be applied."[18]

The rigidly enforced rule forbidding the use of the Kiowa language proved the most difficult trial for students to overcome. Punishments for speaking their native language included paddlings, holding quinine tablets in their mouths, or brushing their teeth with lye soap. Annie Bigman also attended school at Rainy Mountain, and she remembered the ridicule of her teachers when she tried to speak English. "I liked a couple of them," she told an interviewer years later, "the rest are mean." Teachers punished students for violating the rules in a variety of ways. Some teachers spanked the students' hands with a ruler, forced them to stand on tiptoe with arms outstretched, or locked them in a dark cellar or closet for a period of time. Indian children responded to schooling in many ways, but the disciplinary measures were foremost in the mind of one Kiowa woman when she remembered her school years: "You get punished. Everything you do you get punished. You'd get tired and get punished."[19]

Some Kiowa families willingly sent their children to the government and mission schools in spite of the poor facilities and their fears about abusive treatment.

A few of the more acculturated leaders such as Lucius Aitsan, who had been educated at Carlisle Indian School in Carlisle, Pennsylvania, and Big Bow, believed that an education in reading, writing, and speaking English would help their children deal with the new life ahead. School also provided food, clothing, and medical attention especially necessary for orphans and the poorest Kiowas. Eventually, boarding school represented the opportunity for displaced Kiowa families to associate with other Indians. They continued to follow the tradition of early marriages (at about fourteen years of age) for their daughters, however, and this bothered many officials. Agent James Randlett preferred on-reservation education for Indian children with the exception of the most highly qualified young men. He believed that boys sent to off-reservation boarding schools often returned home and preyed upon, rather than helped, their less-advantaged associates. In contrast he insisted that young women ought to be transferred to non-reservation schools at an early age in order to discourage their marriages. Randlett thought removal at thirteen years old was suitable and "not too early."[20]

Another scourge wracked the Kiowas in 1892, when a measles epidemic struck the agency. Negligently, the Kiowa School superintendent sent sick children back to their home camps where they spread the disease. The death toll reached over two hundred, most of them children. The Kiowas reacted in the only way that gave them comfort, but it horrified non-Indians, who had been sent there to educate them. Mothers and fathers expressed their grief by cutting off their long hair; gashing their shoulders, arms, and legs with a knife; sometimes amputating a finger joint; and screaming, wailing, and crying in hysteria. The name of the dead person could not be spoken again, and all of his or her possessions and animals were broken, given away, or destroyed. Some Kiowas found temporary comfort in the peyote religion or the Ghost Dance, claiming that they communed with their dead children in this way. School teacher Lucy Gage, a person unusually sensitive to the struggles of the Kiowas, felt repulsion when she observed such a dance. She censured it as a "barbaric exhibition of human frenzy and unnaturalness." Hunger, disease, and death stalked many camps.[21]

Apiaton, one of the most trusted Kiowa leaders, traveled northward to meet with the Sioux and to discover the truth about the Ghost Dance. The original Ghost Dance ideals, as taught by the Paiute holy man Wovoka, of peace and restortion of the natural world through meditation, chanting, prayer, and dancing, had changed. The practice among the Sioux included insurgency, and the possibility of violence increased the likelihood of military retaliation. Disillusioned with what he saw and heard, Apiaton rejected the Ghost Dance as an answer to the problems confronting the Kiowas. Apiaton, the younger Lone Wolf, Belo Kozad, and I-See-O all became influential peyote leaders. The peyote ceremony served many purposes for these suffering people. The sacrament gave them emotional strength in time of illness and mourning, a sense of unity and hope, and, eventually, an avenue of accommodation.

The younger Chief Lone Wolf sent word to Reverend Joseph S. Murrow of the American Baptist Home Mission Society that he needed to talk with him. According to one account, the Kiowa chief told Murrow that the Great Spirit divided the world into two seasons; the warm season brought light and life, and the cold season brought death and desolation. He continued: "You Christian white people are like the summer. You have life and warmth and light. You have flowers and fruit, growth and knowledge. We poor, wild Indians are like the winter. We have no growth, no knowledge, no joy, no gladness. Will you not help us with light and life, that we may have joy and knowledge and eternal life hereafter?"

While this account may involve a great deal of exaggeration, misunderstanding, and wishful thinking, Morrow's answer to the request brought a surprisingly large number of women missionaries to the reservation to work among the Kiowas. Some collapsed under the strain and left after a year's service, a few married local ministers or businessmen, but others stayed and had a significant impact on Kiowa lives.[22]

Marietta J. Reeside and Lauretta Ballew, recent graduates of the Female Baptist Missionary Training School in Chicago, Illinois, arrived at Lone Wolf's camp at Elk Creek (near present-day Hobart, Oklahoma) in 1892, but soon accepted the offer of Chief Gotebo's house at Rainy Mountain located fourteen miles to the east. Reeside and Ballew worked there in conjunction with Reverend C. H. Clouse and his wife, Mary, to establish a mission station, chapel, and school. Using their home as a base, they traveled to the nearby Kiowa camps, visiting in the tipis, assisting with births, comforting the bereaved, holding Sunday school classes, and spreading the Christian message. Julia Given, daughter of the great deceased chief Satank, acted as their interpreter.[23]

George Hunt and several other Kiowas repeated a story, perhaps apocryphal, to retired army officer William Sturtevant Nye that illustrated the difficulty the young missionaries had in overcoming the religious traditions of the Kiowa past as well as the impact of the peyote religion. The missionaries had succeeded in converting Sanko, a local medicine man's assistant, to Christianity. The shaman, Tone-a-koy, also observed the peyote ritual. When Tone-a-koy found out about Sanko's defection, he threatened to kill Sanko with his special medicine. He ordered the day of execution to be announced so that the Kiowas would gather at Rainy Mountain and find out whose god had the greatest power. The terrified Sanko fled to Reeside and Ballew's cabin. The two missionaries lightly assured Sanko that the threats were just superstitious nonsense and that nothing would happen to him. Sanko remained unconvinced and begged for some kind of antidote to Tone-a-koy's power. Julia Given finally persuaded the missionaries that they could not just dismiss these fears and that to Sanko the medicine man's powers represented a very real threat. Reeside, Ballew, Given, and Sanko knelt for a long time in prayer and asked for divine intervention on his behalf.

The evening of confrontation arrived, and Tone-a-koy made a frightening and horrible appearance in paint and costume as he danced and chanted the death prayer. In the middle of the performance, Tone-a-koy fell to the ground, suffered a seizure, and died. The crowd grew frenzied as Tone-a-koy's wives and sister cut themselves and screamed in mourning while blood ran down their clothing. Reeside and Ballew had refused to attend the ceremony, but when they heard the telltale wailing, they rushed to the site to comfort the women. Sanko's god had prevailed, and attendance at the chapel increased. Whether these events actually happened as they were told to Nye meant less than the image of cultural upheaval that they evoked. Reeside, Ballew, and other missionaries to the Kiowas needed alternative means of access to the hearts and minds of the people—techniques beyond the usual appeals to follow the Jesus Road.[24]

One method of gaining the acceptance and trust of the Kiowas lay in becoming intimately acquainted with their daily lives. Isabel Crawford, more than any other missionary among the Kiowas, met this requirement and consequently experienced success in helping the Kiowas to shape a reconciliation to a United States government-imposed way of life. She came to the reservation, she believed, following a divine call to bring the message of God to the Plains tribes. She soon discovered, however, that she could gain greatest acceptance in the lives of the Indians through participation in female activities. Women missionaries could go into the tipis and touch the basic routines of life as men could not. Crawford made female activities the center of social exchange, and Kiowa men joined their wives in group projects fostered by Crawford that enabled them to regain a measure of control of their existence. She became so influential among Kiowa women and men that she shaped some Kiowa behavior to be more consistent with acculturating goals. Her downfall within the church came when she crossed the gender line drawn by her own culture and placed herself in conflict with white male authorities over land ownership and the holy sacraments of her denomination's hierarchy.[25]

Isabel Crawford, a new graduate of the Female Baptist Missionary Training School in Chicago, Illinois, reached Indian Territory in 1893. At the age of twenty-eight she had already acquired a lifetime of training for the mission field while growing up in Canada. Her father, John Crawford, had been a minister and theology professor at several remote locations in Canada and in North Dakota. Crawford had been baptized at age ten and had promptly proceeded to recruit her own boys' Sunday school class from the city streets. As she grew older she served as her father's assistant. Her parents educated her at home in Bible study, music, French, and art in addition to her regular studies at school. At age sixteen Crawford contracted tuberculosis and was forced into a prolonged period of bed rest accompanied by massive doses of quinine. The illness left her almost completely deaf. She carried a hearing device for the remainder of her life and referred to it good-naturedly as her "conversation piece."[26]

Crawford's father's death left the family virtually penniless. Believing that advantageous marriage was unlikely, Crawford gave painting lessons and music performances to earn the money to enter the missionary training school. Mary G. Burdette, corresponding secretary for the Women's American Baptist Home Mission Society, exerted a powerful influence over Crawford, and they continued to be close friends for the remainder of their lives. From conversations at the school with Burdette, Crawford developed a keen sense of the importance of women in the mission field. Burdette was "the first person I ever heard emphasize the fact that *God called women* as well as men," she remembered, "not to go into all the world and *preach* the Gospel, but to go into the world and *teach it in a simple womanly way*." At the end of a long career as a missionary, fund-raiser, and speaker, Crawford amended this belief. Her experiences among the Kiowas convinced her that "God calls *women* into full service as well as men."[27]

The two-year program of missionary instruction included theology and Bible study, rules of order, physical and vocal culture, kindergarten methods, and temperance. Physicians also instructed the trainees in basic medical practices. More importantly, the school sent the young women out in pairs on the streets of Chicago's slums to proselytize and minister to the poor. Crawford had seen poverty on the Canadian and American frontiers, but in Chicago she encountered violence, prostitution, alcoholism, drug abuse, disease, and starvation. She quickly learned that no one took her spiritual message seriously until she had won their trust with food, clothing, firewood, or medical attention. Crawford proclaimed that she met these challenges with a "castiron constitution, a Scotch backbone, a fully developed Irish funny-bone—which equipment, if properly used, should land one, if not on Canaan's shore, then surely on some other." Her field appointment, announced upon her graduation, shocked and disappointed her. She had dreamed of an exotic assignment in China, India, or Africa. Instead, the Women's Missionary Society sent her to Indian Territory. "I did not want to go to the 'dirty Indians' and nearly cried my eyes out over the thought of it," she wrote. "However, I gave in and went to the Kiowas."[28]

Reverend Joseph S. Morrow escorted Crawford and her coworker, Hattie Everts, to Lone Wolf's camp at Elk Creek in 1893. He explained to the assembled crowd that the young women wanted to tell them about Jesus and would not take their land or their money. Condescendingly, Crawford also made a brief speech that she hoped set the theme of her work. "We have come to love you," she told them, "to tell you all about Jesus and teach you everything we know." In the following months Crawford more likely learned more than her native hosts. Only thirty-seven Kiowas resided at Elk Creek, and these were divided into three camps under the leadership of Lone Wolf, Little Bow, and Komalty. The initial response to the two strangers seemed precarious; neither of the women spoke Kiowa, and Crawford could not hear. She taught their interpreter, Paul, to shout into the large end of her hearing trumpet to communicate with her. He taught her sign language, and this became her chief method of communication. The missionaries began work by sitting outside the tipis singing hymns and reading the

Bible. The Kiowas ignored them. A Que Quoddle, wife of Chief Lone Wolf, told her great-granddaughter years later that when Crawford and her partner first arrived, their singing, praying, and crying seemed very strange. The Kiowas referred to them as those "poor, crazy old white women." Crawford finally entered a tipi and asked the woman inside if they could come in and hold a prayer meeting. After this initial contact, Crawford and Everts moved from tipi to tipi bearing the Word. Not all of the Kiowas accepted this intrusion, however, and on one occasion, Everts and Crawford scurried out when the husband came home and threatened them with a knife. Like most missionaries, Crawford was frightened by the peyote ceremony, and she saw it as a threat to her own message of Protestant Christianity.[29]

Crawford put her Chicago training to good use. When a baby was sick, she entered the tipi and gave it what nursing care she could, or she cleaned and washed for the mother. Alma, Komalty's wife, was one of the first to welcome Crawford's attempts at friendship, and after the wives of Lone Wolf and Little Bow accepted her, Crawford felt more secure. When the missionaries opened a kindergarten, Crawford gave each child a bath, and Everts mended their clothes. They encouraged the mothers to send children over seven years old to the Rainy Mountain School. Unfamiliar with Kiowa culture, Crawford expressed grave concern to Burdette that Kiowa girls were "sold, stolen, or given away," and she felt that to stop this more Christian women were needed to "win the hearts of the mothers and try to instruct them in a better way." Crawford combined Bible lessons with sewing lessons, and she expected good work. If they failed to sew neatly, she pulled out the stitches. "They don't like me to rip up their work," she wrote in her journal, "but when it is bad, out it comes, and when their noses go up, mine follows." She also insisted that they mend their worn garments although "several of the women contemptuously refused," preferring to buy new things. She noted that "those who mended and those who refused, however, listened to the Gospel."[30]

How Crawford presented the Gospel message to the women, in view of the physical, cultural, and linguistic barriers, and what the Kiowa women understood about Baptist theology, defies comprehension. If the responses Crawford recorded in her diary are any indication, however, it is clear that one of the incentives she proffered for acceptance of Christianity lay in alleviating the misery associated with the deaths of children. Crawford attempted to console the bereaved parents, even though the agony of their mourning ritual appalled her. She made coffins, helped dig graves, and adorned markers, painting them with calla lilies and the words, "Gone to Jesus." References in her reports abound with professions of faith based on the desire of parents to be with their children. The following excerpt serves as a poignant example:

> We cannot understand English, but the white ladies make us understand exactly what the Bible tells us. . . . A long time ago I had several children and because I was a great sinner Jesus took them away with Him. After they died I suffered very much and kept thinking and thinking, for I wanted to see my children again some place. After a while I heard the gospel about everlasting life and how Jesus had my children with him, and I believed in my heart.[31]

Dealing with the hunger rampant during 1893–95 required most of Crawford's energy and courage. Crawford expressed her anger toward both the govern-

ment for their failure to make good on promises to the
Kiowas and toward the greedy white opportunists who
cheated the Kiowas out of what little they had. The two
women missionaries survived on beans for weeks when
supplies failed to arrive, and at times hunger made
them too feeble to work. Crawford tried to supplement
their diet with fish, but she was usually unsuccessful.
On more than one occasion she fed starving Kiowas the
scraps she had prepared for her dog. Hattie Everts left
after the first year. Crawford never forgot these years
of deprivation, and she spoke of this time frequently on
her lecture and fund-raising tours. "The Indians know
more about starvation than any other people on the
earth," she announced, "and after this winter I have a
sympathy for them that will always be ripe for action."
She also used the experience to encourage Kiowa men
to provide better for their families. During one
Christmas celebration, Crawford called all of the men
who had plowed, fenced, or hauled wood for their wives
to stand at the front with her. She delivered a lecture
on the value of labor and how it would make them as
prosperous as white people, and she ended her remarks
with the reminder, "Jesus' book says, No work—no
chuck-a-way [food]." She then rewarded those men
standing near her with homemade fruit pastries. Later
she confided to her journal this postscript to the scene:
"What's the use of our coming out here to teach the
women how to do more work while the men bask in the
sun?"[32]

Crawford recognized the limitations of the Elk
Creek location and asked for placement in an area
where she could reach more people. In 1896 she made
arrangements to move to Saddle Mountain, thirty
miles east, where nearly one hundred Kiowas were
camped. Crawford had some doubts about joining this
group. A few years earlier the camp at Sugar Creek

Isabel Crawford and Lucius Aitsan.
From Hugh D. Corwin, *The Kiowa
Indians, Their History and Life Stories*,
p. 189. Photo courtesy Western History
Collections, University of Oklahoma
Library.

had armed themselves and driven off government
contractors who were hauling in wood for a school.
When she inquired about safety, officials at Anadarko
sent the ambiguous message that the location "is all
right if you can stand it." Zotone and his wife Un-ga-
day, who had been converted at a camp meeting at
Rainy Mountain, accompanied Crawford to Saddle
Mountain and assured her of the help of Chief Hunting

Horse and Lucius Aitsan, who would be her interpreter. The Kiowas seemed surprised that she came all
alone, telling her, "We like this. One Jesus woman
among so many Indians, and no skeered." Many,
especially the peyote leaders, remained suspicious,
however, and warned that "We will let this Jesus
Woman sit down with us because the Great Father has
sent her, but we will give no land to Jesus for we do not
want a church in here. White men are dangerous."
Crawford set out immediately to persuade the Kiowas
that they really did want a church of their own.[33]

The first few months at Saddle Mountain tested
Crawford's courage and vitality. She lived in a tent
fighting off invading chickens, pigs, and dogs. When
the creek overflowed after a rain, muddy water soaked
her possessions. Food and fresh supplies arrived from
Fort Sill irregularly, and for days at a time Crawford
survived on bread and syrup. At one point when she
saw Mabel Aitsan rounding up a litter of pups that she
intended to cook for supper, hunger overcame
Crawford's objections, and she shared in the feast. Her
only relief came when she traveled by wagon to Rainy
Mountain for visits with Reeside and Ballew, rest, food,
and a hot bath. She confided in her journal, "There are
different kinds of hardships and those of the heart and
spirit are harder to bear than those of a physical
nature." When word arrived that her mother had died,
the Kiowas offered her their sympathy and prayers, but
the news devastated Crawford. "At that moment, the
brown arm and nasty blanket were repulsive to me.
The whole life was horrid. I hadn't a taste in common
with it. I couldn't love the Indians, but I wouldn't give
them up because I thought God had called me to give
them the gospel," she wrote. Lucius and Mabel Aitsan
offered to share their two-room house with her, and
Crawford was touched by this generous gesture.[34]

Crawford ingratiated herself with the Kiowa women at Saddle Mountain in the same way she had at Elk Creek. She gave them lessons in baking bread, sewing, and cleaning, all accompanied by prayers and Bible lessons. Crawford insisted that acceptance into church membership required that they give up the practice of polygamy. This was an especially hard decision for older families who had lived together happily for years. Polygamous marriages usually represented two sisters married to the same man. For a man to give up his wife meant for him to "throw her away" or abandon her, and it implied discreditable behavior on her part. Botone posed the dilemma to Crawford: Why should he be forced to treat a good wife in this way? A male minister had refused Botone and his two wives admission to church membership, but Botone thought Crawford might have an answer. "Men's hearts are hard like stone. Women's are not hard. They pretty soon cry," he told her. "I want you to think wisely and tell me what road I am on." Although sympathetic to the situation, Crawford offered no other resolution. Regretfully, Botone told her, "I will try to keep close enough to Jesus every day so that I can hold onto him with one hand and pull my two wives behind me with the other, and with all our ten papooses on our backs. When we get to the wonderful door it will open without a key and the Great Father will say 'Come in! You got here with all I gave you. You did not throw any of them away. I will not cut you off.'" Occasionally, a Kiowa wife resolved the issue and slipped silently away with her possessions to her own tipi on her own allotment—freeing her husband, her sister, and herself for church membership.[35]

Crawford's true goal became the establishment of a church. As early as January 1897, Crawford gave a gold one-dollar American coin and a ten-cent silver

Canadian coin to the daughter of Lucius and Mabel Aitsan, along with a letter telling her that one day the Kiowas would change their minds and want a church of their own. "This money is to be put by for that church so that you, a little baby girl, just two years old, are the very first to start a church for the Kiowas at Saddle Mountain." Crawford devised a scheme to forward that goal and one that would draw in the men of the camp. Reverend Joseph S. Murrow contributed quilt lining and batting, and boxes of donations from Crawford's contacts with national churches came filled with scrap material. Crawford began a sewing circle among the women that was designed to make quilts and sell them for money. The singing, refreshments, and good-humored activity attracted the men, who joined the women in the sewing projects. Crawford modestly reported, "Our quilt meetings were always well attended by both men and women, the sociability as well as the work attracting all within reach."[36]

By the end of the year Crawford had converted the sewing circle into a missionary circle that the Kiowas named Daw-kee-boom-gee-K'oop, or God's Light Upon the Mountain. Crawford wrote to the officials of the Women's American Baptist Home Mission Society for permission to allow male members into the group, but the president of the missionary group, Pope-bah, was a woman. Under Crawford's tutelage, Pope-bah advised her group of male and female quilters, "I am head and I want you all to work together for Jesus and then we can do something." Pope-bah and her husband, Kokom, and a small group of Kiowas accompanied Crawford on a lecture and fund-raising tour across the Midwest. Anticipating the hostility that they would face along the way, Crawford issued each of them a washcloth and a bar of soap, and she instructed them to keep clean and not to chew gum or eat raw green onions. The trip terrified the Kiowas. Pope-bah told Crawford, "I am skeered of white people and I'm skeered everytime I see a train." The train passengers acted equally alarmed at the presence of the colorful Kiowas. At Chickasha, Oklahoma Territory, the hotel manager refused to allow them to eat in the dining room until Crawford reprimanded him: She told him they were Christians and, showing the soap, said, "We are all very clean and particular; we carry soap and washclothes." That settled it. By the time the group arrived in Topeka, Kansas, however, they insisted on eating at what Crawford described as an "uninviting colored restaurant." Kokom reassured Crawford, "Black men are our friends, They have kind hearts and never laugh at us like white men."[37]

Crawford convinced the group to put the money earned from the quilt sales into two barrels, one to send to help poor Indians of other tribes and one to put aside in a bank for a church building of their own. Mary G. Burdette located for Crawford a group of Hopi Indians in Arizona who were receptive to a missionary. Lucius Aitsan summed up the feelings of the missionary circle and the urgency with which they worked: "Send this to the Jesus Woman's Society and tell them to hurry up and send a Jesus woman to another tribe, or the old people will die and be losted, and it will be our fault." The Missionary Training School sent Katherine Bare to assist Crawford at Saddle Mountain. Crawford's former assistant, Mary McLean, and the Kiowa quilt money went to Arizona to establish a mission for the Hopis, whom the Kiowas believed to be less fortunate than themselves.[38]

The matter of a church involved more diplomacy. Crawford had to assure the camp that if they built one, white people would not come in and take it away from them. Domot told Crawford that he feared that, "After we old men are dead and gone the white man will come and drive our children out and use the Jesus house for themselves." Land allotment to the Kiowas was almost complete in 1901, and Crawford told them that if the Women's American Baptist Home Mission Society received the allotment of church land, it would always belong to the Kiowas. The band also demanded that the minister be one of their own people, and they chose Lucius Aitsan to train for the position. Quilt production increased, and Crawford scoured the immediate area and the nation for donations. She convinced a Chinese mission in San Francisco to contribute money to the Kiowa fund, and she so impressed agent James Randlett that he took up a collection among wealthy railroad developers and sent her $200 for the church. Crawford hired her brother, Hugh Crawford, and a Texas contractor, C. C. Cooper, to design and construct the church with Kiowa labor. The Saddle Mountain Baptist Church opened on Easter Sunday in 1903 with sixty-four charter members; Crawford was the only non-Indian.

Crawford's joy at the development of a church built by Kiowas, staffed by Kiowas, and filled with Kiowas lasted only a short time. She had alienated the male administration of the American Baptist Home Mission Society (separate from the women's branch of that organization) by insisting on a full 160-acre allotment under the auspices of the Women's American Baptist Home Mission Society. Crawford secured a promise of 80 acres at the church site and an additional 80 acres at another location. She lobbied agent James Randlett and commissioner of Indian affairs W. A. Jones. They both assured her that, although the other missions objected, the full allotment had been registered. The remaining three Baptist missions on the reservation, under the direction of the American Baptist Home

Saddle Mountain Baptist Church. From Hugh D. Corwin, *The Kiowa Indians, Their History and Life Stories,* p. 115. Photo courtesy Western History Collections, University of Oklahoma Library.

Mission Society, had 160 acres divided among them. The administration resented Crawford's success even more when the government set aside an additional 40 acres adjacent to the Saddle Mountain church for a cemetery. However, neither Crawford nor her adversaries discovered until 1952 that the second 80 acre allotment had never been recorded.[40]

Officials of the American Baptist Home Mission Society and the Oklahoma Indian Baptist Association seized on an excuse to discredit Crawford's work. In the

absence of an ordained minister, the Saddle Mountain
Church chose Lucius Aitsan to administer the sacrament of Holy Communion. The deacons of the church
and Crawford assisted him. The Indian Baptist Association passed a resolution condemning the action and
suggesting the possibility of other irregular practices.
The Board of the Women's American Baptist Home
Mission Society expressed concern and disapproval,
and Mary G. Burdette frantically demanded an explanation from Crawford. Crawford assured Burdette that
she had not conducted the service herself and that she
had only assisted Aitsan, but she defended the right of
any unpastored church to celebrate Communion. The
Women's Home Mission Society closed the matter. The
American Baptist Home Mission Society, however,
continued to insist that Crawford should have invited
the pastor at Rainy Mountain to conduct the service,
and they refused to rescind the critical resolution.
Crawford regretfully resigned her position and left
Saddle Mountain in 1906.[41]

Her relationship with the Kiowas never waned,
however, and she returned for several visits before her
death. Harry S. Treat served as pastor until Lucius
Aitsan was ordained. Aitsan led the church between
1913 and 1918. One of the young girls Crawford knew,
Ioleta Hunt MacElhaney, graduated from a New York
college as the first Kiowa woman to receive a
baccalaureate degree and returned to direct the church
from 1949 to 1954. Crawford continued to travel
throughout the United States on behalf of the Women's
Mission Society. When she lectured, she donned a full
Kiowa woman's native buckskin costume and closed
her program with the Lord's Prayer, or the Twenty-
third Psalm, performed in sign language. According to
her wishes, she was buried at the Saddle Mountain
Cemetery after her death in 1961. Her tombstone

Lucius Aitsan
and Mabel
Aitsan. Photo
courtesy of the
Western
History
Collections,
University of
Oklahoma
Library.

contained the inscription, "I dwell among mine own people."[42]

The Kiowas accepted Isabel Crawford and what she had to teach them as they accepted few others. A decade after Crawford's departure, Delos Lone Wolf, nephew of the younger Chief Lone Wolf, spoke at a meeting of the Society of American Indians at Cedar Falls, Iowa. He defended the use of peyote as an instrument for bringing the Kiowas into Christian churches, but his words echoed those of his uncle years before: "Now you Christian people who are trying to civilize the Indians, why don't you take your civilization and your Christianity to the lost Indians who are using peyote. Right there is where the fault comes in," he said. Isabel Crawford took her faith and her culture directly into the homes of the Kiowa people. She ate what they ate, slept in their tipis, wrote letters on their behalf, grieved with them, buried their dead, and rejoiced in their triumphs. Still, when she left, Saddle Mountain remained a Kiowa-centered world. The 1910 federal census revealed a Kiowa population hardly changed in numbers since 1890, only 1,107. Three-quarters of the tribe claimed full blood. Less than half of the women over ten years of age could read, write, or speak English, as compared to a third of the men who could speak English and 40 percent who were literate. The census listed only a single Kiowa woman as gainfully employed, and 79.9 percent of the women over fifteen years old were married. Acculturation imposed by the force of the United States government showed little success. Kiowas clung to traditional patterns. They incorporated new ideas that they found valuable and discarded the rest. They learned from Crawford a sense of the elementary habits of main-stream American life and the fruits of negotiation and cooperative effort with a non-Indian world. Crawford gained cultural entrance through her ministrations to women, and she improved the leadership opportunities and experience for Kiowa women. They, in turn, taught her the power of an indomitable spirit and cultural integrity under the most cruel circumstances. Once inside the tipi, Crawford wedded homemaking, in the truest sense of the word, to survival in the larger, modernized society.[43]

Cherokee and Kiowa women lived very different lives, and each brought a unique perspective of their transplantation and confinement to the piece of American land known as Indian Territory. American officials capitalized on their associations with Cherokee women from the beginning: Government agents encouraged the expansion of agriculture and domestic manufacture, both of which created a greater appreciation of the individual ownership of material possessions. They promoted intermarriage with white colonials and very early identified Cherokee women as an important element in the pacification and acculturation of the tribe. A mixed-blood Cherokee elite emerged, who used identical strategies to first fend off dispossession of Cherokee lands and extinction of tribal sovereignty, and when that failed, used these methods to assert Cherokee hegemony in the affairs of early statehood. Cherokee women who had been educated at the Female Seminary represented the cultural apex. They combined the education and public activism of New England, the refined graces of the South, and access to the land and wealth of the West gained by virtue of their Indian blood. These three components in the person of the elite Cherokee woman reconciled the tensions of class and race in Oklahoma and came to symbolize an image worthy of the state.

In contrast, Kiowa women were seen only as insignificant dependents of a warrior society and failed to receive any attention until the advent of field matrons in the 1890s. Military officers, government agents, and religious officials found little in Kiowa culture to appreciate or upon which to form a basis for interaction. Until 1874, combat, starvation, and death appeared the only constants. Whereas the numerous Cherokees took over direction of their own institutions, the scattered Kiowa bands resisted all imposed efforts to change the way of life they knew. In both cases, however, some of the most profound changes took place as a result of private, personal interventions by non-Indian women: For twenty-six years Florence Wilson shaped the development of a Cherokee female elite, and for thirteen years Isabel Crawford labored among the Kiowas. Indian women faced a bewildering continuum of alternatives that included education toward the Victorian ideal and vocational training for farm life. All of these alternatives aimed at the inculcation of Euroamerican gender-role standards. The choices the women made depended on their past tribal experiences, the position they enjoyed within their traditional culture, and the nature of their confinement in Indian Territory. The Cherokees and the Kiowas followed a different trajectory, but both groups refused to relinquish a sense of their tribal identity in a period of forced acculturation.

6

Lifting as We Climb

Elva Ferguson's memoirs defined the Oklahoma pioneer experience through several exclusive lenses: she presented settlement from the vantage point of white homesteaders in Oklahoma Territory, and she narrated it from a socially limited point of view. By contrast, Native American women responded to a broad spectrum of alternatives thrust upon them by government officials and white agents of acculturation. The extent to which they embraced expected patterns of behavior determined their acceptability in the wider culture.

Some historians have suggested that gender expectations—more than class, ethnicity, race, religion, education, or marital status—shaped the lives of westering women. A multiracial examination of women's experiences, however, indicates the centrality of the issue of race in the settlement of the American

West. The several all-black communities in the Twin Territories of the future state of Oklahoma provide a rich context for an understanding of gender and race imperatives. The concept of pioneer women took on expanded meaning in these communities as black women not only contributed to the development and growth of their towns but also established a new model of black womanhood. Abandoning the historical limitations of slavery and challenging the contemporary limitations of sharecropping and those of a hardening racist American culture, territorial Oklahoma's black-town women constructed a female culture that reinforced the high standards they set for themselves, sustained and unified their relationships with each other, and defied criticism from whites as well as from their black male counterparts. Their experiences in the insulated freedom of the black town provided the nurturing bridge of race, gender, and culture for future generations of Oklahoma black women.[1]

The land runs and lotteries that opened large tracts in Oklahoma Territory for non-Indian settlement and development after 1889 attracted a considerable number of black families. Many came from the South in search of an opportunity to gain land or to escape from increasingly stratified racial politics engineered through Jim Crow legislation. Others moved in from Kansas, adding another temporary stop to a pattern of exodus that was to continue out of the state of Oklahoma to the far West and into Canada. Former slaves Alice Alexander and her husband joined a covered wagon train leaving Louisiana and walked nearly all the way to Oklahoma in search of freedom and opportunity. "We come to Oklahoma looking for de same thang then dat darkies go north looking fer now," she later told a Works Progress Administration interviewer. "We got dissipinted."[2]

These new settlers joined an already-present black
and black-Indian mixed population residing in Indian
Territory, the freed slaves of the Five Tribes. By the
turn of the century, the federal census listed a black
population in both territories of 55,684, or 7 percent of
the population. The total black population increased
two and one-half times in the next decade to 137,612,
but with burgeoning white settlement, blacks continued to be a small minority, showing concentrations
of over 5,000 in only seven counties. Even so, blacks
outnumbered Indians two to one. Throughout the
territorial period there was a nearly even ratio of black
females to black males both in all-black towns and in
the remainder of the territories as well. Sixty-four
percent of the black women over fifteen years of age
were married as compared to 58 percent of the men.
The suggestion of a historically entrenched pattern of
female-headed households did not hold true in these
all-black Oklahoma communities.[3]

Experienced black politicians, town promoters, and
entrepreneurs saw very real opportunities for wealth
and advancement in the Twin Territories, and possibly
even for the creation of an all-black state. Edward P.
McCabe promoted Langston City in 1890–91 as a
settlement supply base for future land openings in the
northern part of the territory. The Fort Smith and
Western Railroad, building across Indian Territory,
purchased the allotment of Abigail Barnett, daughter
of a Creek freedman, and platted a townsite along the
rail line at Boley in 1904. They appointed a recent area
settler, Thomas M. Haynes, as townsite manager and
promoter. These two communities, Langston and Boley,
became the best known of approximately twenty-seven
all-black towns in territorial Oklahoma.[4]

The *Langston City Herald* and the *Boley Progress*
newspapers boasted about the development of the

OKLAHOMA'S ALL - BLACK TOWNS

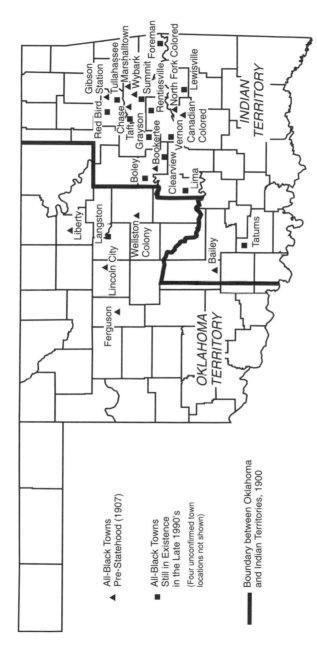

All-black Oklahoma communities. Map courtesy of Oklahoma State University Cartography Service.

towns and sent representatives throughout the South to recruit new businesses and settlers. The male editors chose a female image to project the fertility of the land. In Boley the *Progress* boasted that the area "leaped at one bound to the adult age; a buxom young giantess," who demolished records and astonished the world with the energy of her people and the variety of her resources. To further this "onward march of civilization," the newspaper advertised for the services of several young women to act as agents for its distribution. In return for the highest number of cash yearly subscribers above one hundred, the *Progress* offered to support the winner for one year in the school of her choice. For an agent residing within the territories, the advertisement agreed to send the young woman to Langston University for a school term.[5]

The initial infrastructure of the towns was more anticipated than real. Even though *Herald* editor R. E. Stewart warned that this was a new country "with no ready employment" and that those who came must have "sufficient money to take care of themselves and families until they raise a crop or get into business," hundreds came, by train to Guthrie and by foot or wagon to Langston, ill-prepared for the circumstances. Mrs. Willis Monroe, a homesteader, met one such train and later reported: "It was terrible how those people had suffered to get to the homes they did not own. Some had died on the way." She remembered that few who experienced those times were willing to talk about it; they were so disappointed at what they found. The stalwart and impoverished remained, and Langston citizens cooperated in working an eighty-acre vegetable garden to feed the town and to provide some relief to the new arrivals. The newspapers also made frequent calls for charitable contributions to provide food and clothing for needy families, especially after the death of a husband or wife. Families doubled up in tents and makeshift wooden buildings until suitable housing could be found.[6]

Some women went into the larger, racially mixed towns to secure a few days of domestic work: washing, ironing, cooking, or caring for children earning only pennies per day and totins' (leftover food and clothing). A cultural collision of Indian, white, and black experience became immediately obvious. Chaney McNair, born a slave on the Ratliff plantation near Tahlequah, Indian Territory, experienced the upheaval of the Civil War. In Kansas and later in territorial Oklahoma, she "worked out" in white homes. Although she received both money and land in the treaty settlements after the war, she continued to work. As she explained to a WPA interviewer in 1939, "I'se always been a workin' woman, no matter where I is." She humorously shared a story that she said showed her ignorance, but which in fact illustrated the challenge of crossing the lines of race and culture in this type of domestic arrangement. In her first position, her employer sent her away because she did not know how to make a fire with coal in the stove. McNair's only familiarity was with a wood fire in a fireplace. When her employers told her to fill the stove "reservoir" with water, "malgamate" the eggs, and clean the "balcony," she stared in wonderment. "I didn't know white folks language," she said. "They used so much different language, those northerners, I thought I'd never learn it." Another former slave remembered an important piece of racial etiquette: "White folks now don't want you to tech 'em. . . . You kin cook for 'em and put your hands in they vittles and they don't say nothing, but jest you tech one!" Black women quickly learned such distinctions during the transition from slavery to domestic service.[7]

Many black families sent out daughters at an early age to do domestic work. An employment service in the neighboring white town of Paden advertised in the *Boley Informer* for "one small girl about ten or twelve years old to assist around the house." The advertisement listed no wages, but stated it was a "good place to stay, guarantees good treatment, and stay as long as you want to." As a young girl, Mrs. George Busby hired out to a northern couple who owned a grocery store in Chickasha. Her employer taught her how to manage a house and cook and made sure that when she went to parties her "clothes and ribbons were just right." Busby claimed that since the couple had no children, "they treated me nearly like I was their own." Still, she was considered hired help rather than family, and the nature of her employment denied her access to education and economic independence, attributes black-town leaders prized. Better-educated women took jobs as teachers and enjoyed both greater status and independence. Mrs. C. M. Hollensworth, for example, commuted to Guthrie, where she taught in the public schools. She went home to Langston on weekends and during summer vacations.[8]

In Indian Territory animosity existed between the freedmen, who had land allotments, tribal citizenship, and, in some cases, tribal wealth and leadership positions, and the influx of new immigrants often referred to as "State Negroes." Tribal freedmen had been fighting for some time for full implementation of the rights guaranteed them under treaties made between the Five Tribes and the United States government following the Civil War. The treaties granted incorporation of the former slaves as full citizens of their respective Indian nations with rights to land, access to education, and full political participation. The Creek and Seminole tribal governments met those requirements right away, but the Cherokee, Choctaw, and Chickasaw Nations resisted the demands for another thirty years. The Choctaws and Chickasaws enacted "Black Codes" similar to those passed in the South, and they harassed blacks and broke up settlements within their boundaries. The Dawes Commission took determination of citizenship out of the hands of the Indian governments, and the commissioners allotted lands on the basis of their decisions, creating resentment among tribal leaders. Freedmen native to Indian Territory feared the loss of lands to these outsiders through fraud and the deterioration of their own status as the number of black newcomers increased. They blamed increasing racial antipathy from both full-blood Indian and whites on the large numbers of new black arrivals, whom they criticized as poorer and more subservient in their demeanor. Boley matron Alafair Carter Adams contributed a different perspective on the problem: She believed that the Indian freedmen expected an easy life and that they were not as progressive in outlook as the new settlers coming in. She thought the freedmen were lazy and usually "lived up everything before they wanted to do anything." Former Indian Territory slave Polly Colbert agreed; she felt that because of the rich land, "us niggers dat was owned by Indians didn't have to work so hard as dey did in de old states." Women exchanged epithets over seemingly backward behavior: When a woman refused to take an expansive attitude toward the new freedoms, as compared to the security of slavery, she was called a rag-head. Adams pointed out, however, that a number of intruders "claimed they were natives that weren't, just to latch onto a free piece of land here." This increased the tension between the two groups.[9]

In spite of the complex racial relationships and the initial hardships and disappointments, the black towns boomed in the early years. Booker T. Washington's inspiring rhetoric and example of "uplift," carried to the West with the migrants and reinforced in newspaper editorials, forged a unity of effort among the residents to build a showcase of black prosperity, self-determination, pride, and culture. This attitude encouraged the possibility of female entrepreneurship, and black-town women confidently seized the moment to move female work beyond the world of domestic service. Less ostentatious than the first banks or cotton gins, which required large capital outlays, were the small service businesses. These concerns proved just as important to the growth and well-being of the towns, and women often operated the businesses or owned them outright. Black-town newspapers gave equal space to publicizing female enterprises and often applauded the skills of working women in the communities.

A brief survey of newspaper advertisements between 1905–15 indicates the diversity of enterprises operated by black women. Mrs. Lulu Smith owned the Pioneer Milinery [sic] Store, Boley's first, and in the *Progress* she advertised seasonal stock selections and her expertise at dressmaking. Her competition included Mrs. A. E. Gates and Miss S. A. Montgomery, who advertised in the *Boley Informer*. Mrs. William Romby owned the Elite Cafe, and Mrs. M. C. Haynes catered refreshments to special events, such as meetings of the Constitutional League and state Teachers Association, in Boley. Some of the more prominent women coowned or managed businesses separate from their husbands' primary establishments. Hilliard Taylor owned the Boley Cotton Gin and marketed lumber, while his wife advertised hair-care products as the local agent for the French System of hair straightening. California Taylor Turner managed the drugstore owned by her banker husband, and Mrs. O. H. Bradley, wife of the *Progress*

editor, shared ownership in the Boley Burial and
Funeral Association. In the neighboring black town of
Clearview, Maggie Aikens's boarding house was well
publicized, as was Mrs. B. Goens's Ice Cream Parlor.
Mothers and daughters often worked side by side in a
store as, for example, Mrs. J. H. and Miss Amanda
Cummings, who advertised their Clearview sundry
store.[10]

In addition to providing opportunity for female
investment and management, the black towns offered
a variety of other employment positions. The 1910
federal census recorded 37.2 percent of black Oklahoma women over ten years of age as being gainfully
employed. Boley townsite manager Thomas Haynes
placed an advertisement in 1906 for a "lady 'stenographer' and 'typewriter'" offering good wages and a
twelve-month contract. Other businesses, especially
law firms, employed young women in clerical work on
an as-needed basis. While she was single Ollie Robinson
Bacon occasionally worked for Jones and Peters law
firm, and after her marriage she managed the Bacon
and Bacon General Store. Hallie Q. Jones and Eliza
Dolphin Paxton were both postmistresses of Boley, and
Annie Peters worked in the telephone office. Mrs. C. M.
Brock advertised her services as a notary public,
operating from an office located in Turner's Drug
Store. Clerking in the grocery stores also seemed
acceptable employment, and the Clearview Patriarch
singled out Miss Rebecca Grayson for special praise. A
Langston Herald advice columnist voiced the community reinforcement of this work ethic when she
counseled young women that teaching was not the only
career available: "It is now almost impossible to find
any business in which a woman is not engaged," she
wrote, "if not as principal as assistant. Although she is
not always paid as good a salary as the opposite sex."[11]

In these all-black communities working women were considered as vital to survival and success as working men, and newspapers celebrated the accomplishments of both sexes. When Boley city attorney E. O. Tyler rewrote the city's ordinances in 1911, the city council and the *Boley Informer* distributed congratulations for the work evenly between Tyler and his stenographer, Miss Scott Herriford. In a page one article the *Informer* described Herriford as "quite an intellectual young lady" who was a recent honor graduate from the business course at Western University in Kansas City. The column praised her assistance to Tyler as proficient and thorough. On behalf of the community, the *Informer* wished her success and assured her of their "hearty patronage." New jobs and busy, working men and women meant prosperity.[12]

Most of the women mentioned in the Boley newspapers united to organize the Boley Ladies Industrial Club in 1908 to serve social, economic, and benevolent needs. These women were prominent not solely by virtue of marriage, but because they were economically productive, and they shaped the black-town cultural life. The Ladies Industrial Club founded the Boley Public Library, assisted in local relief, and introduced newcomers and young single women into society. Members functioned as the arbiters of manners and morals, but they also stimulated financial growth through their investment and their labor.

Agriculture constituted the backbone of black town prosperity, however, and survival depended on good crops and high prices. Women had no control over the latter, but they could contribute to the former. Like other farm women all over Oklahoma, black women went into the fields, adding their labor to that of their husbands and children. The 1910 federal census listed 6,043 Negro females ten years of age and over employed

Mrs. C. M. Ruff cultivating her cotton field near Wellston. Photo courtesy of the Archives & Manuscript Division of the Oklahoma Historical Society.

as laborers on home farms in Oklahoma, as compared to 6,330 males. Most often the women combined homemaking, childbearing, and field labor in a seasonal cycle of hard work: They tilled the family garden and canned and preserved the harvest. They sewed, washed, and cleaned with limited resources. They bore and reared children, and they lost some in death. They planted, chopped, and picked cotton and corn, always hoping for a better crop next year. The seeming ordinariness of their days masked private sacrifices and quiet heroism, as well as joy and pride in accomplishment. Anna Aldridge Hamm, for instance, who had been blind since the age of sixteen, farmed in the Boley area with her ten children after the death of her husband.[13]

Sometimes the hard work exacted a heavy toll. The *Boley Progress* reported the details of the death of Estella Tomlin in 1908: While she was helping her husband pick cotton in the field, her long skirt swept too close to the warming fire, and she was soon enveloped in flames. Family from Texas, friends, and local doctors ministered to her, but she died two weeks later. The newspaper mourned her passing and praised "Sister" Tomlin's record of church work and her courage in the face of intense pain.[14]

The cases of black women who broke down under the strain, became alienated from community life, or suffered mental collapse were less publicized or documented, but well-known to black-town residents. The *Boley Beacon* included a brief note of sympathy in its "Local Mention" column in 1908 when a local woman was taken to the insane asylum. The same issue asked for aid for a widow with an "insane daughter," a baby, and three other children to feed. Another black newspaper reported on the incarceration of a vagrant black woman, found wandering near Guthrie, who gave her address only as Fort Smith, Arkansas. The article described her as a very large, muscular woman about thirty-five years old. She had been hiding in cornfields and living in secluded locations for two weeks, coming close to houses only to beg for matches. When area residents reported her, the sheriff made the arrest, and the county insanity board ordered the woman to be taken to the insane asylum.[15]

Mabel Irene Bridgewater, a young college student at the University of Oklahoma, made a study of female insanity among Oklahoma women for her senior thesis in sociology in 1911. She reported approximately five hundred women incarcerated at the two state institutions, which were located at Norman and Fort Supply at that time. Male officials followed a standard procedure that involved the arrest and detention in jail of those believed to be insane. The county courts or a local board determined each case, and upon their decision the woman was institutionalized. Bridgewater complained that the "detention of women without attendance by persons of their own sex" was "indecent" and intolerable. At the hospitals, the patients were segregated by sex and race, and the "hardy" were put to work on maintenance chores. Although they ranged in age from ten to sixty years old, the majority of the female patients were fifteen to thirty years of age. Of the women admitted to the two institutions in 1910, 83 percent listed their occupation as housewife. According to Bridgewater most came from the rural and poorer districts of the state, and she concluded, "The principal cause of female insanity in Oklahoma is overwork and deprivation."[16]

Bridgewater's observation about overwork and deprivation as a detriment to female health appeared to voice a commonly held concern. Evidence in black-town newspapers reflected a shared interest with racially-mixed communities about female health problems. Newspaper pages headed "Of Interest To Our Women" contained, in addition to local society reports, columns of advertisements for tonics and cure-alls aimed at revitalizing the female consumer. Oil of Peruna seemed to be a popular general tonic, but Dr. Pierce's Favorite Prescription was designed specifically for women, and the advertisement left little to the imagination. This elixir, so the text read, had been developed by an experienced and skilled physician for the cure of the "delicate, intricate, and obstinate ailments" peculiar to the female sex. It was formulated to invigorate the whole body, but especially to impart strength to "the womb and its appendages." Not wanting to exclude any buyer, Dr. Pierce suggested it be used by "'worn out,' debilitated teachers, milliners, dressmakers, seamstresses, 'shop-girls,' house-keepers, nursing mothers and feeble women generally." The newspapers also extensively recorded illnesses, recuperation reports, and neonatal deaths. The inclusion of these articles and public advertisements reflected the immediate and personal community recognition of an anxiety that would be documented by 1930 as a demographic trend: Blacks in Oklahoma had a stillbirth, maternal death, and infant death rate that was nearly three times higher than that of any other racial group in the state.[17]

Education presented an avenue of escape from drudgery and poverty and a yardstick of racial advancement. Families struggled to build and operate local schools and sacrificed to keep their children attending. Langston women sold pies, box dinners, and sandwiches at picnics, auctions, and public gatherings to supplement the funds their husbands raised to buy the land and to equip a school. They wanted a college to educate black teachers and to offer agricultural, mechanical, and industrial training. After years of politicking and pressure on the territorial legislature to create such a school, the Langston-led Oklahoma Association of Negro Teachers forced a confrontation by attempting to enroll a black student, Cynthia Ware, at the white normal school in Edmond in 1896. This enrollment challenge, along with Langston founder E. P. McCabe's political support of the successful Republican candidate for governor, Cassius Barnes, influenced the legislature to establish the Colored Agricultural and Normal University at Langston the following year.

The school opened in September 1898 with forty-one students and a faculty of four in addition to the president, Dr. Inman E. Page. Students attended classes in the Presbyterian Church for several months until the main building was completed, largely through the donated labor of Langston citizens. Both

Attucks Dormitory for Women, Langston Colored Agriculture and Normal University, 1900. Photo courtesy of the Archives & Manuscript Division of the Oklahoma Historical Society.

students and faculty boarded with local families until dormitories were constructed. By 1899 women students resided in the newly completed Attucks Dormitory for Young Women. Tuition was free to Twin Territory students, but room and board cost $6.00 per month. In addition, each student was required to perform work on the school grounds. The fees proved exorbitant for many students, and it often took years to complete a course of study. Most of the early students were unprepared for college-level work. To meet basic educational needs and to provide on-site teacher training, the university opened elementary and high-school components, and the majority of students attended the lower grades.[18]

Langston campus life promoted the highest aspirations within a structured environment available to young black women of territorial Oklahoma. The female curriculum offered courses in domestic science and teacher training. Women students awoke at 5:30 A.M.

to begin work sweeping dormitories, cleaning rest-
rooms, and preparing the dining hall. At the sound of
a gong, they marched into the dining hall to the chords
of piano music, and they sang the morning prayer.
Mealtime lasted twenty-five minutes; at long tables
young men sat on one side and young women sat on the
other. Women students waited tables and then washed
the dishes. Mandatory chapel services began at 11:45
A.M. each day, and attendance at Sunday school and
worship was required. Over time informal friendships
developed into organized clubs. Bessie Floyd Dungee
started the Literatae Club, whose stated goal was the
"development of better womanhood" with an emphasis
on "deeds, not words." The Philomathean Club was a
debating society with the motto, "Knowledge is the
Key to Success." Female students in the Teacher's
College founded the Phyllis Wheatley Club. Women
students signed in and out of the dormitory when they
went anywhere other than to classes, and the rules also
prohibited them from leaving campus without a chap-
eron. After Sunday vesper services, faculty-supervised
socials allowed students to mingle with each other. In
this environment, school officials molded the image of
a wholesome, educated, respectable black womanhood.[19]

All-black communities supported the public school
as well. When the labor demands of harvesting the
cotton crop diminished public school attendance, angry
editors denounced black parents, declaring, "Our
watch word at this time is [to] see that your child is in
school. . . . the first day and every day up to the last
day. Let no excuse keep you from doing your full duty
to your children." Common-school attendance was high
in these towns for both boys and girls between the ages
of ten and fourteen (84.8 percent of males in this age
group attended school, as did 86.8 percent of females),
the highest rate for black children in any southern

Black women and children pose in front of the homestead they struggled to develop. Photo courtesy of the Archives & Manuscript Division of the Oklahoma Historical Society.

state. This compared to a 92 percent attendance figure for white children. The decline in illiteracy in this age group dropped precipitously from 30.7 percent in 1900 to 6.2 percent in 1910, the lowest rate for this age group of any southern state. Illiteracy in native-born white children of the same age hovered around 1 percent. Above the elementary level, black school attendance declined by one-half. Black parents, like others in agricultural states, more often kept their daughters in school than their sons. Girls could not earn as high a wage as boys could, and black parents hoped their daughters would advance in life by staying in school and becoming teachers. Langston University enrollment reflected this preference; female enrollment in the Teacher's College amounted to twice that of male enrollment.[20]

Female teachers occupied a conspicuous social position among the elite women of the town. Because they represented role models for young black women, their movements and activities underwent careful scrutiny. Teaching in the first schools required long hours in crude classrooms with pupils ranging in age from six years old to the mid-twenties. Books and basic supplies were in short supply. Providing instruction and keeping order demanded planning, organization, and innovation. In addition to these career demands, the town leaders expected female teachers to engage in activities that were devoted to community and moral improvement. While these expectations were also true of female teachers in white communities, black teachers carried the additional burden of setting the standard for the female gender of the black race. Wives of the town patriarchs, women who were often schoolteachers themselves, determined the social climate and introduced new teachers to the community. When Mrs. Myrtle Webb and Miss Maud Smith arrived in Clearview in 1911 to take up their duties as school principal and assistant teacher, they were hosted at parties in the homes of Mrs. Bessie Warren, wife of the local newspaper editor, and Mrs. Neva Thompson, wife of the town founder. The Clearview newspaper publicized their parties and published reports of the participation of the teachers when they attended womens' club meetings, provided musical accompaniment at town gatherings, served refreshments at parties, and, of course, led church functions. Indeed, the *Clearview Patriarch* carefully documented the activities of two young teachers, Miss Georgie and Miss Matty Taliaferro. Whenever they traveled away from town, to attend normal training schools in Boley, to visit Okemah on business, or to shop, the newspaper commented on their industry and their value as ambassadors of the town.[21]

Teachers provided more than just social dignity, however. They also performed services in community outreach and local continuing education. Both of the Taliaferro sisters delivered instructive papers at a farmers' conference in 1911, and their lectures focused on the benefits of educating farm girls. Langston teachers, too, traveled to outlying black communities and provided practical demonstrations in the latest farm procedures taught on the campus. The university served as the base for home-demonstration agents after 1910 and held an annual community free fair each fall between 1916 and 1923. Annie Peters of Boley became the first black female home-demonstration agent in the United States in 1912. By 1921, four black women agents in Oklahoma reported that they had met with 817 girls in various canning and sewing clubs and had provided 732 home demonstrations to adults in that year. The agents' other achievements included repair to septic tanks, building screen doors and windows for farm houses, and the purchase of dairy and kitchen equipment. The teacher, the society matron, the farm wife, and the businesswoman were united in the survival and productivity of the black town. They played key roles in establishing the institutions that promoted a sense of permanency for the communities.[22]

Beyond this commitment to the community, however, there existed a determination to seek a resolution to the long-standing virulent assumption of black inferiority. Issues of race more often superseded those of gender for black Oklahoma women. Throughout the early years of Langston University, Dr. Inman Page, the surrounding townspeople, and black territorial leaders fought to exercise autonomy over the kind of education offered and the direction of their school. The struggle revolved around the different ideological approaches of the two most prominent

national black leaders, Booker T. Washington and
W. E. B. Dubois. Booker T. Washington proposed a
program of education concentrating on agricultural
and vocational skills while Dubois insisted that only a
traditional, classical college education would lead to
equality. White Oklahoma political leaders favored
Washington's approach. However Page, who was himself
a graduate of Brown University, and most Langston
citizens, while admiring much of Washington's self-
help philosophy, worked to create a curriculum with an
emphasis on the liberal arts. Their vision of the
university encompassed an institution that represented the highest scholastic standards and one that
would serve as the cultural center of the state.

The first faculty included a professor of English
literature; a mathematician; Page, who taught history
and philosophy; and Zelia N. Page (later Breaux), the
president's daughter, who directed the music program.
Educators Mary McLeod Bethune and Carter Woodson,
poet Langston Hughes, and contralto Marian
Anderson each responded to invitations to appear on
campus during the early years. Contact with these
black persons of such high stature in their professions
transformed the ambitions of some students. Longtime
Oklahoma activist and editor of the *Black Dispatch*
Roscoe Dunjee attended Langston during these years,
and he later remembered that it was there that "I got
the inspiration to do big things."[23]

The cultural influence of Zelia Page Breaux, first at
Langston and later in Oklahoma City, held national
significance. American novelist Ralph Ellison paid
tribute to Breaux in an eloquent essay. Ellison characterized Breaux as "an agent of the broader American
culture" and as a person who helped to "widen our
sense of possibility and raise our aspirations." Breaux
organized a seven-piece orchestra at Langston in 1902

Zelia Page Breaux, director of the music program at the Langston Colored Agriculture and Normal University and, later, Douglass High School, Oklahoma City. Photo courtesy of the Archives & Manuscript Division of the Oklahoma Historical Society.

that grew to twenty-three members by 1904. She formed a choral society and developed a three-year vocal-music curriculum and piano course that required students to play Bach, Liszt, Chopin, and Mozart. After statehood Breaux added a band and a glee club, and as director of music, she supervised an instructor in pedagogy and vocal music, George Porter, and an assistant, Luther L. Henderson. Throughout her career Breaux insisted on the discipline of training in classical music and on the exposure of black youth to an appreciation of a variety of other arts and of European cultures. She later became supervisor of music for Oklahoma City's segregated schools, where Ellison encountered her, and she discouraged her students from playing the then-popular jazz. Yet, she also owned the Aldridge Theater, the only black theater in Oklahoma City, and she brought in the finest black blues singers, jazz orchestras, and drama groups to perform there. In both endeavors, Breaux demanded quality performances. Some of her students from the Douglass High School band became prominent jazz musicians: Jimmy Rushing sang with the original Oklahoma Blue Devils that formed the nucleus of Count Basie's orchestra, and Alva Lee "Bo" McCain, Sr., played saxophone for Duke Ellington's band.[24]

Ellison credited Breaux with providing a "cultural nexus" in which both classical and vernacular styles comingled to produce a music-oriented culture. He concluded:

So just as her father transmitted the ideals which he'd gained at Brown University across the color line and down the annals of our unwritten history, so did his daughter bring together and make possible an interaction of art forms, styles, and traditions. Interesting enough, it wasn't until years later that I learned how unusual this was, or the extent to which it cleared away the insidious confusion between race and culture which haunts this society.[25]

Distinct from their interests in community and racial improvement, black-town women also created binding ties to each other. These bonds endured times of tragedy and loss, economic boom and decline, and racial oppression. Most significantly, black-town women promoted a public image of unity in the face both of white castigation and of criticism by men of their own race. They developed strategies to protect young, single women from the dangers of white harassment. They challenged black males to treat them with the same respect accorded white women. They applied pressure through the newspapers to guide moral conduct toward a standard that placed black women within the "protected" realm of wife and mother, and they organized into clubs to lobby more effectively for the interests of black citizens in the state. At the root of these actions lay the belief that they were responsible for the future of the race. Black pioneer women believed that they occupied a significant historical position as the bridge from slavery to equality and that by their efforts the dignity of the race would be proved.

W. E. B. Dubois encouraged just such an ideology of female importance. In his writings Dubois continued the championship of women's rights begun by Frederick Douglass half a century earlier. Dubois supported women's suffrage and the advancement of women in professional and vocational positions, and he also upheld the right of birth control: "The future woman must have a life work and economic independence," he wrote. "She must have knowledge. She must have the right of motherhood at her own discretion." Black women, forgotten in a "world that wills to worship womankind," had emerged from a history of insult and degradation to hold out promise for the future. They represented a group whose "strength of character, cleanness of soul, and unselfish devotion of purpose" rivaled any group of women in the world. From black women came the groundswell of new revolutionary ideals. Their determination to raise the status of women and to solve the problems of the color line would, in the future, have a significant impact on the "thought and action of the country."[26]

The Supreme Court's decision in *Plessy v. Ferguson* in 1896 legitimized the enactment of a series of measures aimed at enforcing segregation in Oklahoma. These laws eventually separated schools and public transportation along racial lines, made intermarriage illegal, and effectively disenfranchised black male voters. Long before segregated transportation codes became legal, however, black-town women took action to protect themselves when traveling outside of their communities. Black-town newspapers scrupulously recorded the comings and goings of their citizens. In most cases, women traveled in groups of twos and threes unless escorted by a male relative. Prominent married women of the towns often accompanied young single women on shopping expeditions to Guthrie or Oklahoma City, to and from schools, and even to visit relatives in another part of the state. Clearview matrons Neva Thompson and Bessie Warren, for example, frequently chaperoned Miss Georgie and Miss Matty Taliaferro, two of the town's most active club women, when they left town. This action became even more necessary after statehood when legislation pertaining to the railroad provided no penalty for failure to establish equal accommodations on such lines. Even though black newspaper editors pleaded for first-class cars for "respectable" women, a Meridian, Oklahoma, citizen described the waiting rooms as small, filthy areas, littered with whiskey bottles. The Jim Crow car was just a dirty smoking car with a toilet at one end for both men and women.[27]

Black women were intimately acquainted with the potential for violence in their own lives: violence associated with white domination and also with abuse at the hands of their own husbands and leaders. Langston and Boley residents read with indignation about the beating of a fifteen-year-old schoolgirl in the racially-mixed town of Guthrie: Professor I. F. Scott at the segregated black school ordered two large teenage boys to hold down Josephine Lyle while he beat her with a leather strap until her shoulders were bruised and bleeding. Lyle was unable to attend school for the rest of the term, and black newspaper editorials demanded Scott's removal. The Langston *Western Age* reported the outrage of area residents when, during an argument with his wife, a black homesteader ordered her to kneel down in the wagon and pray. When she finished the prayer, he shot and killed her instantly and then escaped into the woods. The Guthrie *Oklahoma Guide* devoted an entire column to the brutal slaying and to the funeral of a prominent woman who held office in the Daughters of Tabor. Her husband had beaten her, cut her throat, and locked her in the house to die. She crawled out a window to a neighbor's home, but even with medical attention, she succumbed three days later. These incidents, lurid in description, appear as exceptions to the incessant boosterism of most black newspaper copy, but they indicate that domestic violence occurred and that such incidents reflected badly on community reputation.[28]

Most often, black male newspaper editors, in a manner similar to that of their counterpart white editors, assumed the paternalistic duty of advising women about their obligations and about appropriate patterns of behavior. They printed directives admonishing women to be frugal and hardworking, strict in the upbringing of children, but gentle, yielding, and generous in their relationships with their husbands. They also reprinted prayers by theologian Walter Rauschenbusch and essays by philosopher John Ruskin on the function of women in the creation of "The Ideal Home." Some young women responded to such heavy-handed instruction with an independence that illustrated both gender and racial tension.[29]

In 1904 the (Guthrie) Oklahoma Guide featured a special New Year's edition under the direction of Elmira S. Ridley, niece of Guide publisher George N. Perkins. Ridley printed an invitation in late December to the "Ladies of Oklahoma" to send in articles on any subject to be published in the January 7 issue, which would be dedicated to women. On page one, Ridley placed the submission of Carrie Lynwood from the all-black colony of Wellston, Oklahoma Territory. Lynwood's article, entitled "Negro Man's Ideal of Womanhood," attacked black men who sought women whose only virtues were fair skin and long, straight hair. Lynwood knew that at least some black women held ambivalent attitudes about their racial characteristics. They used hair straighteners and skin lighteners and wore long-sleeved garments and hats in the sun. In 1910 three Boley women organized a club emphasizing proper English, good housekeeping, and social accomplishments. The group admitted only light-skinned members. The community reacted immediately by forcing them to disband.[30]

Lynwood blamed the soul-crushing experience of slavery for having shaped this ideal of beauty, but she believed it to be so deeply ingrained in some men that even the danger of white vigilante action failed to prevent them from seeking the attention of white women. She praised those editors who supported an image of racial dignity for black women, but she insisted that they were working at the wrong end of the problem. "The Negro do not need better women," she wrote, "half so much as men who appreciate good women." Within their communities black 'own women insisted that their husbands and sons exhibit the same respect and appreciation for black women that they gave to white women.[31]

Lynwood's essay failed to provoke a male response, but an article in the *Western Age* of Langston, Oklahoma Territory, echoed this same resentment with less bitterness and more instruction. *Western Age* editor S. Douglas Russell placed the senior oration of the only black member of the 1906 Topeka, Kansas, high-school graduating class on the front page of his newspaper. On the editorial page he wrote that this speech was one of many "Negro Classics," and "should be read in every Negro school in Oklahoma." The address, entitled "The Position of the Colored Girl in Society," by Ada Upshaw, explained that surrounding the much-publicized homage that men paid to women, men drew a color line that black women could not cross. Because of prejudice, the black girl had to overcome more obstacles, endure more hardships, and suffer more insults than any other. Her task was the elevation of the status of her race, and yet, some men of her own race held the same "degrading opinion" that white men held. Consequently, they treated her "too cheaply."[32]

Upshaw insisted that the black girl was as pure, innocent, noble, and beautiful as any other. She must be encouraged "to do whatever [work] her hands find to do," and "she should be loved, honored, and protected in doing it." If the men of her race responded to her in this way she would "command the recognition and respect of all the world." These young women extended the boundaries of female appreciation beyond the white feminine ideal of beauty, and they insisted on evaluation on their own terms. Skin color and hair texture had nothing to do with a woman's quality. The womanly virtues were not ends in themselves, they believed. Black women placed female ideals within their commitment to service to the race.[33]

Recognition and respect came through dignified conduct as well, and black-town women used the newspaper as a forum to monitor their own social behavior and to suggest the correct moral standard. Metella Clement, Nettie Carlisle, and Mrs. J. E. Robinson frequently contributed articles to the Langston *Herald* on a wide variety of topics from housekeeping tips, child-rearing techniques, and the evils of female snuff-dipping to the importance of inspirational reading. Sometimes these essays appeared under the heading "Household Column," but often they were printed as independently signed articles. After Clement launched a particularly lengthy diatribe on the use of tobacco, the *Herald* editor joked, "Look out ye young snuff dipper, the ladies column is after you."[34]

Carlisle taught Sunday school and often participated in the formal debates among male and female members of the Langston Literary Society. On one occasion she argued the affirmative position on the topic that men and women should be guaranteed an equal education. Carlisle also published articles on the value of personal grooming and cleanliness. She wrote that bathing once a day was an absolute necessity; it contributed to good health and eliminated offensive body odor. "When a young lady assures me that she can dress in ten minutes," Carlisle insisted, "I feel confident that the most important part of the toilet [the bath] must be neglected." Poor personal hygiene indicated a disorderly character; therefore, black women must be scrupulous in this area.[35]

Mrs. J. E. Robinson's essays concentrated on advice about strengthening a positive attitude toward life, inexpensive ways to add touches of beauty to a humble home, and the importance of maintaining a cheerful outlook even in adversity. These three contributors did more than write advice, however. They put their words into action in 1895 by organizing a society to benefit needy girls in the county. As Robinson explained, "Some of us has Mrs. prefixed to our names, but we are working in the vinyard in the interests of our young girls." Membership in the society could be obtained by contacting the *Herald* office. These female writers set the boundaries of appropriate behavior for black-town women and used their columns to reinforce community standards. They provided the discourse that set standards by which black men judged black women and black women judged themselves. They also expressed the goals to be achieved—those of respect and honor.[36]

The growth of the all-black communities in territorial Oklahoma coincided with the coordination of a national black-women's movement in the 1890s. The National Federation of Afro-American Women, led by Josephine St. Pierre Ruffin, and the Washington, D.C., National League of Colored Women, under the direction of Mary Church Terrell, merged in 1896 to form the National Association of Colored Women (NACW). Ruffin and Terrell had both experienced discrimination in their dealings with the white General Federation of Women's Clubs. The catalyst for a national movement, however, stemmed from a letter by Missouri Press Association president, James W. Jack, that had been circulated among black leaders. This letter, issued in response to Ida Wells-Barnett's lecture tour in England on antilynching legislation, characterized black women as liars, thieves, and prostitutes. Ruffin, Terrell, Margaret Murray Washington (Mrs. Booker T. Washington), Fannie Barrier Williams, and Ida Wells-Barnett joined forces to create the NACW, an organization largely composed of middle-class women, to defend the honor and meet the needs of all black women in the United States. In less than twenty years, the NACW represented more than fifty thousand women in twenty-eight federations and over one thousand clubs.[37]

Territorial Oklahoma's black-town women seized upon the words of national black women leaders for inspiration and encouragement, and they organized numerous reform groups aimed at improving the lives of black women. The *Langston City Herald* printed Margaret Washington's call to "women who see the needs of our sisters and will seek to find a remedy" through local organizations for reform across the nation. Washington supplied information on how to organize local chapters and affiliate with the national NACW group. She closed her essay by repeating the goals of the association: to work through social, economic, and moral reform for "enlightened motherhood, intellectual development, individuality and with all a steady growth of the development of noble womanhood." Fannie Barrier Williams, another NACW leader, devoted her essays to the black "woman's sphere," and these also appeared in the local newspapers.[38]

Hundreds of women's groups formed in the black towns. Some of them had specific goals and activities;

others were strictly social in nature; and many, like the Boley Ladies Industrial Club, performed a variety of services. The Boley Women's Club emerged in 1906, and many of its first meetings were devoted to gathering and sharing information about the activities of clubs in other cities. *Progress* editor O. H. Bradley encouraged women to organize and join local clubs. Indeed, Bradley saw the advantage of using women's clubs for town-improvement projects, and he attempted to capitalize on their activities. For example, he suggested that the women organize a "Boley Beauty Club" to decorate the city. This group would be responsible for removing all rubbish from alleys and property, whitewashing fences and outhouses, and planting flowers and shrubs along the streets—work he had previously scolded men into doing. He also pressured women to spend some of their leisure time in uniting a group to support the "discipline, management, and general progress of the school." Men and women alike recognized the value of female support to community institutions and upkeep.[39]

A number of female organizations such as the Order of the Eastern Star and Daughters of Tabor lent support to the male fraternal lodges. The Sisters of Ethiopia functioned as the female auxiliary of the Patriarchs of America in Clearview, Oklahoma. This organization was dedicated to the improvement of conditions for the black race through economic and political unity. At the annual meeting in 1912, during a time when the Oklahoma black towns faced social, economic, and political assaults engendered by the racist environment of the state, the members of the Sisters of Ethiopia debated a colonization scheme to resettle black families outside Oklahoma. Several "Sisters" read papers calling for renewed dedication to the goals of the organization and increased support for town leaders. They proclaimed that men always worked harder in a cause when joined "heart and hand" by women: "If it [the relocation] makes the men masters of their affairs it will make women mistresses of the entire situation."[40]

Also in Clearview were the Alpha Club, the Self-Enterprising Club, and a social club led by Neva Thompson and Bessie Warren for "ladies of good moral standing," organized with the object of encouraging "literary, social and industral [sic] attainment." Beneath the formation of these groups lay a complex motivation that had little to do with imitation of the trappings of white society. Unity, cooperation, and activism set a standard for racial advancement, and women's clubs laid the foundation for the elevation of both race and sex. As Margaret Washington wrote, "we accept only the theory that we are inferior in opportunity, and not in capacity or ability. . . . The American colored woman is not going to live beside the American white woman and remain any the less a woman."[41]

Some of these black-town organizations antedate by more than a decade the formal incorporation of Oklahoma clubs with the National Association of Colored Women. Although territorial Oklahoma sent representatives to the national conventions as early as 1896, when members of the Guthrie Woman's Club attended, state chapters did not affiliate with the national organization until 1910. At that time Harriet Price Jacobson, a public schoolteacher who was president of the East Side Culture Club of Oklahoma City, issued a call to local clubs in the state to form the Oklahoma Federation of Colored Women's Clubs. By 1920 the federation had grown from the original seven clubs with a membership of 111 to thirty-four clubs containing 518 members, including groups in Boley and Langston. Two of the first seven presidents of the state organization, Anna H. Cooper and Adelia Y. Young, received their education at Langston University. Jacobson recalled the formative years of the federation and described the founders as busy women with little time and less money. They believed that they were "laying the foundation of an organization which would in a few years be the most helpful that could have been planned for making better conditions among our people of the state."[42]

Perhaps one of the best examples of the influence of the federated clubs can be seen in the success of the group in the small black town of Bookertee during World War I. In February 1919, local president Mary Carr Edwards announced the results of the Tag Day competition to raise funds for a social charity center. Thirteen clubs with names as diverse as the "Merry Matrons," the "Phyllis Wheatley Domestic Science Club," the "Renaissance Club," and the "Stand Ready To Help Club," reported their combined total of $1,000. Edwards praised the wonderful spirit of cooperation among club members, team captains, and the community that made this success possible.[43]

A close, reciprocal relationship existed between the national NACW and the Oklahoma federation. NACW president Elizabeth C. Carter visited Oklahoma in 1911, as did president Mary B. Talbert in 1917. The official emblem of the Oklahoma federation, designed by Manilla Johnson, was adopted as the insignia of the national organization. The badge depicted a woman leading a young girl by the hand up the side of a mountain, and it included the motto, "Lifting As We Climb." The local Oklahoma clubs organized programs around civil rights issues. Some of these programs included: an examination of women's property rights, the endorsement of women's suffrage after 1914, and talks on community development, prevention of juvenile delinquency, and youth and adult education. The meetings went beyond a sharing of information and an encouragement of benevolent activities. The clubs promoted political activism through lobbying and petitioning for the economic and social advancement of blacks in Oklahoma. The federation founded and supported two seminaries, located at McAlester and Sapulpa, for black girls and established education and training facilities for delinquent boys at Boley and for delinquent girls at Taft. They created rural health clinics and developed Mothers Clubs to disseminate information on better child care. They also organized fund drives for playground equipment, parks and cemetery beautification, and hospital furnishings and equipment. The club women kept alive a continual negotiation of racial issues that reinforced the legal challenges that black male leaders pursued through the courts under the direction of the Oklahoma branch of the National Association for the Advancement of Colored People. They launched legislative letter-writing campaigns for citizenship rights and for full integration into American life. They also provided financial support to the Oklahoma NAACP and to the Constitution League, a lobby group working for state legislation on behalf of black citizens.[44]

Time and freedom ran out for these oases of black independence in the desert of Oklahoma racism. After statehood in 1907 the very existence of all-black towns represented a political challenge to state Democratic supremacy, and every effort, legal and illegal, was exerted to retard further black-town growth or development. The first state legislature enacted Jim Crow laws that created an inferior status in public education and transportation and led to segregation in all areas of social contact. The state passed antimiscegenation

laws and used the the Grandfather Clause to extin-
guish black voting rights. White officials gerryman-
dered districts to secure the white town of Okemah,
instead of Boley, as county seat of Okfuskee County.
The home of the only black resident of Okemah was
dynamited, and Okemah deputies made frequent
sorties into Boley to intimidate its residents.[45]

These expressions of power affected the lives and
safety of black men and women and eventually erupted
into mob violence. When an Okemah deputy sheriff
went to the Nelson farm near Paden in 1911 to make
an arrest, he was shot by the suspect's terrified
thirteen-year-old son, who guarded the home in his
father's absence. Deputies took the boy, his mother,
Laura Nelson, and her infant into custody. Before they
could be tried, a mob dragged them from the jail,
separated the baby from its mother, and hanged the
woman and her son from a bridge six miles west of
town. The *Crisis* reported that some members of the
mob raped Mrs. Nelson before they hanged her. A black
woman who watched the lynching from a place of
concealment remembered: "After they had hung them
up, those men just walked off and left that baby lying
there. One of my neighbors was there, and she picked
the baby up and brought it back to town, and we took
care of it." Although white county newspapers
expressed token regret at this vigilante action, a grand
jury could not gather enough evidence to return an
indictment. Black women had experienced this power-
lessness before, and they realized that the hopeful
walls of security they had built around their all-black
communities could be breached at any time.[46]

As historian Norman Crockett pointed out in his
study of Oklahoma black towns, these experiments in
separatism were destined for failure because of the
economic realities at work in the nation. Forces of

industrial concentration and modernization, combined with a national movement of population from rural areas into the cities, dictated their decline. The small towns could not survive without access to large sources of capital. The Fort Smith and Western Railroad located its line at Coyle, nearly two miles from Langston, insuring that the town would not grow beyond a small service community for the college. White farmers organized Farmers' Commercial Clubs in Okfuskee County to restrict any further black agricultural development through discriminating restrictive covenants. The final blow came with the depression of the cotton market in 1913 that continued into the 1920s.[47]

The towns might have stabilized in spite of these social, economic, and political assaults had it not been for the lure of a new frontier and an ancient homeland. Black-town families faced the decision of packing up and moving to the open lands of Canada to begin the homesteading process again or of following the siren song of Chief Alfred Sam back to Africa. Either decision brought population loss to the black towns after 1910. In that year Jordan W. Murphy and his two sons, from Wellston, Oklahoma, moved north to Pine Creek, Edmonton, Alberta, Canada, and established homesteads. Young Jefferson Davis Edwards saved enough money to follow Murphy the following summer. He worked shoveling coal, digging basements, and hauling freight until he had enough money to send for his sweetheart back in Wellston, Murphy's daughter, Martha. Mrs. Edwards and Martha then joined their husbands in Canada. The Murphy, Edwards, and Toles families formed the nucleus of Amber Valley, an all-black community of transplanted Oklahomans. A larger group of emigrants, recruited in Clearview by Henry Sneed, followed later. Mattie and Joe Mayes and

Essie Matthews and her future husband, Walter Lane, joined another large group that established black communities near Maidstone, Saskatchewan. The women had raised and sold chickens and pigs and the men had done carpentry and farm work to get the necessary traveling money.[48]

Once in Canada they began to build again: clearing land, constructing homes, forming churches, and starting schools. Martha Murphy Edwards and her husband, J. D., recalled their newlywed days and their first home of rough-cut logs and clay plaster that leaked for days after a rain. She remembered, too, the births of her children and the midwife who stayed with her: "We didn't have a doctor, but Mrs. Broadie was a fine midwife. She would come to the house two or three days early, and stay a couple of days after the baby was born. She took care of ten of our eleven children." The distance of years softened the memories of long, bitterly cold weeks when Martha stayed at home with the children while J. D. hauled freight to make enough money to survive another year. On one occasion J. D. was falsely arrested on the charge of trying to cash a stolen check; it was a case of mistaken identity. The terror of this brush with the law subsided as they developed their land and reared their children. Once again they worked to establish roots.[49]

Canadian government officials became concerned about the sudden influx of blacks into Canada that continued until 1912. They feared that large numbers of poor black settlers would deter white farmers from moving onto the land, and they mobilized to stem the flow. Immigration authorities required blacks to produce increasing amounts of cash as guarantees of solvency, and they insisted on a thorough inventory of immigrant luggage. They added a medical examination to entry requirements, and they detained livestock for inspection. Government agencies published reports designed to discourage any further black settlement. The Canadian Pacific Railway discontinued to blacks its lower fares for prospective settlers. Finally, the Canadian Department of Immigration hired G. W. Miller, a black Chicago doctor, to travel through the black communities of Oklahoma and speak against emigration to Canada.[50]

In his speeches across Oklahoma, Miller outlined the difficulties of farming in the frigid northern climate, the complex entry requirements, the expense of beginning again, and, just as importantly, the racist opposition to black settlement already manifest against the original black settlers in Canada. He emphasized that blacks would not find greater opportunity, prosperity, and freedom there. By mid-1911 Miller believed that the "unfavourable reports" he had been circulating were having an effect, and he stated that "The Canadian Boom is rapidly dying out."[51]

An even more extensive movement of Oklahoma black-town citizens occurred after the exodus to Canada. This time it was in response to the orchestration of a back-to-Africa scheme. Alfred Charles Sam arrived in Oklahoma in 1913 amidst the turmoil of black disfranchisement and harassment. He claimed to be an African chief from the Gold Coast, and he offered $25.00 shares in the Akim Trading Company, Ltd. The company's ships would transport American blacks to an African paradise with sugarcane as high as stove pipes and then return to America laden with cargo. Hundreds sold their belongings, land, and homes and set up camps on the outskirts of Weleetka to await word of the success of the first advance party of sixty. A local woman remembered both the fervor of the meetings in Boley and Clearview and the hardships of the campers, who poured all of their money into the expedition and waited months through cold and sickness for the ship to cut through the bureaucratic obstacles and set sail. "I wanted to go so bad," she said, "I could have walked." Other black-town women remembered less the promise Chief Sam offered than the destruction his plans wreaked upon the communities. "Chief Sam almost broke Boley up. . . . He broke up families, and some people left and never came back," a Boley pioneer remembered. Alafair Carter Adams agreed: "He tore up the county among the colored people. . . . They were looking to someplace where there was no opposition. Chief Sam was just a good con man." The scheme failed miserably, and the destitute survivors of the original group struggled back to the United States over the next two years. Campers in Weleetka and emigrants who had managed to get as far as Galveston, Texas, dispersed into western cities or spread out in multiracial Oklahoma towns. The remnants of the black towns survived, but the dream of a separatist Oklahoma showcase—of prosperity, self-determination, and cultural pride—had ended.[52]

For a brief time in Oklahoma history all-black communities provided an incubator for female advancement. Pioneer women seized this opportunity to assert their abilities and to weld a network of relationships that commanded respect, improved their circumstances, and increased their opportunities. In the end they saw their own array of alternatives diminished, but the experiment armed them with survival strategies to meet the demands of life in the racially mixed urban environment of Oklahoma. In spite of the failure to attain social and political equality in Oklahoma and the eventual economic collapse of most all-black towns, black-town women exercised greater freedom in determining their own destinies for a historical moment.

They found in the insulation of the black towns the opportunity to expunge the degraded image of black women that had been created by slavery and to advance a new model of black womanhood based on race and gender accomplishments.

7

In Love with an Ideal

Newspaper editors occupied an important position in territorial politics. Party lines were closely drawn. The success of a slate of candidates at the county level carried with it the contracts for printing that sustained many a small weekly newspaper. The partisan editors fiercely debated the issues affecting the new settlers: land legislation, herd laws, schools, railroads, the placement of county seats and governmental institutions, and political appointments. Weekly newspapers kept the people informed of national events, but also supplied larger-city daily newspapers with the news from the outlying communities.

The weekly newspaper editor was a local man, a known personality whose word could be trusted. It was up to him to convince the voting citizen to support a candidate for territorial or national office. Consequently, the editors often served as campaign managers and members of territorial committees. The Democratic and Republican Parties competed for Populist support to win elections and to determine the political direction of the territory. Thompson Ferguson once compared Oklahoma politics to riding a bucking bronco; he and Elva used the *Watonga Republican* to catapult themselves into the saddle in 1901.

Politics fascinated Elva Ferguson. Since the couple's arrival in Oklahoma Territory, she had managed the newspaper when Thompson traveled out of town to support Republican candidates. In 1900, he managed the Dennis Flynn campaign for Congress from Guthrie, leaving Elva in charge of the newspaper for three months. As she explained in her memoirs, most people believed that women did not have the intellect to write editorials, especially political ones. Looking over copies of the *Republican* years later, she noted with satisfaction that the newspaper maintained its usual standard under her direction. More importantly, this experience built her confidence and sparked her enthusiasm for political involvement.

The assassination of William McKinley in 1901 propelled Theodore Roosevelt into the presidency, and he immediately removed the Oklahoma Territory governor, William Jenkins. Thompson Ferguson was away in Hitchcock establishing a branch newspaper when Elva received the telegram from Roosevelt offering Tom the office. Without consulting her husband, Elva sent a return telegram accepting the appointment. She packed his bag, bought his railroad ticket to Washington, and met him at the door with the news upon his return home. At first he balked and ordered Elva to send another message declining the offer, but by morning Thompson was on the train headed to Washington to accept his commission as governor.

During the next four years, the Fergusons directed the government of Oklahoma Territory as the clamor for statehood grew. Elva, as First Lady, presided over the social life of the capitol at Guthrie, but she also continued to write the political news for the *Republican* throughout her husband's tenure. Frank Greer, editor of the *Oklahoma State Capitol*, wrote about her: "She is just the woman to make an able helpmate to such a man as Tom Ferguson in the governor's chair. Intelligent, capable, businesslike, yet womanly to the last degree and accomplished in all things."[1]

Valuable as she was, she functioned as a power behind the candidate. She saw her duty as helpmate, not as officeholder. That distinction fell to another intelligent, accomplished, compassionate woman, named Catherine Ann (Kate) Barnard. When Ferguson wrote about those transition years to statehood, she recalled, "It seems to me that perhaps we were in love with an ideal created in our own minds of the greater privileges we would enjoy under statehood, without realizing that greater problems would surely follow." Kate Barnard mounted the political bronco and experienced both the privileges and the problems.[2]

Nationally, the period 1890 though 1920 represented an age of expanded activism and organization-building by women. Jane Addams and the settlement-house movement typified a progressive thrust that allowed certain upper-middle-class, educated women to turn the humanitarian, nurturing, and compassionate qualities attributed to the Victorian female into a profession. William O'Neill, in his book, *Everyone Was Brave: The Decline and Fall of Feminism in America*, gave the name "social feminists" to those women whose efforts concentrated on service to others and society as opposed to feminists who advocated individual opportunity. More recent scholarship has challenged O'Neill's dichotomy, questioning whether all public-spirited women should necessarily be classified as feminist. In an attempt to enunciate more clearly a definition of feminism, historian Nancy F. Cott proposes a model that includes a broad range of women's consciousness. One component is feminism, with a critique or challenge to male supremacy implicit. Also included are aspects of female consciousness derived from social constructions of women's tasks and of communal consciousness based on the solidarity of a defined group. Oklahoma women, like their national counterparts, drew from all three of these aspects of women's consciousness as the motivation for public action. Each level of awareness could be applied as the need arose, and each rationale could be used by diverse women to promote contradictory political, economic, and social positions.[3]

Kate Barnard exemplified the public woman who shaped opinion and policy to reflect her benevolent beliefs. She identified herself with causes that promoted the well-being of the poor in Oklahoma: compulsory education; child-labor reform; protection for Indians, orphans, prosoners, and the insane; and improved conditions for the worker. Barnard embraced politics and proved particularly adept at initiating legislation and securing grassroots support for the measures. She claimed to be working for the betterment of life for women, yet she conscientiously opposed women's suffrage as a measure to help them achieve their goals.

The brief political life of Kate Barnard, 1905–15, represented an enigma. The newspapers hailed her as Saint Kate, the good angel of mercy, the defender of the poor and helpless. She shared the spotlight with William H. ("Alfalfa Bill") Murray, leader of the Farmer's Union, and Pete Hanraty, president of the Twin Territories Federation of Labor, in developing and

Kate Barnard, Commissioner of
Charities and Corrections. Photo
courtesy of the Archives & Manuscript Division of the Oklahoma
Historical Society.

implementing state constitutional planks favorable to
labor and social-justice issues. She gave emotionally
charged speeches to appreciative crowds all over the
state. For a time contemporary politicians feared the
influence that she exerted at the polls. Inasmuch as
Oklahoma remained an all-male electorate until 1918,
this power was indeed significant. Serving as commissioner of charities and corrections, the first woman to
be elected to statewide office, she believed that she had

introduced "scientific statecraft," that is, professionally designed legislation, in the first four legislatures following statehood. By 1915, however, Barnard could not obtain any local press coverage and received little national attention for the issues on which she had campaigned for ten years. Completely excluded from political action, she lived out the rest of her years in obscurity, broken health, and mental instability. Near the end of her life, she bemoaned, "No One knows . . . but God . . . how much I might have accomplished for Human Progress during these twenty years I have been forced into Silence . . . forced into Idleness . . . banished into Obscurity."[4]

Kate Barnard's notable achievements received recognition in her own time, and historians, too, from Joseph Thoburn in 1916 to Danney Goble in 1980, have credited her as being the driving force behind the social-justice reforms of Oklahoma Progressivism. Her fall from political grace, however, revealed much about the contradictory elements within Oklahoma politics, the whimsical effect of personality in politics, and, most significantly for this discussion, the limitations of female activism based on a philosophy of separate spheres. Kate Barnard represented a convenient ornament and a useful tool for the political ambitions of the triumvirate of William H. Murray, Pete Hanraty, and Charles N. Haskell, men who orchestrated the formation of Oklahoma state government. However, she misjudged the nature of her importance to them and overestimated the strength of a personal following. When she alienated those men who controlled wealth, patronage, and votes, her only constituency consisted of unenfranchised women and the powerless poor.[5]

Kate Barnard was born in Nebraska in 1875 to John P. and Rachel Shiell Barnard. Her mother and infant brother died before she was three, and her father left her with her maternal grandparents and half-brothers while he sought work as a surveyor and a lawyer in Kansas. John Barnard remarried in 1881, and for a time Kate lived with them. The marriage ended in divorce soon after the birth of a son, and Kate went back to her grandparents. When land in Oklahoma Territory opened up after 1889, John Barnard staked a claim near Newalla, and Kate joined him there. She lived alone in a frame shanty in fierce poverty, holding down the claim while her father practiced law in Oklahoma City. When Barnard proved up on the claim, he moved Kate to a home on Reno Street in Oklahoma City, and she attended school at Saint Joseph's Academy. She retained the Newalla homestead, the Reno Street house, and other real estate investments her father made until her death. Her father represented the single major influence in her life, and in later years she frequently paid lavish tribute to his memory. Her reminiscences record: "My love for my father and a desire to help the poor became the two great dominant factors of my life." His example provided the "moral strength behind every sacrifice for principle, every struggle for liberty, every achievement recorded" in her career.[6]

Financially unable to attend college, Barnard taught in rural schools for a time, then she took a short business course and secured a job as a stenographer for the territorial legislature. By 1904 she had wheedled a clerical-booster position as a representative of Oklahoma Territory to the St. Louis World's Fair. While in St. Louis, the gregarious and energetic Barnard visited innumerable exhibits, listened to speeches by the leading exponents of Progressivism, toured the slums of the city, and made friends with the officers of a variety of benevolent organizations. As her biographer, Julia Short, noted, Barnard "returned to Oklahoma fired with the zeal of a militant reformer." This zeal coupled with a devout Catholic religious faith carried her into a career of public service.[7]

Barnard accepted another stenography position in the office of city attorney Gus A. Paul, but he soon fired her. According to one account, Barnard performed her duties diligently, enthusiastically, and consistently, but she did so with a strikingly independent attitude, and when "her timidity departed," she became "sagely self-assertive." She refused to work overtime on a Sunday, and Paul terminated her employment. Setting a precedent of courage and righteous indignation that she continued to exemplify in later work, Barnard appealed her case before the City Council.[8]

Following her dismissal, she embarked on a crusade to bring relief to the poor of Oklahoma City. She assumed leadership of a struggling benevolent organization known as the Provident Association of Oklahoma City and made her home on Reno Street into a distribution center for food, clothing, money, and job-placement information for the needy. She published eloquent pleas in the *Daily Oklahoman* describing the ragged, hungry children and the homeless families. She also solicited contributions for the association from business leaders, churches, and civic organizations. All of these efforts resulted in surprising success as thousands of garments and supplies arrived at her door. During the next three years as matron of the association, Barnard claimed to have helped three thousand destitute families and provided the resources for five hundred children to be placed in schools. These years changed her attitude about charity work, however, and led her to adopt a new approach toward the alleviation of poverty: In the course of discussions with the unemployed, she discovered that "what men need is not charity but justice, and the chance to do an honest day's work for a fair wage." Charity was the "weakest of weapons" with which to combat the problems of poverty, crime or disease.[9]

From this moment of awakening, Kate Barnard left the acceptable pattern of female activism that remained quiet, cooperative, modest, and devoted to good works and, as she wrote, "embarked on the maelstrom of politics, where contending ideas of statecraft eddy unceasingly, and where the tide of personal ambition is always in motion." She retained the rhetoric of charitable works as women's mission in the world, but she entered the exclusively male arena of political action. Kate Barnard became an agitator. Barnard's success in early Oklahoma politics resulted largely from her ability to tap the support of a wide range of interest groups, all of whom identified her as a suitable spokesperson. She offered to each a message that unified and called to action, rather than fragmented or alienated. Her political party affiliation, the Democratic Party, was that of her father and, fortuitously for her, was the one that dominated the creation of state government. By serving a mainstream party, Barnard could capitalize on the Populist converts in that party and represent the interests that fueled the growing Socialist Party in Oklahoma without the stigma of radicalism. Her own background of poverty gave her currency with the poorest Oklahomans, and her disregard of suffrage united her with the concerns of prominant groups of organized women.[10]

Barnard's combination of beauty, intelligence, energy, and intensity captivated those she approached with her ideas. First impressions recorded by her admirers revealed surprise that she was as professional as she was attractive. Five feet tall, less than one hundred pounds, she was strikingly beautiful with thick, curly dark hair and flashing eyes. As one reporter noted, "she talks very fast, with gestures and smiles and frowns and sometimes with tears." Indeed, her strength lay in her ability to influence individuals and groups. She had a strong, pleasant speaking voice, and she filled her speeches, in true muckraking style, with graphic descriptions of poverty, waste, and abuse, never flinching from placing the blame where she thought it belonged. When detractors claimed that her appeal was "largely personal" and that she "swayed the emotions" of her audience, she responded that she intended to do exactly that.[11]

On one occasion she spoke to a large crowd in an Oklahoma town where a recent coal-mine fire had killed fifteen men. She pointed her finger at the owner of the mine and reproached him, saying: "The diamonds you are wearing in your shirt-front were bought with the blood of fifteen men. . . . You made their wives widows; you made their children orphans; you are responsible to Almighty God for the long, weary lives of poverty and ignorance which they face." Barnard clearly aligned herself on the side of labor, and she became one of its most prized advocates and eloquent publicists. "She looks like a schoolgirl; she talks like an idealist; she is, perhaps, a visionary," one admirer gushed, "but she works with practical efficiency and common sense."[12]

Using the Provident Association as her base of operations, Barnard engaged in a variety of civic improvement activities, attacking the deteriorating slum conditions in her own neighborhood and promoting the unionization of labor. In 1905 she helped create a chapter of the Women's International Union Label League and served as its recording secretary. She lobbied for shorter hours, higher wages, and better working conditions for unskilled laborers, and she organized and represented a union of two hundred of these workers at the Oklahoma City Trades and Labor

Assembly in 1907. As she told a journalist, "the best way to help workers is to get into their organizations and work with them; instead of standing aloof—above, in some instances, and trying to work for them."[13]

Barnard also aligned herself with prominent women's groups. She appealed to the Oklahoma Territory Federation of Women's Clubs, a powerful if unenfranchised lobby, under the leadership of Frances F. Threadgill, and to Edith C. Johnson, society columnist for the *Daily Oklahoman*. She implemented a broader network of women by forming the Oklahoma City Child Labor League and, along with its president, Mrs. D. M. Thorpe, organized groups of receptive women in other communities. Not content to rely solely on local assessments of urban problems, she traveled to several major cities to observe slum and factory conditions and interview leading authorities, such as Jane Addams, Edwin Markham, Jacob Riis, and Luther Burbank, on effective preventive and ameliorative measures. Armed with letters of introduction from territorial governor Frank Frantz and money from the *Daily Oklahoman* editor, Roy Stafford, Barnard gained firsthand knowledge and national exposure, and she made valuable contacts with leading progressive organizations such as the National Child Labor Committee.[14]

By 1906, then, Barnard had earned a legitimate reputation as a labor activist, social reformer, and advocate of the poor. As statehood approached, her priorities included the elimination of child labor, a call for compulsory education, and the establishment of a governmental guardian agency under the direction of a commissioner of charities and corrections. She joined the meeting of the Territorial Federation of Labor, the Railroad Brotherhoods, and the Farmer's Union at Shawnee, Indian Territory, in August 1906, and lobbied for the planks that she was committed to accomplishing to be included in the convention report. The "Shawnee Convention" representatives intended to dominate the upcoming state constitutional convention and to incorporate their demands into state government. Along with proposals for the Australian ballot, referendum, eight-hour work day, mining controls, and a labor commissioner, Barnard led the other women delegates in calling for the inclusion of child labor and compulsory education statements. The Democratic Party endorsed the creation of the position of commissioner of charities and corrections at their convention. Following the Shawnee Convention, Barnard went on the political circuit beside Pete Hanraty and William H. Murray, speaking on behalf of those delegate nominees to the constitutional convention who supported the twenty-four farm-labor planks. Barnard moved audiences with her stories of suffering, hunger, and privation; she delivered a total of forty-four speeches before the election in November. The farm-labor reform coalition successfully elected 70 supporters out of the 112 delegates; of that total, 99 were Democrats. Murray, Hanraty, and gubernatorial hopeful Charles N. Haskell recognized Barnard's effectiveness as a speaker as well as her ties to labor and her connections to the women's lobby.[15]

Barnard did fail to support one of the most significant issues of the time, and, considering her political acuity, the oversight warrants explanation. Sentiment in favor of women's suffrage in the Oklahoma territories had been building since the mid-1890s, when Margaret Rees of Guthrie prepared a bill for representative Cassius Barnes to submit to the territorial legislature. National American Women's Suffrage Association (NAWSA) organizer Laura Gregg coordinated newly formed suffrage organizations across the territory in applying pressure for passage of the bill. In spite of Populist support bolstered by the Women's Christian Temperance Union (WCTU) and a spirited debate, the issue met defeat in the territorial council in 1897. Suffragists continued to submit petitions and to pressure sympathetic legislators to introduce suffrage measures and to attach suffrage riders to innocuous legislation such as county boundary adjustments. Prominent national leaders such as Carrie Chapman Catt and Anna Howard Shaw toured territorial Oklahoma provoking interest in women's suffrage, but another drive for passage failed to gain momentum until the prospect of statehood became imminent in 1905. The Oklahoma Socialist Party included women's suffrage in its platform beginning that year, and the WCTU devoted an issue of its official newspaper, the *Oklahoma Messenger*, to suffrage news. The Oklahoma Suffrage Association, led by Kate Biggers, reopened a headquarters in Guthrie and brought in another national organizer, Ida Porter Boyer, to improve press coverage and speakers' bureau effectiveness.[16]

Throughout 1906 and 1907, when the suffrage lobby increased its efforts to influence the members of the constitutional convention to provide for women's suffrage in the new state constitution, Kate Barnard's aid was conspicuously absent. The leading state social reformer did not believe in women's suffrage. According to one admirer, Barnard's beloved father opposed women's suffrage, and she refused to challenge his position until after his death. Chicago reformer Charles Zueblin claimed that she was so "hampered by the laborious masculine logic of her grateful supporters" that she acquiesced to their resistance to the measure. Neither Haskell nor Murray advocated the vote for women, although Pete Hanraty proved a loyal ally of suffragists at the constitutional convention. A story circulated that Barnard had said she did not need to vote as long as men did whatever she wanted them to do anyway.[17]

Barnard knew that the majority of the men in her political party, the Democratic Party, and the majority of the women from whom she drew support opposed the franchise for women. While the members of the Oklahoma Federation of Women's Clubs supported Kate Barnard's measures advocating protection for women, children, and the unfortunate, they had not yet accepted the legitimacy or even the propriety of a woman in politics. Publicist Kate Pearson Burwell described club membership in an article in *Sturm's Statehood Magazine* in the following revealing way:

> It is noteworthy that from the very beginning the movement has been made up of women with domestic ties, home lovers, keeping up with the development about them, and growing ahead of their children, letting things alone that have nothing to do with the home or its interests. They are not strong-minded women seeking political favors, or begging the ballot, but simply demanding and accomplishing better conditions under which to live."[18]

The Federation hierarchy and individual clubs and members lobbied the constitutional convention with resolutions, letters, and petitions in support primarily of measures for the protection of children. Frances Threadgill, Federation president, wrote a letter to convention president William H. Murray outlining the organization's requests. The territorial club women wanted five clauses incorporated into the constitution. With the exception of forestry protection, the issues were identical to Kate Barnard's priorities: regulation

Pete Hanraty, president of the Twin
Territories Federation of Labor and,
later, inspector of Oklahoma mines.
Photo courtesy of the Archives & Manuscript Division of the Oklahoma Historical Society.

of child labor, compulsory education, juvenile courts,
and reform schools. Escorted to the convention
platform by Pete Hanraty, Barnard addressed the
whole membership of the convention in December 1906
and the labor committee in January 1907 on behalf of
these measures and the creation of a charities and
corrections department. She also marched in a well-
publicized farm-labor parade of delegates in Guthrie.

When the convention completed its work in April 1907, Barnard and her allies had secured all of her desired goals.[19]

The floor debate for women's suffrage also took place in December and January, and Kate Barnard remained silent on this issue. The Oklahoma Suffrage Association believed that they had the support of the same delegates who signed the Shawnee Convention demands. Association president Kate Biggers worked tirelessly alongside Pete Hanraty and Robert L. Owen (who was not a delegate, but who commanded great respect at the convention) to rally support. Murray and Haskell, however, undercut these efforts by arguing behind the scenes to change delegate sympathies. Murray went so far as to fire two of the convention clerks for speaking out on the issue. In the final debate the traditional arguments, as well as a few local variations, dominated the moment. Delegates argued that most Oklahoma women did not want the vote, that men revered women and placed them on a pedestal and protected them, that voting would "unsex" women, that extending the franchise to women would legitimize opportunities for further Negro intrusion into the electoral process, and finally, that passage of women's suffrage would mean socialism and the destruction of the home.

Haskell delivered one of the most persuasive speeches, quoting long sections from the Bible to support his opposition. Then resorting to a trump card, he concluded his remarks with: "Katie Bernard's life is a lesson that every suffragist should study and profit by, and let me appeal to every mother that is in this audience to go back home to your boys, and continue to rock the cradle, and through that well-known medium continue to rule the world." At thirty-two years old Kate Barnard was unmarried and childless, but

Haskell used her, as an extended example of motherhood, to defeat suffrage: Women should attend to their
mothering responsibilities and follow Barnard's practice of petitioning men to bring about necessary
reforms. The final vote on the issue salvaged only the
right of Oklahoma women to vote in school elections.[20]

For one more year Kate Barnard rode the crest of
popularity as the associate of Murray, Haskell, and
Hanraty during the euphoria accompanying statehood.
The convention delegates deliberately worded the
article creating the office of commissioner of charities
and corrections to leave open the possibility that the
position could be held by either a man or a woman.
Barnard campaigned for the office and made hundreds
of speeches in support of her own candidacy and for her
benefactors. In one speech she explained her ideas
about her role in state-building: "Men have reason and
aggression; women, intuition, sentiment, ideals and
tact. Together they succeed." She won the September
election polling more votes than any other candidate,
including the governor, Charles N. Haskell.[21]

Barnard immediately began to consult national
authorities to help her draft legislation to implement
her altruistic goals. Samuel J. Barrows of the International Prison Commission and Colorado judge Ben
Lindsey drafted prison and juvenile court legislation.
A. J. McKelway of the National Child Labor Committee helped with compulsory education and child-
labor bills, and Barnard contacted Alexander Johnson
and H. H. Hart of the Russell Sage Foundation for the
latest advice on the care of the insane and the "feeble-
minded." She knew the legislative routine; she had
been successful in influencing the Shawnee Convention and the constitutional convention. She believed
that she commanded a large electorate, and she had
every right to expect a successful first term. The strain

Guthrie Statehood Day, November 16, 1907. Photo courtesy of the Archives & Manuscript Division of the Oklahoma Historical Society.

of such furious activity began to show up as illness, however, and even the advisers she consulted warned her to slow down, to be more patient, and not to expect to accomplish everything at once.[22]

The difference between Barnard's perception of her own importance and of the significance of her duties as commissioner of charities and corrections and the perceptions of the political leadership of the state became immediately obvious. On statehood day she had no place in the official program, and her position in the parade disappointed her. After waiting an hour, she boarded a "broken down, battered, and frayed buggy," in marked contrast to the elegant carriages holding state officials at the front of the procession. Angrily retreating to the state office building, she searched for her name on a door. She finally located her office on the third floor, "a tiny 'pidgeonhole' . . . hidden away in a recess or alcove of the attick," next to a door with a large sign labeled "Men's Toilet." Barnard claimed that state officials refused to remove the offensive toilet and reconstruct the office to join the Labor Department until she threatened to publicize her predicament, through the Federation of Women's Clubs, as an outrage on public morals. "Many referred to me as the Spiritual Life of the Statehood Battle," she later wrote "I was grateful to the Party Leaders who placed me on the State Ticket. I loved and believed in them and I supposed they returned that Trust and that Affection. . . . I expected Happiness when I reached the State House . . . but they hid me away."[23]

Near the end of her life Kate Barnard wrote bitterly about a score of political enemies whom she felt had persecuted her and had driven her from office. Some of the actions she remembered were deliberate, others reflected indifference, and many resulted from the disintegration of the farm-labor coalition. Murray and Haskell believed that their debt to Barnard had been paid with the nominal political position. Once in office, they expected her to be quiet, to cooperate, to submit reports, and to work cheaply. By contrast, Barnard envisioned her office as the point of leadership for the elimination of serious social problems: "I want to do good," she earnestly wrote for *Sturm's Magazine.* "I want to feel that the world is better because I have lived in it. I am especially interested in that class of legislation that will best protect the tiniest and frailest bit of humanity who is intrusted to our care." In outlining the work of her department for the *Survey*, she wrote that its goal was "to stop human waste and to elevate and ennoble society by directing dominant thought into humanitarian channels." Her perspective and that of the political leadership clashed openly in the first legislative session over the issue of child labor. William H. Murray, now speaker of the Oklahoma House of Representatives, advanced the interests of farmers who depended upon the labor of all members of the family. They resented governmental interference that attempted to place restrictions on hours worked. The contest grew into a personal feud, however, when Murray attacked the appropriation for Barnard's office as unnecessary and publicly scolded her for lobbying for her measures on the floor of the House. Barnard left the chamber indignantly. The child-labor bill passed, but Murray interceded with Haskell, who vetoed it claiming that it was too stringent.[24]

Kate Barnard became Murray's nemesis. She used her influence with labor leaders to inspire a public censure of Murray at the Oklahoma Federation of Labor convention in 1908. She traveled throughout the state performing her duties inspecting jails, poor farms, orphan homes, and mental institutions, never failing to include scorching speeches condemning

William H. Murray, speaker of the
Oklahoma House of Representatives.
Photo courtesy of the Archives &
Manuscript Division of the Oklahoma
Historical Society.

Murray and his associates as enemies of the humanitarian work that she was attempting to accomplish. For his part, Murray railed back about grafters, socialist ideas, and state officials who wanted to assume the role of parent. In response to the rumors of his discourteous treatment of Barnard, Murray stated that "the word woman is by me recognized as sacred, and I have the profoundest respect for the modest, chaste, and virtuous womanhood of our state." Barnard contradicted that description for him the moment she became a public officeholder, and he made no apology for not treating her any differently than he would treat a man. Perhaps Murray's personal memoirs provided a better understanding of his difficulties with Barnard: "Women have always embarrassed me," he wrote. "I know the peculiarities of women, but know very little of their society, because when I was in my youth and young manhood, I had no associates among women, and therefore, do not understand their peculiar Society, System or Humors." The enmity between the two continued in 1910 when Murray ran for governor, and Barnard placed a front-page, notarized denial in the *Daily Oklahoman* that she supported his candidacy. "I will never be for him as long as he opposes measures calculated to better conditions for laboring people of this state," she stormed. Lee Cruce defeated Murray's gubernatorial bid, but Murray remained a force in Oklahoma politics, and Barnard made him a bitter foe.[25]

Wherever Barnard went in pursuit of her official duties, she exposed to public awareness the short-comings of the institutions of the new state. She publicized the filth of jails and the brutal treatment of prisoners and the insane. Following the graphic disclosures, she demanded appropriations to create new, modern public-welfare institutions. Although Governor Haskell attempted to remain above the Murray-Barnard controversy, he too grew weary of her tirades and embarrassed at increasingly negative public attention focused on Oklahoma.

The Kansas-Oklahoma penitentiary scandal of 1908–1909 illustrated his waning support. In the absence of a state penitentiary, Oklahoma sent convicted criminals to the Kansas State Penitentiary in Lansing. At the cost of forty cents per prisoner per day, Kansas provided food, clothing, and incarceration

Charles N. Haskell, first governor of
the state of Oklahoma. Photo courtesy
of the Archives & Manuscript Division
of the Oklahoma Historical Society.

for the 562 male and 13 female Oklahoma prisoners.
Part of the contract also allowed private entrepreneurs
to use convict labor in coal mining and in furniture and
twine factories. Barnard examined the facilities in
August 1908. She first paid a small fee and anony-
mously toured the penitentiary with a group of other
visitors. Then she returned, identified herself to
Warden William H. Haskell (no relation to Charles
Haskell), and demanded a thorough inspection. The
conditions Barnard observed horrified her, and she

returned to Oklahoma and submitted a private report to the governor. Barnard uncovered evidence of an utterly inadequate diet, harsh work schedules and dangerous conditions in the mine, and sexual abuse of young inmates. She heard convincing stories of vicious punishments, such as confinement in a small wooden crate known as the "crib," a water torture in which guards sprayed high-pressure water in the face and on the body of a shackled prisoner in the crib, and the practice of placing a ring in the foreskin of the penis of sexually active prisoners.[26]

Barnard's official report did not become news until mid-December, but Haskell's response between September and late December revealed his alienation from Barnard. Historian Irwin Hurst has suggested that Haskell prevailed upon Barnard not to make a full disclosure of the politically explosive issue until after the November elections in order to protect the already-damaged Democratic coalition. When Kansas governor Edward W. Hoch suggested in a September letter to Governor Haskell that Barnard's findings were exaggerated, Haskell wrote back, "I believe I took the same view of the report you mentioned that you did and therefore I did not give it any further thought." As late as December 14, after the story made headlines in the Kansas capitol, a Topeka paper quoted Haskell as delivering a conciliatory public statement in which he patronizingly noted that Barnard would like to see the prisoners "treated as if they were guests at the Waldorf Astoria." He continued, "I have no doubt that she thought she saw those things about which she reported, but I am not inclined to give them much heavy thought." In Oklahoma, Haskell praised Barnard as "a good industrious official," but "her kindness of heart would make things look cruel to her that an ordinary citizen would consider proper and necessary."[27]

Because of the public outcry, Governor Hoch selected a Kansas-based committee to investigate Barnard's charges in late December, and Haskell was finally moved to act. In response to a letter from Hoch, Haskell explained his change of mind. Until that time "there was nothing to warrant a communication," but now Haskell had received an additional report from "one of our prison board, a prominent and careful state official . . . who is now very decided in his belief that there are just grounds for criticism." Haskell chose a five-man committee to join the Kansas investigation. Significantly, he included in the membership William H. Murray, although Murray later resigned, and he did not participate in the investigation. Kate Barnard attended the hearings and produced witnesses and depositions to support her claims. After a series of bitter and gruesomely explicit confrontations, the Kansas committee and the Oklahoma committee issued separate reports. The Kansas delegates exonerated Warden Haskell and the facility, but appended a list of eighteen recommendations that became the basis of future Kansas state penal reform. The Oklahoma members found Barnard's charges justified, and Oklahoma prisoners departed for home in 1909. They arrived at a temporary barracks in McAlester, Oklahoma, and under the direction of Warden R. W. Dick, they set to work building the walls and cell blocks of a new state penitentiary. As a result of the publicity surrounding this crusade, Arizona officials sought Barnard's expertise in their own prison reform campaign in 1912 and the *New York Times* carried articles applauding her efforts.[28]

While she received acclaim outside the state as a speaker and reformer, Barnard assured her ruin when she embraced the cause of Indian orphans. She fought for legal guarantees against the pauperization of

Indian minors with land allotments until her forced retirement from public life in 1915, but her fortunes began to decline as early as 1910. Barnard's father died in 1909, and she experienced desperate loneliness and physical and emotional breakdown. "My father's death," she later wrote, "is the One thing from which I never recovered." She suffered a series of respiratory illnesses that required extended periods of care at hospices, such as Montcalm Sanitorium in Colorado. Barnard spent several weeks there in 1910 to "gather fortitude for the great trials of life." Barnard campaigned for reelection in 1910, and because of her feud with William H. Murray, she confided to one friend that she was truly frightened. Influential Republican publisher Walter Ferguson (Elva and Thompson Ferguson's son) claimed she had not accomplished much during her tenure except to make political speeches for the Democrats: She was "a nice bright girl and in her press dope you can almost hear the flapping of wings," but her office appropriation was too high for the people "to pay for her as a stump attraction." Barnard faced Kate Biggers, former Oklahoma Suffrage Association president, as the Republican candidate in the election, and women's suffrage was this time an issue on the ballot. At the close of the election, Biggers and women's suffrage went down to defeat, but the weary Barnard was left to brave the budget-conscious administration of the new governor, Lee Cruce, and the disarray of the once-strong Democratic farm-labor coalition.[29]

Barnard lobbied the Third Legislature for an increase in salary, hers being the lowest for state officials with the exception of the lieutenant governor. The legislature raised her salary to $2,500, but this act violated the state constitution and proved to be an issue that would be used to embarrass her later. In the

next session Barnard moved to place her office in a
guardianship role with regard to Indian orphans.
During 1910 and 1911 she secured bills that gave the
commissioner of charities and corrections authority
over the Oklahoma State Orphan Home and made her
office "next friend" to all orphans and minors. Barnard
once again publicized the necessity of this action in
graphic terms. In 1908 the federal government had
terminated its responsibility to Indian minors by
placing authority over their affairs in the county
probate courts of Oklahoma. Barnard witnessed the
flagrant theft of Indian land and money by court-
appointed "guardians" for these minors. She found
children who had been heir to valuable estates living
in orphan homes and wandering neighborhoods beg-
ging for food. She observed three dirty, abandoned "elf"
children with matted hair, who belonged to a guardian
with rights to fifty-one other scattered children, and
one fourteen-year-old girl who worked cleaning tables
in a sleazy restaurant while her absentee guardian
dissipated her wealth.[30]

To help Barnard prosecute these cases, she pushed
a bill through bitter congressional debate to create a
public defender to be appointed by her office. Governor
Cruce vetoed the bill, but her legislative supporters
added additional money to her appropriations ear-
marked for legal work. Barnard hired Dr. J. H. Stolper
to pursue the cases in the courts, and by the end of
1912, Stolper claimed to have prosecuted 1,361 cases
and returned nearly one million dollars to Indian
orphans. Stolper estimated that the cost of each case
averaged slightly more than $3.00, whereas private
attorneys charged between $25.00 and $100.00 for
similar cases. Historian Angie Debo has pointed out
that these cases represented only a small number and
only the most notorious of the abuses of Indian rights

that were rampant across the state. Stolper exaggerated his own achievements and often alienated Barnard's supporters through callous responses to less dramatic appeals for aid. Barnard's health had declined to the degree that Stolper and her longtime assistant, Hobart Huson, carried on most of the office work. The sordid exposure of the corruption surrounding Indian dispossession led to investigations by members of the Board of Indian Commissioners in 1912 and 1913 and to an embarrassing report to Congress made by M. L. Mott, attorney for the Creek Indians.[31]

The Fourth Legislature, led by Speaker J. H. Maxey, put an end to Kate Barnard's career. Angered by Barnard's political wrangling, the adverse publicity, and her interference with lucrative oil and coal land transactions involving Indian lands, her political enemies seized the opportunity to end her influence. They first forced the resignation of J. H. Stolper in February 1913 on a spurious charge of influence peddling. Barnard replaced him with former county judge Ross Lockridge. They then launched an investigation of Barnard's office and charged her with excessive absences, extravagant spending, and negligible results. The final report recommended that her office be abolished and her illegal raise in pay returned. In the midst of this turmoil, attorney Frank Montgomery approached Barnard with a deal. He suggested that if she would replace Lockridge with him, he would use his influence with Maxey and legislators E. P. Hill and J. E. Wyand to end the controversy. When Barnard refused, the legislature cut the appropriations to her office down to funds for only her salary and that of a stenographer. Barnard appealed to Myrtle Archer McDougal, current president of the Oklahoma Federation of Women's Clubs and an ardent suffrage worker, but McDougal could only respond with sympathy. Barnard revealed the whole dismal story to the public on the front page of the *Daily Oklahoman* on May 8. She blamed the politicians who she said threatened to destroy her politically if she continued the Indian work, and she claimed they were determined to "get charge of the department and control it or wreck it." Pathetically, she justified her absences from office as the result of "overwork which I did for you and your children," and she promised her constituents, "I have no home and no social ties and as soon as I am well again I shall put in sixteen hours again a day working for you."[32]

Discarded by her political party leadership and bereft of a power base, a beaten and seriously ill Kate Barnard abandoned hope of reelection in 1914. She stumped the state to defeat Maxey, Hill, and Wyand, and she launched a "people's lobby," endowed by eastern philanthropists, to evaluate further legislation regarding state Indian matters. In October 1914, she made an impassioned plea before the Lake Mohonk Conference of Friends of the Indian in New York for publicity and funds to help her fight for her department and her work. She told the delegates that "7,000 men will act with me during the Legislature," but, in truth, Barnard was effectively silenced in Oklahoma. Friendly national periodicals and newspapers carried discussions of her plight, but Commissioner of Indian Affairs Cato Sells denied her dire assessment of Oklahoma affairs, and the state press either ignored her or ridiculed her. As she wrote years later about her attempts to correct false press reports about herself, editors told her that no one really cared any longer and that she should not take herself so seriously, "and the air of finality with which this was uttered was all the evidence I needed to know that I was definitely dismissed."[33]

Barnard died in February 1930 embittered and alone in an Oklahoma City hotel room. She had been obsessively writing a history of the founding of the state. For many years she had searched for a cure to a serious, disfiguring ailment that caused her what she described as "hysterical pain." The newspaper account of her death stated that hotel employees considered her "unusually eccentric." She wanted her estate to provide a home for the aged and friendless, but the courts divided it instead among her three half-brothers. Her friend columnist Edith Johnson memorialized her as a woman of true moral courage who had enjoyed a colorful career but had ultimately lost influence because she "made bitter enemies in places of power." In her last attempt to understand the tragedy of her own life, Barnard's memoirs—sometimes lucid, sometimes not—blamed a host of villains including Haskell and Murray. Among her thoughts also ran this admission: "This persecution must have come from . . . my failure somewhere because I was ignorant of Politics." Her accomplishments she credited to a strength of character inherited from her father that enabled her to "forego love, home, and other material pleasures, and become a Voice to those who suffer in the gutter of human life."[34]

8

Public Pioneering

In 1921, Thompson Ferguson died leaving the management of the *Watonga Republican* to his wife. Elva remembered how doubtful her friends were that she could handle the full responsibility, and they encouraged her to sell the newspaper and retire. She steadfastly refused this advice and continued to write the editorials and operate the newspaper for another ten years. "Women have always had an uphill climb in public pioneering," she wrote in 1937, and no doubt she recalled those first difficult days without her husband and partner. Ferguson accepted this responsibility, however, at the same time that other state women made their entrance into the area of public political pioneering. Many of them had a lifetime of experience in building the institutions of American society: schools, churches, and civic organizations. Few had the political expertise of Elva Ferguson. The

challenges for women had changed since the days of
Kate Barnard, but few precedents existed to guide the
novices. Looking back, Ferguson wrote, "Statecraft in
those days required a man of iron will and the courage
to say 'no.' . . . To say no at the right time, to possess
honor, integrity, and aggressiveness . . . is not an easy
task." Alice Mary Robertson came to understand
Ferguson's remarks, better than any other woman,
during her brief political career following the passage
of women's suffrage.[1]

Alice Robertson shared the same reputation for
extended motherhood that Kate Barnard had, but
where concern for Indian affairs came as an after-
thought to Barnard, it was the unifying theme of
Robertson's life. She never escaped the legacy of her
illustrious missionary ancestors, and she proclaimed
every success in her life to be a result of that heritage.
Her life was full of paradox. Unmarried, she pursued a
successful career as an educator, reformer, and businesswoman. In spite of these life choices, she stub-
bornly clung to a philosophy that simultaneously
glorified and limited other women to a single facet—
motherhood. Her 1920 election to the office of United
States congresswoman for the Second District of
Oklahoma stunned her contemporaries and fascinated
historians because of her avowed opposition to women's
suffrage and any to organization that promoted an
expanded public role for women. The social attentions
of the wealthy and powerful in Washington, her innate
political conservatism, and her inexperience influenced Robertson to cast votes that alienated her male
and female Oklahoma constituents alike and ended
her influence in state affairs. Illness and dire poverty
marked the final years of her life, and she was reduced
to selling her family historical treasures in order to
survive.[2]

Born in 1854, Mary Alice Robertson was the second daughter of Ann Eliza Worcester Robertson and William Schenk Robertson, Presbyterian missionaries to the Creek Indians in Indian Territory. Her maternal grandfather, Samuel Austin Worcester, had accepted imprisonment by the state of Georgia rather than abandon his missionary work among the Cherokees. The Supreme Court case *Worcester v. Georgia* provided for his release, and Worcester moved his family west in 1835 to a location on the Illinois River in Indian Territory. He established the mission station known as Park Hill and began to publish a newspaper in the Cherokee language. He later translated the Bible and a hymnal into Cherokee. Ann Eliza Worcester also exhibited considerable talent in linguistics. After her marriage to Robertson in 1850, when she joined her husband's work at Tullahassee Mission near present-day Muskogee, Oklahoma, she learned the Creek language and translated the New Testament for their use. Alice Robertson later gave both of these Bibles, Creek and Cherokee, a prominent display wherever she lived and included mention of them in every interview. Almost like a talisman, her family's religious heritage somehow provided her with a sense of distance and security from criticism.[3]

Just prior to the Civil War, Tullahassee employed twelve teachers and enrolled over one hundred students at the boarding school. When southern factions of the Creek Nation threatened the mission, the Robertson family fled to the safety of the North and did not return until 1866. The oldest child, Ann Augusta, continued her education in Ohio, and Alice assumed the house-keeping responsibilities for her weakened mother and younger sister and brother. The family devoted all of their resources to rebuilding the riddled structures of the school. Cholera took the lives of her twin baby

Tullahassee Mission School, home of Alice Robertson and her missionary parents, was destroyed by fire in 1880. Photo courtesy of the Western History Collections, University of Oklahoma Library.

brothers, and for the next years Alice worked alongside her family and studied with her father and mother. After Ann Augusta's graduation, Alice attended Elmira College in New York on a scholarship. In one of her student essays she speculated about what she would do with an imaginary fortune: "I think of the many privileges and advantages enjoyed by the students of this college, and decide that a part of my riches shall endow a similar institution in the far southwest that the black-eyed daughters of the forest may have opportunities to cultivate the equal talent Providence has given them—While it has denied the means of culture bestowed upon their fairer sisters." Until the day that this fortune should arrive, however, she committed herself to a life of hard work.[4]

After two years, the family needed her financial assistance to send her younger sister to school, and

Robertson accepted a clerical position in 1873 in the Indian Office in Washington, D.C. She carried the regret of leaving school for many years, but this was assuaged in 1886 when Elmira College awarded her an honorary Master of Arts degree. While in Washington, she studied shorthand and typing to ready herself with the skills to earn money as a stenographer. She also studied domestic science and social-welfare work to make herself more useful as a teacher at Tullahassee. After a few years she found the Indian Office stifling, and she secured a position as secretary to Capt. Richard Pratt at the Indian School in Carlisle, Pennsylvania. Tragedy struck the Tullahassee Mission in 1880 when a fire destroyed the main building. Robertson convinced the Indian Office to pay the expenses for twenty-five of the most promising Creek students to attend school at Carlisle, and she solicited donations for free railroad passes for the students from Russell Sage and other wealthy benefactors. The shock of the fire proved too much for her father, and he died six months later. Robertson's mother continued to teach at the mission until the Creek government turned over the remaining buildings to the Baptist Home Mission Board for a school for Creek freedmen.[5]

Robertson resigned her position with Pratt in 1883 and began an extensive campaign to raise support for a new school for the Creeks. These efforts met with surprising success as she honed her oratorical skills. Of her meeting-to-meeting fund-raising speeches she stated, "I made people laugh. I made them cry and best of all I made them give." One of those who contributed was the wealthy philanthropist Mary Copley (Mrs. William K.) Thaw in New York. She and Robertson formed a lifelong friendship, and Thaw provided money and clothing to Robertson in times of financial distress. Working through the Presbyterian Home Mission

Board and tapping all of the contacts she had made in Washington and through Pratt, Robertson quickly acquired the funds to build Nuyaka Mission School (near present-day Okmulgee, Oklahoma). Robertson's sister Augusta served as superintendent of the new school, and she and her husband, N. B. Moore, a Creek official, operated Nuyaka for seven years. Nuyaka accommodated seventy Creek students in frame buildings organized along the cottage plan.[6]

Robertson settled in Muskogee and took charge of the Minerva Home, a home for Indian girls from all of the Five Tribes. Mary Thaw and Robertson's cousin Loring Andrews Robertson made sizable contributions to the Minerva Home. The school also operated under the cottage plan. When Robertson attended the 1889 Lake Mohonk Conference of Friends of the Indian, she described the success of her program: The house mother "endeavors to train the girls under her care as though they were her daughters," she told the delegates. "They receive lessons not only from books, but in needlework, in cookery, and in the various womanly accomplishments." A student at the Minerva Home later remembered that Robertson "tried to be a mother to all of us." She tucked each girl into bed with a prayer and a kiss every night. Robertson "mothered" many young Indian girls during these years, and she bought wedding trousseaus for more than a dozen. Although she never married, she adopted one orphaned Indian girl and raised her as her daughter. Robertson reported at the 1889 conference that her previous year's advanced class of girls attended school in Ohio because "I believe in sending them East to finish their studies for the lessons in life they cannot otherwise learn." She also admitted that most of her students married white men rather than Indian men and that this caused some Indian opposition.[7]

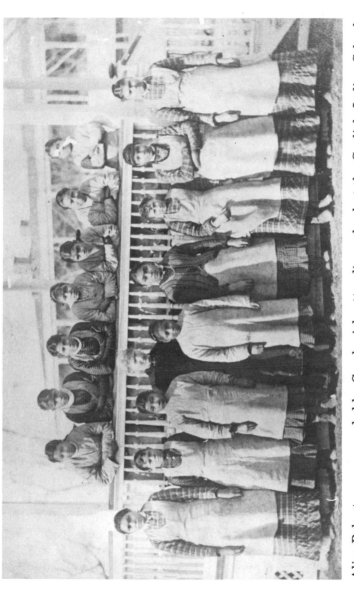

Alice Robertson surrounded by Creek girls attending school at the Carlisle Indian School, 1881. Photo courtesy of the Archives & Manuscript Division of the Oklahoma Historical Society.

In 1894 the Minerva Home combined with the Timothy Hill School in Muskogee to form the Henry Kendall College, a coeducational institution. The college relocated in Tulsa in 1906, and in 1920 it became the University of Tulsa. Robertson taught English, history, and civics at the school until 1899. To supplement her income during these years, she also operated a photography studio. Robertson had met Theodore Roosevelt at the Lake Mohonk Conferences and had established a warm friendship with him. Although she did not share some of his more progressive political ideas, she became a loyal Republican supporter. When the Spanish-American War erupted in 1898, she wrote to Roosevelt on behalf of two of her students who wanted to join the Rough Riders. For each Muskogee boy who volunteered for the war effort, she packed a kit of personal supplies, eating utensils, and a New Testament, and she continued to champion their welfare after they returned home. Roosevelt mentioned her contributions in his book *The Rough Riders*, and he assisted her on several occasions in her charitable work.[8]

At the turn of the century, a burgeoning white population in Indian Territory brought increased pressure to unite the Twin Territories into one state. In 1898 the Curtis Act directed the suspension of tribal governments by 1906 and provided for the allotment of the lands of the Five Tribes that had been previously excluded in the Dawes Act of 1887. Robertson had advised the Lake Mohonk Conference delegates a decade earlier that the most important thing to be done for the Indians was "to press the education and Christianization of these people until they shall be prepared for American citizenship." To that end, she applied for the position of federal supervisor of Creek schools, and in midlife she moved away from the acceptable female endeavors of teaching and charity work and into the highly competitive, male-dominated world of political patronage. She sent letters to President William McKinley, influential senators, and Creek officials citing her family background and her own record of service. A supportive letter from Vice President Theodore Roosevelt advanced her candidacy.[9]

Robertson gained and held this supervisory position until 1905. She traveled alone by buggy all over the Creek lands inspecting schools, appointing teachers, gathering statistics, and preparing reports. Most often she stayed in the homes of Creek friends. John D. Benedict, superintendent of schools of the Five Tribes, reported deplorable conditions in the Creek schools. Favoritism guided tribal appointments of teachers and administrators, and this resulted in shabby business accounting, waste, and incompetence. In spite of pretensions, the boarding schools, with the exception of Nuyaka, operated at the common-school level. Robertson set to work to remedy these practices by professionalizing the selection process and by insisting on teacher participation in summer training "normals" (training schools for elementary teachers). Robertson made it a rule to appoint only properly certified teachers and to promote applicants to choice positions on the basis of merit examinations and attendance at the normals. These policies created resentment, however, and Robertson complained that a large number of teachers found the new requirements distasteful. "Some teachers have been appointed by the Creek superintendent without taking examinations," she wrote to Benedict. "I feel my position should be clarified." Mary Thaw sent a large donation to Robertson in 1902 to pay for the services of instructors in pedagogy, textbooks on teaching methods, and inspirational evening entertainments. By 1903, Robertson reported that fifty-four white teachers and forty black teachers attended separate normals in Eufaula and Muskogee, and she exalted, "Pressure on the supervisor to secure good appointments has ceased. Now everybody knows that opportunity and advancement comes on merit."[10]

With her aged mother near death, Robertson began a new letter-writing campaign to get herself appointed to a more lucrative and less strenuous position as postmistress of Muskogee. Her old friend, now president, Theodore Roosevelt by-passed the patronage courtesies usually given to local politicians and sent her name to the Senate. Robertson held this position until 1913, but not without difficulty. She irritated a Muskogee editor by halting one issue of his newspaper because it advertised a bridge party that offered prizes, and Robertson deemed this gambling. She also alienated women's suffrage groups with her outspoken criticism of their cause. At a postal convention in 1906, as the only woman to hold such a position in Oklahoma, she asked just one favor: that the members refrain from smoking cigarettes in her presence; cigars were acceptable. Otherwise, she wanted to be treated as "one of the boys." She insisted that she was not a suffragist and stated that "The exchange of a woman's privileges for a man's right is too much like bartering the birthright for a mess of pottage." Local politicians objected to her reappointment in 1910; her former male assistant charged her with inefficiency and misconduct, and Republican representative Bird McGuire filed an official protest of her confirmation. A thorough investigation by the Post Office Department revealed no foundation for criticism other than political motivation.[11]

During her tenure as postmistress, Robertson established her first permanent home since Tullahassee. She built a spacious wood and native-stone

residence on fifty-five acres atop Agency Hill northwest of Muskogee. She called the farm "Sawokla," a
Muscogee term meaning gathering place. Here she
displayed her Indian artifacts and family treasures,
and she entertained reunions of war veterans and
friends from all of her past endeavors. After 1913
Robertson directed a highly successful farming operation at Sawokla. She raised dairy and beef cattle, hogs,
and chickens; cultivated vegetables of all kinds; and
preserved a variety of fruits. These crops provided the
food for a cafeteria she opened in downtown Muskogee.
In an effort to help young, single working women, now
more numerous in the growing city, Robertson established a club in the McKibben Building that offered a
cafeteria lunch, reception rooms, and rest and bath
facilities. The women paid a small membership fee, and
a man might only be admitted as the guest of a female
member. The fame of the lunchroom spread rapidly,
and Robertson expanded her service, with additional
personnel, to a full-time cafeteria catering to local
businessmen as well. The establishment closed only on
Sundays in keeping with Robertson's lifelong strict
observance of the sabbath. She enjoyed the financial
success and the social limelight of the farm and
cafeteria, but she believed that those accomplishments
had a price: "Men are not particularly attracted to
women in business," she told a reporter, "and they
must be prepared to sacrifice the wonderful joys of
motherhood and the blessings of grandchildren."
Concerning her influence on young women, she stated,
"My greatest ambition has been to do all in my power
toward the establishment of happy homes . . . I have
always held myself up as a warning and not an
example to my girls."[12]

    Robertson made another foray into politics in 1916
when she campaigned for the office of Muskogee

County superintendent of schools. In spite of almost certain defeat in the Democratic stronghold, Robertson asked voters to elect her because, "As a woman who combined thorough and practical knowledge of domestic affairs with a man's business training and ability I claim special qualifications. . . . I'm not a politician or a suffragette, but I love the homes and the children of my county." The Democrats stood solid, however, and won the election.

With the outbreak of World War I, Robertson extended her professional mothering. When troop trains began to pass through Muskogee, Robertson loaded up her car with sandwiches, donuts, snacks, and coffee to pass out to the weary servicemen. She and her chauffeur met every train without fail, and the reputation of the motherly woman with the generous heart spread. The railroad company eventually provided a coach on the siding, and Robertson took charge of Red Cross workers in the operation of a canteen—one copied by communities throughout the state. She also entertained soldiers at Sawokla, made small loans to them, and fed uniformed men and their families at her cafeteria free of charge. These acts of charity began to drain the resources of Sawokla, but when friends cautioned her, she replied, "What was a little food, when a man was willing to give his life."[13]

At the age of sixty-six years, when many other women retired to lives of seclusion and anonymity, Alice Robertson shocked her associates by declaring herself a 1920 candidate for Second District representative to the United States Congress. Many factors made this new endeavor highly questionable. The incumbent, William W. Hastings of Tahlequah, had served three consecutive terms with distinction. Hastings drew prestige from his Cherokee heritage, Vanderbilt law degree, and notable service as an officer of the Cherokee Nation, and he had the support of political backing and finances from the strong Democratic party. Alice Robertson had no political organization except for a few Muskogee friends, and her financial affairs had not successfully recovered from her wartime generosity. More importantly, Robertson had actively opposed women's suffrage in Oklahoma.[14]

Suffrage activity lay dormant in Oklahoma after the ignominious defeat of a referendum in 1910. By the advent of World War I, however, the climate had shifted in Oklahoma, as well as the rest of the nation, to a more receptive attitude toward women's suffrage. The Oklahoma Federation of Women's Clubs endorsed the measure in 1914, and this organization, along with an invigorated Oklahoma Suffrage Association, campaigned to bring about a state constitutional amendment in 1918. These groups combined suffrage publicity with women's war work in the Red Cross and Liberty bond sales to inspire a reputation of patriotism and respectability. Alice Robertson had not changed her mind, however, and she accepted the office of vice president of the newly formed Oklahoma Anti-Suffrage League. The "antis" accused the suffragettes of advocating socialism and free love and of having pro-German sentiments. In spite of a number of obstructionist tactics by the Election Board, such as insisting that the suffrage question be on a separate ballot and then somehow failing to provide that ballot at polling booths, the women's suffrage amendment carried by a vote of 106,909 to 81,481. The Anti-Suffrage League filed a protest against the election-return certification, but Governor Robert L. Williams declared the results valid.[15]

In explaining her opposition to suffrage, Robertson declared, "I've always done a man's work, carried a man's burden, and had to pay the bills." She had fought women's suffrage as an added burden to women, but now that the men had given women the vote, she intended to see if they meant it. She saw political office as another duty for women, and she compared the situation to a time when, as a young woman, she had been forced to chop wood in a blizzard to keep her family alive. "I didn't like to do it," she told a journalist. "I didn't think it was work for a woman to do. But it was my duty—the nearest one."[16]

Few took her campaign seriously at first, but she devised an original method of political publicity that soon captured the imagination of her district: She bought classified advertising space in the local newspapers and combined the menus of her cafeteria with political statements. A typical advertisement read, "Watermelons better everyday. Fried chicken extra good tonight. Our campaign seems to be going very well, even if we are not neglecting our customers." Readers soon turned to the want-ad section each day to see what the lady politician had to say. The curious packed her restaurant, and the proprietor greeted her guests at each table, taking time to shake hands and to discuss politics. She handed out paper flyers with her photograph in a Red Cross uniform, and she left a calling card that stated: "There are already more lawyers and bankers in Congress than are needed. The farmers need a farmer. I am a farmer. The women need a woman to look after their new responsibilities. The soldier boys need a proven friend. I promise few speeches, but faithful work." All told she spent $2,940 on campaign expenses. She won the November election by a few more than two hundred votes.[17]

The most important reasons for Robertson's victory lay in the political division engendered by President Woodrow Wilson's League of Nations fight, the cultural discontent following World War I, and the increasing agricultural woes in Oklahoma. For the first time since statehood, the citizens voted for a Republican presidential candidate, Warren G. Harding, and sent a majority of the state's eight representatives, along with the state's first Republican senator, to the Republican side of Congress. Robertson's platform appealed to voters because of its simplicity and its foundation in traditional values. She told her constituents, "I am a Christian, I am an American, I am a republican." They believed "Miss Alice," as she was affectionately called, when she assured them, "I cannot be bought, I cannot be sold, I cannot be intimidated." She promised to work for the interests of Indians, soldiers, and women and children.[18]

It seemed ironic that in the first national election in which Oklahoma women were allowed to vote, Robertson won. The irony could be explained, however, by Robertson's revised attitude toward women in politics: Women had always been the "conscience keepers and conscience quickeners" of life and the "custodians of all that we mean by Americanism. . . . In politics, as well as in the home, women of today need the pioneer virtues: courage, industry, self-forgetfulness, loyalty, honesty, strength, housewifery, neighborliness, love of country, of children, of God." Women's new duties, then, revolved around an extension of household responsibilities, and she advised her constituents that without conflict or undue aggressiveness the new voters should quietly assume their duties.[19]

Robertson's election did not signal a victory for women as independent political beings. Rather, many perceived it as the triumph of the "right kind of woman" over the selfish and divisive suffragette minority. Mary Thaw wrote to Robertson congratulating her, as an anti-suffragist, on her success and praising her "practical commonsense notion." In the

following weeks, Thaw sent a one-hundred-dollar check
and clothing suitable for the congresswoman's new
position. Robertson did not stand as the lone example
of an anti-suffragist's elevation to office. Neither of the
two women elected to the Oklahoma legislature that
year had been active suffrage workers. In addition,
Governor J. B. A. Robertson (no relation to Alice
Robertson) appointed the president of the now-defunct
Anti-Suffrage League, Sallie Stephens (Mrs. T. H.)
Sturgeon, to serve as the first woman on the state
health department's sanitary inspection board.[20]

Naturally, political observers compared Miss Alice
to the first woman elected to Congress, Montana's
Jeannette Rankin, and to the sole woman in the
British parliament, Lady Astor. *Daily Oklahoman*
columnist Edith C. Johnson wrote a scathing attack on
Rankin's tenure, claiming that she was a "much made-
over and flattered woman" whose career was remarkable only for her disgraceful failure to cast her vote in
favor of World War I. Johnson also criticized her for
wearing fancy clothes and "getting her hand kissed."
The stout, plain Robertson dressed in shapeless black,
wore sensible shoes, and preferred cotton stockings to
the more fashionable silk ones. Mary Thaw often sent
hats, clothes, and money to improve Robertson's drab
wardrobe, and the congresswoman referred to Thaw as
her "fairy godmother." Johnson predicted that since
Robertson was at the age when "the passions have
cooled," she would "bring to her work pure reason, a
heart whose interests will be undivided and a nature
undisturbed by romantic excitement." When questioned about international affairs, Robertson assured
Johnson that she would not hesitate to vote for war and
that she opposed Wilson's League of Nations, but
stated that on most issues, she knew "absolutely
nothing. . . . I have not formulated any definite policies,

Congresswoman Alice M. Robertson, 1921.
Photo courtesy of the Archives & Manu-
script Division of the Oklahoma Historical
Society.

but I have very decided ideas about right and wrong
and before deciding any questions I always will try to
put myself in the place of others." She chose as her
secretary a Muskogee war veteran, Benjamin E. Cook,
because "men like to talk things over with a man."[21]

When Robertson took office she reveled in the
attention national dignitaries paid her, but she was
woefully unprepared for the grueling schedule and
competitive tactics of legislation. Mary Thaw arranged
a Press Club reception and banquet for over a thousand

people, and she included Robertson at the speaker's table. Robertson mingled among the politically conservative and wealthy elite, and she met such luminaries as secretary of the treasury Andrew Mellon. She wrote to her sister Augusta about Mellon, "Imagine, please, poverty-stricken me sitting next to that wealth, but he was 'plain as an old shoe'—quiet, keen, and giving a feeling of great power." When she first met President Harding, he presented her with a rose. Later during her term, he sent her to Portland, Oregon, to represent him (with full presidential honors) at the annual Rose Festival. Robertson and Mrs. Harding became good friends, and Alice was frequently invited for expeditions on the presidential yacht and for quiet dinner parties at the White House. She dined with Lord and Lady Astor when they visited America. Reporters delighted in comparing the appearance of the two lady politicians: Lady Astor, slim, attractive, and impeccably groomed, and Robertson, white-haired and plain. Organizations and clubs all over the United States besieged Robertson with invitations to speak. "A woman can do anything she sets out to do," she told her audiences, "if she keeps her mouth shut and her ears open. . . . If people think I am going to do something sensational they are mistaken. I am a conservative." The whirl of social affairs and speaking engagements dazzled her as well as tired her, and she referred to this period as "Alice in Wonderland."[22]

Robertson received professional courtesies as well. The Senate allowed her access to its chamber, and at one point the Speaker of the House of Representatives turned the gavel over to her as a gesture of honor. She received appointments on the Indian Affairs Committee, Department of Interior Expenditures Committee, and, ironically, the Woman Suffrage Committee. Robertson wrote of her early experiences, "The men are simply beautiful to me and everyone seems sure that I'm going to 'make good' because I do not push myself."[23]

Not surprisingly, she voted with the conservative wing of the Republican party. She opposed social legislation and favored high protective tariffs and restriction of immigration. She sent her views on immigration to her Oklahoma constituents in a letter stating, "Atheism, bigotry, fanaticism, defiance of American ideals—all are evils attendant upon the poison stream of immigration." Consistently, she opposed any pardon for Socialist war resister Eugene V. Debs.[24]

Although she petitioned for the construction of a veteran's hospital in Muskogee, Robertson destroyed the endorsement of much of her political base by voting against the Adjusted Compensation, or soldier's "Bonus Bill." The American Legion pressured Congress for legislation providing pensions for war veterans. The measure passed, but it failed to survive President Harding's veto. Robertson not only voted against the bill, she urged the other Oklahoma legislators to oppose it as well. She gave a most unfortunate address to the New York Republican Women's Club in which she was quoted as saying that the country could not afford this legislation and that the veterans were trying to "put a dollar sign on their patriotism." Letters of protest flooded her office, but Robertson refused to reconsider her position. At a meeting with the Veterans of Foreign Wars in Muskogee, she tried to defend herself on her past record, but she made the situation worse when the only reason she offered for her opposition to the bill was that President Harding did not believe the treasury could support the bonus. "I believe him, I will stand by him," she said. A number of American Legion posts condemned her action, as did the Oklahoma state executive committee of the Women's Legion Auxiliary.[25]

Robertson also offended her female constituents on several occasions. She identified the new League of Women Voters with her old suffrage enemies and opposed almost any measure the League supported. At a speech at Elmira College she voiced her distaste for the league "or any other organization of women which tries to influence legislation, as dangerous and liable to give rise to class distinctions." She particularly angered this group when she refused to urge the appointment of a woman as a delegate to an international disarmament conference in 1921. Robertson asserted that no woman had the credentials to qualify for such an important responsibility. Mrs. Richard Edwards, vice president of the league, blasted Robertson as a "political accident." She regretted the press attention that Robertson received because of her "contempt of women and their ability, her total ignorance of women and women's affairs." Edwards continued, "The women in my part of the country know that she never responded to the demands of women nor concerned herself with the things women's organizations were developing throughout the country."[26]

Indeed, Robertson insisted that women's political efforts be linked to the interests of the home. "The most wonderful place in the world is a home," she said, and "the sanest women active in political work are wives and mothers accustomed to think for the future of their children." A new mentor joined Mary Thaw in influencing Robertson. Emily Lowell (Mrs. William) Putnam, sister of poet Amy Lowell and Harvard president Charles Lowell, represented the Women's Municipal League of Boston. Exceedingly wealthy, Putnam dispensed money to Robertson for the remainder of her life, but like many philanthropists of the time, she adamantly opposed what she considered paternalistic legislation by the federal government.[27]

Putnam encouraged Robertson in her opposition to the Sheppard-Towner, or "Maternity" Bill. This legislation provided for federal- and state-funded centers to offer free instruction and information on maternal and child health care. Almost all of the major women's organizations lobbied for its passage, and a majority of the Republican legislators backed it, but not Alice Robertson. "Women in politics must not be afraid of unpopularity," she told a journalist. "They must do what they think is right, not what they think will please people. There is only one important question: 'Is it right—or is it wrong'?" Despite pleas from the Oklahoma League of Women Voters, Robertson spoke against the bill on the floor of the House. She believed it to be a threat to the American family, a possible source of birth control information, and another attempt at a "Bolshevistic" extension of federal power and bureaucracy. To a reporter, she criticized as "absurd" the "sob stuff" claim of Florence Kelley, general secretary of the Consumers League, that hundreds of babies died every day. The centers, she argued, would not provide the kind of tangible help the general public believed, but instead would be centers of propaganda. The measure passed by a large majority, and because of her stand, Robertson alienated a substantial number of her female voters. A prominent Muskogee woman told the Pan-American Women's Congress in 1922, "Please do not judge Oklahoma by Miss Robertson . . . she is entirely out of tune with Oklahoma ideas and progressiveness."[28]

Robertson campaigned for reelection in 1922, but the voters remembered that she had promised to work for Indians, soldiers, and women and children. She had accomplished nothing for the first group and had voted against the interests of soldiers and of women and children. The Second District and the city of Muskogee returned Democrat W. W. Hastings to office by a large margin. Robertson was extremely bitter about this failure to secure a second term. Nearing seventy, she urgently needed to find a source of income since the Sawokla Cafeteria had not survived her absence. She felt especially insulted by Muskogee's betrayal, and she threatened not to return. She told reporters, "I've got to do something. . . . I haven't a cent of income after I leave Congress. . . . I have learned that politics is a good thing for a woman to keep out of." Through the intercession of Mary Thaw with Secretary Mellon and President Harding, civil service requirements were waived, and Robertson gained a position as a patient adviser at the Muskogee veterans' hospital. She quarreled with the superintendent, however, and the next year her appointment provided no salary. Compounding her distress, her beloved Sawokla home burned to the ground in 1923.[29]

For the remainder of her life Robertson borrowed money from family and friends and sometimes sold family heirlooms to pay her bills. Mary Thaw and Emily Putnam continued to send checks from time to time. The Oklahoma Historical Society endowed her for one year with a small salary in compensation for archival help, and a group of wealthy Oklahomans solicited donations for a fund to support her after the beginning of the Depression. Oil millionaire Lew Wentz sent her $100 a month, but a satisfactory level of contributions never materialized. Alice Robertson died of cancer in July 1931. Emily Putnam paid all of her hospital and funeral expenses. Her friend and supporter columnist Edith Johnson praised Robertson's life of unselfish service and moral courage. Johnson predicted that "Future generations will bestow upon her memory tributes and honors that should have been given her while she lived." Of her own paradoxical life, Robertson once modestly said, "If my hard working life has seemed one of accomplishments, as I know it has been of earnest, sincere effort, it is no credit to me, but simply something I could not help because of the blood in me."[30]

Robertson's life was one of sacrifice, hard work, and dedication to benevolent causes. She achieved success as an educator, fund raiser, reformer, and businesswoman. She enjoyed the friendship of women of like mind in the state and across the nation, and her accomplishments supported both herself and her family dependents for most of her life. Robertson's political endeavors, however, posed for her the same type of conflicts facing many other women in the early twentieth century. So bounded was she by the heritage, traditions, and gender understandings of her nineteenth-century ancestors that the demands of political office and the cultural changes surrounding her left her stranded between two worlds. Alice Robertson was unable to relinquish the known and unwilling to embrace the new.

9

Grand Work in Newspaper Fields

Twentieth-century Oklahomans faced bewildering changes as the pioneering period came to a close and the state became integrated into the economy and social life of the nation. After statehood women's interest columns in Oklahoma newspapers grew in popularity and reflected the cultural tumult surrounding women. The columns expressed an anxiety about male and female relationships, the nature of power within the home, the conduct of family life, and a negotiation of status for women in the public world. Middle-class female columnists offered a variety of responses to this anxiety. Not surprisingly, they drew upon their partici- pation in the recent pioneer history of the state to form a context for respectability and security. Wrapping about themselves the mantle of the pioneer woman, they attempted to create an "Oklahoma lady." The prescriptive recommendations revealed a legacy that contained a commitment to traditional domesticity, a productive feminine ideal, and an incipient feminism. "Among the many women who are now doing grand work in newspaper fields in Oklahoma," Elva Ferguson wrote, "there are two who have accomplished great things and are nationally known columnists." These two were Ferguson's own daughter-in-law, Lucia Loomis Ferguson, and Edith Cherry Johnson. The popular columns of these three journalists guided the women of the state through the first three decades of the century.[1]

The *Watonga Republican* was from the beginning a joint enterprise. Thompson Ferguson usually wrote editorials, but Elva worked as reporter, typesetter, paper folder and mailer, subscription and advertisement clerk, and local feature writer. As Thompson became increasingly involved in Oklahoma politics, Elva assumed more responsibility in the management of the paper. The Fergusons returned to Watonga and full-time newspaper work in 1906, when their tenure as governor and first lady ended.

In 1914 Ferguson created and edited a society page for the *Republican* that contained news of local citizens and events, church and school announcements, club meetings, entertainment, and commentary. Her page was titled "Local News Items, Personals, Social Observations and Remarks, by Mrs. T. B. Ferguson," and it included her telephone number. After the death of her husband in 1921, she assumed complete control and management of the newspaper, but she continued to personally edit her special feature. The page reflected not only the intimacy of a small community weekly but also Ferguson's personality, her position as an Oklahoma matriarch, and her expertise in political affairs.

Commenting on fashions, Ferguson quipped that one of the "most amusing street sights" was watching a short woman in a tight skirt trying to keep up with a tall man. She announced that drugstore cosmetic sales had fallen off because no one could afford to apply "any sort of expensive stuff" to the outside when food for the inside cost so much. In another issue, she teased a neighboring newspaper editor for commenting that exercise at the washtub was beneficial for more beautiful female arms: Ferguson reminded him that plowing was a "wonderful chest developer" for men.[2]

Ferguson promoted other female journalists working in Oklahoma, whether they agreed with her political positions or not. Edith Cherry Johnson, feature writer for the *Daily Oklahoman*, had for years opposed women's suffrage and female involvement in the world of politics, yet Ferguson praised Johnson's book of collected columns, *Illusions and Disillusions*, recommending it as an ideal Christmas gift in 1920. Ferguson described Johnson as a "self-made woman" who, because of courage, ambition, and ability, had worked her way up to a position as writer of one of the most widely read columns of the *Oklahoman*. Ferguson wrote that Johnson was especially interested in exposing the shortcomings of "a certain class of women who expect to get through life on the platform of demanding attention and the best things in life because of their sex, and giving no value in return." She was sure that Johnson's direct manner had improved the lives of many of her women readers. Edith Johnson returned the favor years later by writing the introduction to Ferguson's memoirs, *They Carried The Torch*. Johnson declared that Ferguson had "achieved immortality" in Oklahoma and that the word that best described her was "stalwart." She was stalwart in meeting the challenges facing a pioneer mother, as her husband's "mate and partner," and "in her eagerness at all times to stand shoulder to shoulder with him for what they believed to be right." Both columnists shared an understanding of their role as women and, especially, influential women, even though they disagreed about suffrage.[3]

In the early 1920s, Ferguson filled her women's page with coverage of the latest political news. Using an editorial "we," she denounced the national and state Democratic Party and faithfully promoted the Republican cause. Her columns particularly addressed the newly won position of women as voters, and she admonished women to exercise their rights. In a column entitled "How It Seems To Be A Citizen," Ferguson good-naturedly described casting her first vote:

> We have been told so often in the past that should they be allowed to vote our women would change, that no longer would we be refined, gentle creatures, so adored by the men; that we would become masculine in appearance and a lot of other things too numerous to mention. Our first impulse after casting our first vote in a political convention was to feel surreptitiously of our chin to make sure that no whiskers had sprouted.

She noted that her sister voters, also, had not changed into "coarse, loud creatures" and that they had been treated with the deference and respect befitting their rightful place as American citizens. Ferguson scolded the Democratic Party for holding a separate convention, which she called a meaningless, "clearing house talk fest," for its women, and she advised the women that they had been "Jim Crowed."[4]

Suffrage alone was not enough according to Ferguson. In preparation for the 1920 presidential campaign, she wrote that "to be good citizens women must ally themselves with party machinery." Women had learned the value of organization through previous service in club work. When women became active in party politics, they were not only prized as public speakers, but they were more energetic than men and could be counted on to do a good job. Ferguson explained that anything could be accomplished through unity and that "Women are entering upon their political responsibilities, now more fully theirs than ever before, actuated by the same desire to see ideas become laws which has caused voters through past generations to band themselves into political parties."[5]

True to her column's instruction, Ferguson expanded her own political activities after the death of her husband, and with these efforts and her control of the newspaper, she became a leader in Oklahoma sixth district Republican circles. In 1924 she served as chairman of the state delegation to the national Republican convention. In 1926 she was a member of the executive committee representing Oklahoma at the Philadelphia Sesquicentennial exposition, and two years later she became vice-chairman of the state Republican committee, a position she held until 1932.[6]

Ferguson sold the *Watonga Republican* in 1930 in order to travel, campaign for Herbert Hoover, and write her memoirs. Although she had continued to edit her special women's page, her personal commentary became more infrequent in the last years of the 1920s. As she contributed less in this area, she increasingly turned to columns written by her daughter-in-law, Lucia Loomis Ferguson. Lucia's column appeared in the *Republican* under the heading "Woman's Column," by Mrs. Walter Ferguson. Often commentary by both women appeared side by side on Ferguson's page, sometimes discussing the same topic, sometimes differing. Frequently, Ferguson placed "Woman's Column" on page one.

There were, however, subtle topical and generational differences between the two journalists. Elva equated status with pioneer virtues—hard work, endurance, and cooperation within a patriarchal society. She closed her memoirs with the admission that "Women have always had an uphill climb in public pioneering," and she wrote, "I feel sorry for anyone who has never known the fascination of pioneering and starting at the beginning of things." She believed that women had overcome prejudicial public sentiment through sacrifice and perseverance. They had proven themselves in the public arena and yet remained womanly.[7]

Lucia, however, was far more militant in her columns on the position of women's rights, not just in politics but in family affairs as well. She advocated an immediate renegotiation of power both within and without the family on the basis of a recognition of equality. The separate newspaper eulogies, written by Lucia and Elva following the death in 1919 of national women's activist Dr. Anna Howard Shaw, best illustrate the differences between the two women. Elva described Shaw as a "woman with a gift." She had entertained Shaw in her home several years earlier during one of Oklahoma's many suffrage campaigns. Ferguson remembered that during the course of Shaw's public address, she not only converted the men to support votes for women, but gave the wives in the audience pointers on the right way to manage a man. Ferguson wrote, "She did not hammer them over the head to get what she wanted as most suffrage speakers did in those days, but with the most subtle flattery appealed to their vanity." By "paying the utmost deference to men and their convictions," she won them over. Elva praised this example and followed it in her own life. In the same issue of the newspaper, Lucia also paid

Lucia Loomis Ferguson, daughter-in-law of Elva Ferguson and the author of "A Woman's Viewpoint" newspaper column. Photo courtesy of the Archives & Manuscript Division of the Oklahoma Historical Society.

tribute to Dr. Shaw, but her column pictured a different woman. It was Shaw's ability to agitate that Lucia admired most. She wrote that "It takes a really brave woman to drive against the opposition and criticism of men." Shaw was "too far seeing, to rest with favor upon the men of the country," who were intolerant and narrow-minded. She had been a "torchbearer" in establishing equal rights for American women. Both of the

Fergusons agreed with Shaw's position on political equality, but Lucia urged equality in gender relationships and refused to pay homage to patriarchal power.[8]

On the same page that Elva Ferguson cheerfully described casting her first vote, Lucia's column headed "Shameful Tyranny" related an incident in Watonga: When a group of Republican women arrived at a friend's home to accompany her to the primaries to cast her vote, the woman's husband broke into an outburst of rage, denouncing the idea of women voting as "nonsense" and behaving "in a very undignified and altogether disgusting manner." To keep peace at home, the woman did not go. While Ferguson recognized that "the little intricacies of matrimony are often quite complicated," she attacked this man's behavior as well as that of all men who regarded women as "chattel." She declared that no one ever expected a man to give up his desires, mental habits, or customs for his wife, and yet this submission was constantly expected of women. Ferguson wrote that men who treated women in this manner never understood that "a woman, whether she be wife or not, is still an individual with a mind, and ideas all her own" and that she should be allowed to use them as she wished.[9]

In another column Ferguson argued that women had a long history of working for causes to improve conditions for men and women alike. Proclaiming that "Women Are The National Conscience," she outlined a list of reforms that women had fought for and won against overwhelming odds. Ferguson claimed as victories for women: the abolition of slavery, child labor reforms, the temperance movement, free public education, and, finally, their own emancipation by gaining the vote. Women's emancipation had become a reality because, "We have been able to convince the men of the injustice meted out to us, their own women, who have stood by them through the tragedies of pioneer days to the horrors of a world war." When the new generation of women "reared to see their work as national as well as domestic" assumed their duties in public affairs, they would vote for measures to bring about good to the greatest number of citizens.[10]

Lucia Caroline Loomis was born and raised in the tiny village of Boggy Depot, Indian Territory, which was part of the Choctaw Nation's lands. Daughter of a rural doctor, her world consisted of buggy rides around the countryside with her father, the novels of Charles Dickens that her mother ordered from eastern publishers, and temporary "subscription schools," in which neighbors recruited a teacher on a pay-per-pupil basis. To provide for her education, the Loomises sent their daughter to a convent high school in Denison, Texas, and then to Hardin College in Missouri. After two years at Hardin, she transferred to the University of Oklahoma, where she was graduated in 1907 with a degree in Fine Arts. At Oklahoma University she met Walter Scott Ferguson, and they were married in 1908. Lucia's father helped the young couple buy the *Cherokee Republican*, a newspaper in Alfalfa County. Like her mother-in-law, Ferguson adapted her married life to revolve around the routine of the weekly publication of a small community newspaper. Although she had no newspaper experience initially, she began with the duties of subscription and advertisement bookkeeping and eventually moved into writing local items, interviews, obituaries, editorials, and special features.[11]

The younger Fergusons created quite a controversy in Oklahoma when they debated women's suffrage in their newspaper. Walter wrote editorials opposing the measure, and Lucia came out strongly in favor of it in her own column devoted to women's interests. This was rather startling, because the usual procedure at the time was for all newspaper staff to follow the editorial policy. Ferguson remembered, "I was strong for women's rights, something you just don't discuss in Alfalfa county. . . . People just laughed when you mentioned giving a woman the vote, and I didn't like it one bit." She later confessed that "Walter was just as much for women's rights as I was" and that together they sat at the kitchen table at night composing the arguments for both sides of the issue. Their heated public discussion tripled the circulation of the newspaper, but friends privately worried that their marriage was breaking up. Some readers expressed concern at the idea that Lucia would publicly contradict her husband. The volatile issue of women's suffrage called into question the traditional woman's role. The Fergusons had settled this conflict within their own marriage, but their debate both fueled the public imagination and benefited their newspaper. Ferguson wrote that throughout the whole episode, she and her husband "had more fun than can be guessed, from all sides for feminine rights." Surely, part of the fun came from increased exposure for the paper and its editors.[12]

Ferguson believed her newspaper career had ended in 1919 when they sold the *Cherokee Republican* and moved to Oklahoma City, where Walter pursued a career in banking. It was then, however, that her opportunities as a columnist increased. She wrote "Woman's Column" for her mother-in-law, and in 1922 George B. Parker, editor of *Oklahoma News*, asked her to develop a woman's column to compete with that of Edith Johnson. He told her to keep it short, start with a lead-in to capture attention, and end with a good punch line; aside from that, the column was hers. Lucia Loomis Ferguson's "A Woman's Viewpoint" became so popular that it was syndicated by the Scripps-Howard Newspaper Alliance and appeared in thirty-five newspapers across the United States. Edward J. Meeman, editor of the Memphis, Tennessee, *Press Scimitar*, praised her column as "original without being odd," "clean without being prudish," and "feminist without being anti-masculine."[13]

Ferguson wrote her regular column at home and sold individual columns to independent newspapers as they were requested, all the while raising three children. She stated that at first she tried to write only about "purely domestic topics," but confessed that she really was not very domestic. She talked to women and wrote about what they were interested in, and she soon realized that her column had unlimited possibilities.[14]

A theme that appeared repeatedly in Ferguson's columns throughout the 1920s was the controversy over what she called the "restlessness" of the modern woman. Referring to Edith Johnson, Ferguson noted that some authorities on the female sex bemoaned the current state of women and claimed that American homes were decaying, women were worthless, and society was headed to "perdition" because women did not "work as hard nor stay indoors as closely as their grandmothers." Ferguson agreed that their grand-mothers had been tied to the fireside by back-breaking labor, but she insisted that technology had now freed both men and women from many time-consuming, arduous tasks. She felt that this was a sign society was advancing, and she noted that these authorities never recommended a return to primitive and restrictive methods of labor for men. Restlessness was not con-fined to one sex, she wrote: "We do not condemn the man whose restless nature makes him wish to rove out into the world, why should we be less lenient with his sister?" Ferguson lamented that women had been "penned up" too long and "locked" in their husbands' kitchens. If they were restless now, perhaps "hovering spirits of thousands of suppressed grandmothers" were urging them on and they had a right to freedom.[15]

Ferguson returned to this theme when she gave advice about the upbringing of young girls. Denouncing past generations of women trained only to be house-wives, Ferguson stated that they became excellent mothers "from a material standpoint" but that within their hearts there were "buried longings unspeakable, and dreams born but to die." The result of this "unappeased craving" was the current state of restless-ness. Ferguson advocated preparing girls to earn their own living, because too many would have to do it anyway. More than this, she thought that allowing girls to "get a taste of the struggles" of the world would create a nation of happier mothers and happier homes. She wrote, "Girls must be given some freedom so that they may the more fittingly appreciate their home when they shall have attained it." This early freedom would delay marriage for a few years, and Ferguson believed it would reduce later marital problems.[16]

Ferguson resented the fashion of early marriages. Commenting on a seventeen-year-old bride who had given her baby away, she wrote that the girl's action had been charged to radical ideas, "flapperism," bobbed hair, and heartlessness. Ferguson argued that the "crime" was ignorance and a culture that promoted marriage from the time women were in the cradle. She added that some "respectable, but misguided" mothers began to "preen" their daughters for marriage at age six, and the results were miserable youngsters who married too young to care for themselves, let alone their children. Ferguson believed that "the right marriage is and should be the ultimate aim of a girl— but not any sort of marriage."[17]

In another column, Ferguson responded to a young girl's expression of Thanksgiving gratitude that she was unmarried and free to have a good time. Drawing a clear distinction between what brings happiness to a girl and to a woman, she commended the girl for knowing that marriage brought responsibility. She explained that too many young girls got married and expected to keep their premarital "frivolities." She added that after marriage many went "blissfully about for years and years denying children to their husbands" so that they could continue a "giddy round of gaiety." Ferguson warned that this did not bring real happiness.[18]

For women to deny children to some men, however, seemed completely acceptable to Ferguson. She outlined in her column a sordid story of poverty and isolation in rural Oklahoma: The mother of eight small children tried unsuccessfully to keep her husband from assaulting their fifteen-year-old daughter. Ferguson wondered why the woman had not murdered him years ago. She considered all of those little children dependent on the father for food, and she sympathized with the "depths of humility" and "dark abyss" of spirit under which this woman lived. Ferguson described the man as fiendish and depraved, and she pronounced it a pity that one such as he had been the means of bringing eight children into a world where their souls and spirits would be "slowly crushed to death by evil." Ferguson finished her column warning, "Let those who do not believe in birth control think of these things." She also encouraged women to show their opposition to wife-beating. "Men used to like to assert their authority by beating up their wives," she accused, "because it gave them such a swaggering feeling," and this behavior was supposed to remind a woman of her place. She labeled the idea that women liked rough treatment as "insiduous [sic] propaganda" manufactured and promoted by men. Ferguson decided that it would be a fine thing for men to have some of this "excellent discipline" and that they had reason to worry about the restlessness of women, because it showed a new spirit of independence and self-respect.[19]

Contradicting Edith Johnson's advice that a wife should expend extra energy to keep her husband from falling for "designing females," Ferguson suggested that maybe they should first ask if he was worth keeping. A woman who maintained a man's home and bore his children had the right to expect her husband to act with forethought and not to allow himself to be compromised. He was responsible for his actions. Ferguson believed that men had too much love and attention lavished on them. She thought wrong society's "annoying attitude" that women should submerge their lives and ambitions within those of men for love. Love was a big part of life, but not the only thing, Ferguson contended, and when women quit making it so, they would be better off.[20]

Ferguson continued this argument in a later column on divorce. She termed divorce a "menace to the life of a nation." She felt it was especially bad when children were involved, but she believed that it was sometimes necessary. She quoted statistics that showed that 75 percent of recent divorce complaints were filed by women. Ferguson compared the modern woman's attitude to that of past generations: Women had been "skilled in the art of self-sacrifice" and martyrdom. They had been called good, "but quite as often instead of being good they were merely stupid." Because they regarded themselves as the "inferior person in the family circle," they had fostered selfish husbands and sons. The modern woman would no longer countenance this position. She expected men to honor their obligations to wife, home, and children; and she expected her individuality to be accepted. Ferguson even wrote up a column of hints for husbands to follow to make their wives appreciate them more. The list included suggestions on rudimentary cleanliness and courtesy, but it also included the recognition of equality. She instructed each husband to give his wife money of her own, to talk to her, to ask her advice, and not to patronize her. She added, "Don't think that you are better than she is for you're not."[21]

Elva Ferguson's columns and editorials reflected her acknowledged position as Oklahoma's archetypal pioneer woman. They promoted an image of the productive female ideal—the helpmate, responsible in all things, yet still abdicating fame and political authority to men. The reality of her life, however, represented the changing latitude of freedom of action and power for white women. Her personal circumstances and bravery increasingly led her into avenues of prestige and influence and into violation of the traditional roles of women.

The cautious feminism contained in Lucia Ferguson's work indicates the example of her famous mother-in-law as well as her own acceptance of empowerment for women. Lucia represented the twentieth-century woman's courage to break new ground for female equality. Her column provided a counterpoint to the views of Edith Johnson in the *Daily Oklahoman*.

Edith Johnson struggled with the same contradictory forces that shaped the public lives of Kate Barnard and Alice Robertson: How could a woman be an individual of intellectual and economic independence, a complete citizen, without sacrificing the special nurturing qualities that society demanded for the orderly conduct of the home and the nation? Unlike the other two social feminists, Barnard and Robertson, Johnson never pursued a political career of her own, but she used her position as a journalist for the *Daily Oklahoman* to fulfill her commitment to social and

Edith Cherry Johnson, columnist for *The Daily Oklahoman* and the voice of authority to Oklahoma women for fifty years. Photo courtesy of the Archives & Manuscript Division of the Oklahoma Historical Society.

moral improvement. Her daily column suggested a wealth of progressive programs for "municipal housekeeping." She engaged in war mobilization work with a vengeance. She provided commentary on the social changes rapidly transforming the post-frontier state of Oklahoma into part of the mainstream of twentieth-century America. Most often she advised men and women on the affairs of the heart and the construction

of satisfying marital relationships, but she also
provided counsel to the young, single, working woman.
Johnson tried to reconcile her own life and the public
activities of other Oklahoma women that she recorded
in her column with the lingering security of the
traditional Victorian role. She opposed women's suffrage, and she grappled with her own definition of
feminism. She could find no answer to the dilemma,
and by the 1920s she retreated to what historian Jill
Conway described as a "romantic and suffocating"
ethic of domesticity. For the remainder of her lengthy
career, Johnson instructed women to find fulfillment
within the confines of their homes and families.[22]

Edith Cherry Johnson, born in 1879, was the oldest
daughter of an Ohio businessman who had a history of
economic reversals. She exhibited a talent for writing
at Miss Phelp's School for Young Ladies in Columbus,
Ohio, where she edited the school newspaper, and after
graduation she entered Ohio State University with the
intention of becoming a writer. At the end of Johnson's
freshman year, her mother died after giving birth to
triplet daughters, and she left school to take care of the
family. She later wrote, "Not only had I lost my mother
at a time when a girl has a very great need of a mother,
but I was to fall heir to her cares and responsibilities."
She assumed direction of the household and care of her
young sisters.[23]

In 1903 Johnson's father moved the family to
Oklahoma City, in search of better opportunities, but
within five years he had lost a great deal of money and
was terminally ill. Johnson heard about the impending
marriage of the society editor of the *Daily Oklahoman*.
She interviewed with business manager E. K. Gaylord
and editor Roy Stafford, and in December 1908, she
was hired. She described herself as "the greenest
timber that ever stalked into a newspaper office."

Johnson often worked from 8:30 A.M. until midnight, covering social events; serving as music, drama, and literary critic; and occasionally writing special features and interviews with prominent visitors to Oklahoma City. As she waited for the last streetcar of the night to take her home, she braved the catcalls and stumbling bodies of drunken passersby. She remembered that when she went to work for the *Oklahoman*, she was "a timid, shrinking, unsophisticated girl with very little knowledge of the world and the people in it, but with a fiery thirst to find out what was going on." She proved her mettle in 1912, when she convinced the manager of the Skirvin Hotel in Oklahoma City to lock her into the presidential suite so that she might get an exclusive interview with Theodore Roosevelt. The diminutive reporter sat unmoving in the dining room until Roosevelt relented and gave her a story.[24]

In 1915 the *Oklahoman* created a special women's page, under Johnson's direction, for the Sunday edition. The page was eventually discontinued, but Johnson developed her own signed column entitled "The Problems of Every Woman." Editor Stafford placed Johnson's picture and work on the editorial page, and it remained in this familiar location until her retirement in 1958. Johnson became the sole woman to attend the newspaper's daily editorial meetings. She wrote in 1918, "The writers of this country will have a considerable share in molding the ideals of the future. Involving as that does a tremendous responsibility, it will be a very wonderful thing to do."[25]

The public reaction to her column was extremely favorable. One city mother wrote to the editor that Johnson's advice was "a great comfort and help"; two male readers called her "the most potent single moral force and social builder in our community"; and a Missouri fan bragged, "I venture to say that many women never saw the editorial page of the *Daily Oklahoman* [italics added] until Edith Johnson's articles appeared upon it, and then it was the most talked of and eagerly read of the whole paper." By 1930, a Tulsa banker described her as "the most widely read writer of the Southwest."[26]

Johnson opened 1916 with an optimistic message to her readers: "Is it not a very great thing to be a woman in this wonderful era of ours," she rejoiced, "when everyone of us dares to formulate a creed of our own, and to live up to the light of our individual intelligences." She encouraged women to use their talents and wisdom to reconcile the discordant elements of society and to make the world a better place in which to live. Johnson truly believed women to be the superior moral beings, and she claimed for women the power to change the world. "Women, the world over, are the spiritual mentors of their race," she declared. "Every nation rises morally and spiritually according to the character of its mothers and wives. . . . Men are just what their mothers and wives make them." Johnson saw in the women's club movement the engine of democracy. Praising the movement as the finest example of the American spirit, she publicized the 1916 national biennial meeting as a convention where pettiness would be put aside in favor of policies that would work the greatest good for the greatest number. She cheered the business agenda of the meeting, which would focus on issues related to the life of the home. She wrote that "No class of women in this country is more firmly grounded in the belief that the home is the citadel of national life, that woman's first duty is to safeguard the home, to protect its moral integrity and to keep alive its best ideals." Certainly the membership of the Oklahoma clubs appreciated Johnson as well. Federation president Annette Ross Hume thanked

Johnson for her "wise and discreet counsel" in advancing the work of the movement and broadening its scope.[27]

This unbounded enthusiasm for the club movement caused Johnson some discomfort, however, when it came to women's suffrage. The Oklahoma Federation of Women's Clubs endorsed the measure in 1914. Johnson opposed women's suffrage on the grounds that it represented yet another burden for women to carry, it might cause friction in the home, and it appeared to call for a repudiation of women's finer sensibilities. Still, she seemed almost ready to join the advocates as she reported on the insertion of women's suffrage in the 1916 Republican Party platform. She stopped short of endorsing the measure, but she assured her readers that when this major social change occurred, women would use their votes to good ends. Johnson maintained that "all organized bodies of women are first directed toward the benefit of children, second, toward improvement in home and civic life, and finally toward the consideration of their own rights. So it will be with nation-wide suffrage."[28]

By early 1917, she retreated on the issue again, never to come as close to support as she had the year before. In a column entitled "Women's Privileges and Men's Rights" she carefully outlined the dangers she foresaw in women's suffrage as an example of equality of rights. She insisted that women had a wider latitude of opportunity than ever before but that instead of being grateful, they grew more resentful of every limitation. The more conservative group of women, among whom she counted herself, supported any measure that they felt would improve the condition of women, but feared any movement that tended "to foster strife, encourage restlessness and inspire endless contentions between men and women." She thought women were mistaken if they believed that "by a process or will they can circumvent nature." Johnson emphasized her firm conviction that "woman's sphere lies essentially in the moral world, and that her freedom and happiness depend very largely upon her acceptance of this fact." For Johnson, then, and the women she influenced, women's suffrage represented a poor bargain in which they sacrificed their cherished privileges and standards of womanliness for the acquisition of voting rights.[29]

Johnson completely separated women's suffrage from the concept of feminism, and she quoted journalist H. L. Mencken's contention that the "suffrage movement is the intellectual slums of feminism." She moved further to advance a definition of feminism that she could support: Johnson decided that humanism was a synonym for feminism. To her, feminism incorporated all the best elements of the interest in social services that was sweeping the world. Johnson ventured that feminism represented "the eternal feminine raised to the highest degree; . . . woman fully conscious and made aware of herself." Underpinning this "eternal feminine" was, of course, a genuine understanding of love—love of men and of children. Without this love the feminist knew that there could be no personal progress or self-development. "The true feminist's ways are not ways of strife, sex-antagonism or political combat," she advised. "They are the ways of love and peace." She believed that the true feminist, fortified with these idealistic sentiments and the "mother principle," could reach out her arms to embrace the whole world.[30]

This understanding of feminism motivated Johnson's suggestions for personal economic improvement, civic development, and wartime mobilization. Throughout the decade of the 1910s and into the 1920s Johnson urged women to be frugal and to build up savings. Since she believed that women set the family standard of living, made all of the family purchases, and determined the expenditures for social amusements, she thought that they should make it an inflexible habit to save. This personal saving represented a "patriotic service," as a "bulwark of safety for the nation." It would also inspire interest in better politics and the wise disbursement of public revenues. In keeping with this attitude, Johnson rallied support for the newly formed Oklahoma City Housewives' League. This group was organized to force down the high price of staple foods. The League believed that food speculators hoarded products in storage facilities to drive up the prices. Through boycotts, petitions, and political investigations, the membership intended to bring about reform. The president of the league told Johnson, "It is a case of the female of the species fighting for her young."

Johnson supported militancy on other occasions as well, particularly when the influenza epidemic spread through Oklahoma in 1918. Comparing the current commissioner of public health to a "slatternly housekeeper," she blamed the illness sweeping the city to his mismanagement and political trickery, and Johnson cheered the group of irate citizens demanding his removal. She argued that the office should be appointive rather than elective and that scientific municipal housekeeping should be instituted by a competent, trained official with a responsible staff and an adequate budget. Johnson also advocated the establishment of a permanent community food kitchen, municipal baths, and a municipal laundry. She publicized the squalor uncovered during the epidemic and compared the conditions in Oklahoma City to larger cities like New York, Chicago, Singapore, and Hong Kong. Johnson believed the filth to be an expression of character as well as poverty; therefore, she suggested stringent laws to force people to make use of the facilities that she wanted established.[31]

America's entry into World War I and its subsequent demand for patriotic unity dominated Edith Johnson's columns from 1917 until 1919. As early as June 1916, she prepared for the role of women, should war come. First, she suggested the formation of an Oklahoma Red Cross society under the direction of one central committee. She argued that to avoid confusion, friction, and inefficiency, "personal opinions and ambitions must be entirely subordinated to centralized direction and responsibility." The organization would mobilize supplies and prepare bandages, clothing, and hospital necessities. Johnson believed that when the hour arrived, Oklahoma women would provide the vanguard of citizens willing "to give, to serve, and if need be—to sacrifice." Montana congresswoman Jeannette Rankin's failure to cast her vote for war shocked and appalled Johnson. She had previously written a column praising Rankin as a self-made woman whose courageous spirit refused to accept defeat. Now, Johnson regretted, as the eyes of the nation watched to see how a woman would behave in times of crisis, Rankin "has been weighed in the balance, and we fear, has been found wanting." According to Johnson, Rankin had been unable to divorce herself from the personal practice of "feminine thinking" and to accept the universal motivation that necessitated war. Her actions justified the conviction of her male contemporaries that "women are not made of stern enough fiber to stand the strain of political strife."[32]

No one accused Johnson of lacking stern fiber. She engaged in every facet of civilian wartime support and cajoled, challenged, and ordered other women to do

Edith Johnson devoted her column to mobilizing the patriotic efforts of women during World War I. This Fourth of July celebration float was typical of the response. Photo courtesy of the Western History Collections, University of Oklahoma Library.

likewise. Naturally, food conservation topped Johnson's list of patriotic duties. She insisted that all women return to making home-baked bread and that they use "war flour," a practice that would use less wheat than would be used in commercially baked bread. Furthermore, she thought rich and poor alike should don aprons as a symbol that thrifty household management and hard work constituted their pledge to the war effort. Johnson also encouraged women to take over jobs in the field, office, and factory in order to free men for military service. She questioned the opinions of those whom she called "extreme feminists," who asserted that once women experienced the independence, excitement, and money of outside employment, they would not return to the home. She insisted that a woman was by nature and by preference a homemaker, and that the upsurge in female employment only reflected the necessities of war. Johnson predicted that "as long as there are homes, there will be women to do housework, women who will be able to see as much beauty and value in darning and dishwashing as in operating elevators or driving trucks."[33]

Johnson advised young women considering marriage to avoid a man who was a slacker or war protester; any man not willing to accept his duty to his country would surely not adequately abide by his domestic obligations. "The arm that was too flaccid to shoulder a gun, will be too flaccid to protect a woman or a child," she warned. She urged that married women who sent their husbands and sons off to war must vow not to complain about their circumstances or their loneliness; each must keep in mind that she was her man's "spiritual keeper" and that her duty was to assure him of her love and loyalty and "to present to him in every letter the fair and bright side of their mutual concerns."[34]

As the months of war stretched out, Johnson grew ever more virulent in her criticism of those who she believed did not devote their lives, energies, and money to the war effort. Besides food and fuel conservation and Red Cross work, Johnson campaigned frequently for the sale of war savings stamps and Liberty bonds. In 1918, during a bond drive, she abandoned all restraint when she described for her readers German atrocities, stories no doubt circulated to her by the national Committee of Public Information. Speaking of the many "facts" every American citizen ought to know, she asserted that the "horrible mutilation of women, the bestial abuse of young girls, the murder of little babies forms a delightful recreation for the crazed, besotted Hun mind." No excuse for failure to contribute generously to the war effort withstood Johnson's withering judgment. Some foolish men and women thought that they could get away with their "hideous selfishness", she warned, "But, they won't be absolved." In a curious twist of logic, she warned American women not to intervene in peace negotiations. A group of German women had asked Mrs. Woodrow Wilson and Jane Addams to intercede with the diplomats to modify the terms of the armistice, but Johnson stated that for them to do so would be grossly insulting to their Allied sisters, who had suffered so much. "The passions of the German people run riot because the women of Germany know nothing of restraint," she criticized. "Germany has made a science of cruelty because the women have countenanced that." Johnson saw no justification for helping the mothers of such evil people. Many years later she regretted such journalistic excesses. When she wrote her autobiography in 1940, she remarked that her beliefs had changed substantially. She had no "sense of pride" in her efforts "to stimulate what I then believed to be the patriotic sentiment. . . . The experience of the 18 months our country spent in war and the dreadful aftermath have altered my ideals of patriotism."[35]

This "dreadful aftermath" constituted the 1920s. Johnson dedicated her efforts to restoring the peaceful tranquility of the American home, believing it would act as a panacea for all of the problems confronting the nation. Johnson fully believed that men were intellectually and physically superior to women and that while women might exert a powerful moral force, they needed to be schooled in their responsibilities. The role Johnson prescribed for women in the 1920s would have suited just as appropriately the pages of *Godey's Lady's Book* a century earlier: Real fulfillment for women came through dedication to the wholesome service of her family. For Johnson the ideal was a married woman, with children, supported comfortably by her businessman husband. Her columns always used that status as a yardstick of attainment, and any woman who did not aspire to that role was not "normal." This attitude closely corresponded to the cultural climate in Oklahoma and no doubt contributed to Johnson's fifty-year tenure with the *Oklahoman* and to her numerous statewide honors. However, this position must have required extensive intellectual and emotional gymnastics for Johnson personally; she remained unmarried, childless, and dedicated to her career throughout her life. In her memoirs, she wrote that her fate was "to live vicariously in and through thousands of other people's marriages" and to mother no children of her own, but to "strive to comfort and console and guide countless others."[36]

As prominent as she became, Johnson never used her column as a vehicle to personal political office or power. She had opposed women's suffrage so strongly that she continued in the 1920s to berate the political activities of women. Writing about a meeting of the League of Women Voters in 1921, Johnson maintained: "The rule of woman suffrage is, I believe, a minority rule. Where one woman demanded the passage of the nineteenth amendment, ten more did not want it or were frankly indifferent. . . . I am not at all sure now, that the men who gave suffrage to women . . . have not played a joke on all women." She complained that those women who had demanded the ballot ought to be willing to accept military service if there should be another war, but that, unfortunately, this burden would fall on all women and would produce a national hysteria. She declared that the sex that cringed at the sight of mice and worms was not the sex that craved experience on the battlefield.[37]

Johnson included jury duty as another obligation that might eventually fall to women now that they had the right to vote. She opposed this prospect, insisting that women would most likely think with their hearts rather than with their heads and that they would not deal with cases objectively. She also believed that the nature of many court cases would be so embarrassing that jury duty would be "a shock to woman's innate refinement and modesty" and that a woman would be unable to discuss openly the details of the cases in the jury room. The major reason she opposed jury service for women, however, was the possible neglect of their families. "Just imagine what would happen in a family of three or four children, no cook, no nurse, if mother were summoned to sit on a jury in a murder trial," Johnson posed.[38]

Johnson saved her greatest contempt for women who campaigned for political office, and she insinuated that neglect of family was their chief sin. With a bitter reference to Mrs. Robert M. LaFollette of Wisconsin, Johnson compared the modern wife with her predecessor of twenty-five years before: Prospective husbands had looked for a woman with a long list of domestic accomplishments. She had to be able to cook and sew, and "every 'lady' cultivated certain artistic accomplishments." In contrast, the modern wife rarely cooked or "put a smooth darn in her lord's hose." Instead she shook hands, campaigned, and sat at the telephone to solicit votes, Johnson observed. "She studies parliamentary law instead of the cook-book," and she presides over committee meetings instead of "fashioning a frilly bonnet for the baby" or "keeping the angel child's soft hair" in perfect ringlets. Johnson rhetorically speculated that the modern wife might contribute just as much to her husband's happiness as a wife in past generations, but clearly the language of her comparison was unfavorable. Johnson also wrote several columns in the mid-1920s opposing the elections of two widows, Nellie Ross and Miriam "Ma" Ferguson, to the governorships of Wyoming and Texas. While Johnson might admit that Ross "exemplified the highest standard of noble womanhood," she was especially vitriolic toward Ferguson. Declaring that Ferguson's victory was not a credit either to the masculine or feminine electorate, Johnson arrogantly advised that when Texas developed intellectually, it would make better choices in leadership.[39]

Johnson had her own theory about women who sought political prominence. In 1927, Governor Henry S. Johnston selected her to represent Oklahoma at the Annual Luncheon for Famous Women at the Woman's World's Fair in Chicago. When she returned to Oklahoma, she wrote a lengthy column on her observations about women and fame. Johnson only stopped short of describing famous women as aberrations of nature. First of all, she was disappointed to see that the greatest share of admiration and attention was given to women who were successful in political life rather than to women who excelled in the arts, education, or philanthropy. Next, she observed that "ninety percent of them were big women physically," that they possessed a "certain sturdy maleness," and that "they have the masculine quality of self-assertiveness well developed." Finally, Johnson counseled that this kind of woman represented a novelty; she was the exception, not the rule. She believed that the majority of American women preferred love to fame and money. She rejoiced that "Because of this majority with their qualities of gentleness, sweetness, patience, modesty, and unselfishness, society is made safe and kept safe."[40]

Johnson might have personally disapproved of women voting, serving in the military, running for office, or assuming jury duty, but when her sense of propriety was offended, she had no reservations about using her column to rally the support of Oklahoma women who advanced those very ideas. In October 1924, Johnson wrote five separate columns calling for the organization of women voters to defeat senatorial candidate John C. Walton (who had recently been impeached and removed from the office of governor). Johnson criticized Walton's negative record and charged that he promoted conflict; hatred; and racial, class, and religious prejudice. After Walton's humiliating defeat, Johnson praised the women of the Democratic Party who with "superb courage" had broken with party politics and delivered the right man to office. She had employed the same rhetoric to unleash female political power that she had used to spurn it. "Women, as a sex, demand honesty and decency," she wrote. "They are determined to preserve the ideals of the home which are the strength of the nation. Women uphold Christianity, their churches,

Organizations of women like this 1916 gathering of the members of the Knowles, Oklahoma, WCTU gave Edith Johnson a widespread popularity. Photo courtesy of the Western History Collection, University of Oklahoma Library.

and their religious leaders." Johnson believed that it was this womanly instinct that compelled women to seek the "higher and finer things" in the world and that these would be obtained for society by woman's determination to secure them; therein lay the power of women in politics.[41]

Most of Johnson's columns, however, were not about politics. She was much more comfortable dispensing advice on male and female relationships and the proper conduct of marriage. In this area, too, Johnson spoke for her personal vision of acceptable behavior. Early in 1921 Johnson wrote a column critical of the current fashions. She reported that numerous masculine readers had protested against short skirts and low-neck dresses, crying out, "like Adam of old," that they were "the unwilling victims of the wave of immorality that has been precipitated upon men by women's style of dress." Johnson mistakenly forecast a change in fashion within twenty-four hours, since women dressed to please men. She concluded, "Man is woman's king, and she lives for him." Similarly, Johnson advised against women smoking cigarettes: Smoking was not immoral, but it was not a graceful and feminine thing to do. Since the basis of feminine fascination lay in her difference, why should women imitate men? Women were also more affected by nicotine than men since they did not have as much stamina, and a mother who smoked set a bad example for her children. It would be a rare mother who would not "sacrifice the use of tobacco for the sake of her sons."[42]

By far the greatest danger to marriage and home, according to Johnson, were women who sought stimulation outside the home. Echoing the sentiments of a New York City judge, Johnson mourned the passing of family unity because of a new variety of women's interests. When Johnson, on business after nightfall, encountered young girls "displaying a great expanse of gossamer-clad legs" and make-up "plastered" faces, she asked herself, "Where are those girls' mothers?" Johnson urged a back-to-the-home movement in which mothers spent less time on their outside interests and more on creating a pleasant home atmosphere, where they provided good food, cleanliness, and cheerfulness. Johnson had outlined the basic duty of the married woman sometime before. She suggested that every woman should have "graven on her heart," or at least on her wedding band, this motto: "She profits most who serves best." Before marriage each woman should face the situation honestly and repeat to herself: "I have undertaken to serve this man and to make him a home. It is up to me to create order and comfort, harmony, happiness and security, and if I cannot do that, I will not have earned a faithful husband and all the good things of this life." Johnson was adamant about marital commitments. She delivered her judgment about divorce, writing that while some divorces were necessary, society should treat the guilty party as a social leper, and he or she should be legally deprived of the right to marry again.[43]

In 1923 Johnson published a book entitled *To Women of The Business World* that, on the surface, appeared to contradict her long-standing commitment to the domestic role of women. The preface described the book as a series of intimate, straight-from-the-heart talks to women, offering concrete, practical information; advice; and suggestions for success in the business world. She said that she wrote the book for the nine million women in business and industry who had taken as their motto: "What man can do, woman can do likewise." Johnson included topics such as the proper choice of vocation, application for a position, appropriate dress, the importance of a pleasant voice, and adherence to a strict code of manners. Much of this same information about working women appeared in her columns throughout the 1920s. The book almost immediately exposed Johnson's traditional posture. Johnson's advice clearly applied only to white-collar employment in acceptably feminine occupations such as teaching, nursing, clerical work, and sales. "Perhaps, four per cent of women in the United States have very superior intellects," she observed, and only these might pursue professions that placed them in competition with men. She suggested that the majority of women worked best under supervision where they "are not required to display a great amount of initiative," and she concluded that this book was not intended for women with lesser abilities.[44]

In addition, the book reflected Johnson's own sense of class pretension. She fondly used expressions such as "the refined classes," "the better sort of people," and "the better classes." The young woman whom she addressed had the time and resources to choose carefully not only a job that suited her personality but also a considerate and "progressive" employer. Johnson warned that though the young woman might be completely supported by her family and have her whole salary at her disposal, she should be careful not to overdress: Wearing all of her diamonds in the morning or coming to work in a mink coat would make her the target of criticism and jealousy. She must dress tastefully and appropriately for her surroundings, because "a faultily or carelessly attired woman is a liability to her employer." By observing Johnson's rules for dress and behavior, working women would not be socially hampered by a limited pay envelope. She suggested that "If she is a member of a good family; if she succeeds in her work; if she is clever and charming and attractive," there should be no barrier in her social

progress from the office to the drawing-room. Indeed,
Johnson felt that working women who won distinguished positions in society deserved the admiration and support of all women because they were
"pioneers."[45]

Finally, the book spoke mostly to young, single
women. It contained one section devoted to the single
worker with dependents, and Johnson labeled her a
"Superwoman," because she was forced to earn a living
and raise the children. Johnson believed that such a
woman must find her own methods to earn money, but
she outlined a number of income-producing activities
that could be managed from the home. Johnson,
however, could not accept the idea that a married
woman with children might desire a career. In a 1927
column entitled "Enemies of the Home," Johnson
mentioned a wife and mother of two who had asked her
for advice on entering the business world. The woman
told her that she was tired of her housekeeping and
mothering tasks and wanted to try her luck at
insurance or real estate. Johnson was appalled. She
reported that whenever she received this kind of
request, she knew that the woman was keeping a
"pretty poor sort of home. . . . I have visions of dusty
furniture, a sticky, messy kitchen, disorderly closets
. . . and unmade beds in the afternoon." Johnson
warned women not to allow trivial interests to blind
them to their already-taxing triple role of wife, mother,
and homemaker.[46]

Johnson's was not the only journalistic voice
advising women in Oklahoma. Other columnists, such
as Lucia Ferguson, offered alternative points of view.
Johnson's column was the longest lasting and most
widely read, however, and it earned for her the most
honors. In 1930 a panel of Oklahoma businessmen
chose Johnson as a member of the honor roll of the

state's twenty-four outstanding women. She received an honorary doctorate from Oklahoma City University and was inducted into the Oklahoma Hall of Fame in 1935. The Business and Professional Women's Clubs awarded her Woman of the Year in 1948, and she was one of only seven female journalists honored by the Women's National Press Club in Washington, D.C., in 1950. When she retired from the *Daily Oklahoman* in 1958, four hundred friends and associates paid tribute to Miss Edith at a celebration at the Skirvin Hotel. She died at home in 1961.[47]

Elva and Lucia Ferguson and Edith Johnson occupied pivotal positions in Oklahoma society. They successfully entered the male-dominated profession of journalism. They represented the interests of women, and they won acclaim through their work. The columns of each woman served as lenses through which the negotiations of gender interests were viewed. Men and women in Oklahoma depended on the Fergusons and Johnson to provide them with guideposts for the rapid economic and social changes that they saw taking place in the state. Edith Johnson remained the most conservative of the three columnists, because of her insistence on a limited role for women: one devoted to the needs of home, family, and community. Elva Ferguson allowed for a widening circle of participation for women that was based on a productive feminine ideal. Within the work of Lucia Ferguson lay the cornerstone of feminism: the recognition of equality. These three journalists offered the forum of debate for issues concerning Oklahoma women, and they illustrated the spectrum of alternative points of view.

Epilogue

By 1920 Oklahoma resembled most other states in the West. It continued to have a rural, agriculture orientation in spite of expansion of the oil industry and population concentrations in Tulsa and Oklahoma City. The pioneering days had ended, and two cultural artifacts emerged to provide a mythology for the memories and experiences of the women in the state.

In 1927, Oklahoma oil millionaire Ernest W. Marland sent six proposed models of a pioneer woman statue, his bequest to the state, on a tour, for public examination and appraisal, of the major cities of the United States. Not surprisingly, five of the six statues included a child, but interestingly, half of the models depicted the woman carrying an axe or a gun. None of the representations suggested contributions by black or Native American women, and their histories were relegated to obscurity. The most popular model,

The Pioneer Woman Monument in Ponca City and its sculptor, Bryant Baker. Photo courtesy of the Western History Collections, University of Oklahoma Library.

sculpted by Bryant Baker, presented a neatly clad young woman holding her belongings, the Bible, and the hand of her son. The two figures stood with bodies erect, and an aura of courage and determination marked their faces as they strode toward the future. This statue, eventually completed and erected in Ponca City, represented both the pioneering spirit of the past and the future to many Oklahomans.

The writer Edna Ferber produced the second work of art. First as a novel published in 1930 and later as a motion picture, *Cimarron* told the story of Oklahoma development through the eyes of the dynamic woman Sabra Cravat.

Perhaps Elva Shartel Ferguson would not have approved of the history of Oklahoma women presented in this book any more than she did their depiction in *Cimarron.* Looking back over more than one hundred years and including black and Indian women in the context of interpersonal relationships, the story of women in Oklahoma suggests new dimensions that Ferguson might have found difficult to admit. Oklahoma constituted a unique frontier that tested the world views of women in many ways. Theories of domestic ideology, forms of racial interaction, acceptable modes of male and female conduct, negotiation of class status, and accommodation of cultural differences all underwent examination and transformation in an area of the country that struggled into existence as a state while one century gave way to another. Black, white, and Indian women, to greater and lesser degrees, redefined their lives in the context of a new multicultural environment. They crossed boundaries of race and class on a private level to share common interests as women, and they mediated the limits of a middle-class mentality.

Oklahoma women of all races exhibited a wide range of female consciousness in gender awareness,

Poster for the movie, *Cimarron*. Photo courtesy of the Western History Collections, University of Oklahoma Library.

motives for action, and modes of behavior. For some women the needs of the community became the over-riding imperative, and female self-assertion worked toward collective needs and goals. Other women defined themselves and judged others within the limits of a closed set of activities derived from attributes associated with woman's biological and social role expectations. A few women made inroads into the realm of patriarchal power, challenging male authority and proposing female equality. These circles of initiative joined and separated at different moments in disparate women, creating multiple social interactions and shifting levels of empowerment. The points of their concurrency provided the basis for partnerships.

White pioneer women brought to Oklahoma a variety of regional backgrounds and experiences. Some came, under destitute circumstances, with histories of failure in other states. Others arrived with the assurance of economic security and education and with attitudes about social refinement. All faced the challenge of making a home in a new land and insur-ing their families' comfort and survival. While tech-nology made this process easier than it had been for earlier frontierswomen, they still had to make adjust-ments to the land, the water, the wind, and the isolation. They clung to the rhetoric of a past ideal of separate spheres that provided a common language, sense of security, and social acceptability, but they quickly abandoned its practical restrictions. In inter-action with other white women, they made cultural compromises that smoothed relationships still marred by memories of the Civil War. With Indian women, they found levels of common understanding in shared domestic activities. When white pioneer women met black pioneer women on the Oklahoma frontier, they often worked side by side to insure the survival of all, but underneath every action lay an unspoken limitation: Regardless of gender, education, and economic means, black women were considered inferior. As statehood became a reality, that "inferiority" was institutionalized in law and practice.

Black women living in the sheltered environment of all-black communities assumed the challenge of racial improvement. They carried the scars and shame of slavery, but they fervently believed that land in Oklahoma offered them the opportunity to prove the dignity of both their gender and their race. They worked within their towns to establish a new model of black womanhood based on respectable conduct, education, and accomplishment. Seeking middle-class status, black women seized the chance to operate businesses on their own or in conjunction with their husbands' enterprises. They worked in white-collar employment positions and enjoyed the reinforcement their communities gave to their efforts. Farm women sacrificed to build schools and to keep their children attending. They pinned their hopes and dreams of an institution of high academic standards and black cultural pride on Langston University. They organized a variety of clubs to share their commitment and to unify their relationships to each other. Black women protected each other from white male harassment and demanded respect and appreciation from men of their own race. Few of the black towns survived the onslaught of racial prejudice following statehood, but from their experiences in these communities, black women developed survival strategies for life in racially mixed Oklahoma cities.

Oklahoma provided the home for sixty-seven different Indian groups. The histories of selected Cherokee and Kiowa women can be used to illustrate the diversity of life for Indian women in Oklahoma. The

Cherokees became the ultimate example of acculturation and acceptability to the mainstream culture.
They enjoyed the advantages of education at the
Cherokee National Female Seminary, modeled after
the Massachusetts institution Mount Holyoke Seminary. Principal Florence Wilson and her faculty
influenced generations of the Cherokee female elite.
The education that young Cherokee women received at
the school molded their aspirations toward the
accomplishments of the traditional Victorian lady.
They learned Latin, piano, national politics, and
homemaking skills. Graduates of the school, in turn,
spread this educational outlook throughout the tribe,
and many became leaders in early statehood civic,
cultural, and benevolent affairs.

Kiowa women, in contrast, experienced the almost-
complete destruction of life and culture as they knew
it. The alternative life that was presented to them in
government schools reeked of corruption, incompetence, and poor management. Their reservation
overrun by duplicitous whites, they suffered hunger,
disease, and social disarray. Baptist missionary Isabel
Crawford touched the lives of Kiowas as few others
could. She gained their respect and friendship through
her ministrations to women, her commitment to their
survival, and her skill at negotiating a modicum of
Kiowa control over their lives within the framework of
government-imposed acculturation. Both the Cherokee
and the Kiowa women insisted, however, on retaining
recognition of their tribal particularity and culture.

As the twentieth century began in Oklahoma,
some women stepped forward to advance female
activism in public affairs. Three Oklahoma women
achieved national prominence for their activities. The
life paths of Kate Barnard, Alice Robertson, and Edith
Johnson illustrate the ways in which women both

extended and circumscribed their own autonomy. Each built a career from traditional female virtues and rejected what she believed to be the selfish aspects of feminism. All three women assumed a persona of extended motherhood, but found themselves isolated and vulnerable as their efforts pushed against the boundaries of patriarchal power.

Kate Barnard sought the spotlight of politics as a means to further herself and her benevolent beliefs. Armed with beauty, charm, and intelligence, she mistakenly placed her trust in the powerful political leaders of the Democratic Party and eschewed the more receptive Oklahoma Socialist Party. However, the Democratic Party leadership capitalized on her abilities to serve their own ends. Barnard refused to support women's suffrage, and she chose instead to champion the protection of Indian orphans and the commitment of resources to social legislation—issues that challenged the interests of the very men for whom she had previously campaigned. Isolated and powerless, she could not save her career from destruction by her former mentors.

From birth, Alice Robertson accepted a sense of religious obligation to educate Indian children. Later she adopted the welfare of young soldiers as a special cause. Duty and penury prompted her to ever-widening circles of activism, and late in life she used her educational background and impressive credentials to pursue a political career. Republican politicians exploited her gender in 1920, and a variety of interest groups buffeted her from many directions. She failed to grasp the realities of political life and the incipient power of a new female electorate. Robertson's innate conservatism and her political inexperience blinded her to the financial and social bribery that attended her one term in office. National politicians and wealthy

philanthropists influenced her to withhold her support
from highly popular programs for women and veterans—
a stance that destroyed her credibility.

Edith Johnson entered the field of journalism as a
naive and insecure young woman. *Daily Oklahoman*
publisher, E. K. Gaylord, and editor, Roy Stafford,
fostered and promoted her career, placing her column
on the same page as their own editorials. She became
the newspaper's official adviser to married women,
advocate for female concerns, and guiding mother to
young working women. As her own career developed,
she extended what she believed to be the boundaries of
female activism and employed her newspaper column
to advance progressive programs and wartime mobilization. Like Barnard and Robertson, Johnson stum-
bled over the issue of female equality and tried
desperately to fit modern realities into an old-
fashioned separate-sphere domestic ideology. Over
time, she exchanged independence for security. By the
1920s, she had retreated to a position of shrill
conservatism. Her outlook had been checked by the
editorial policy of her employer, the honors afforded her
position, and her own fears of gender confrontation.

The histories of these three women suggest an
environment that allowed upward mobility for less-
advantaged women. In separate ways their lives, by
example, expanded and contracted the possibilities for
an adjustment of women's roles. Kate Barnard, Alice
Robertson, and Edith Johnson all came from humble
economic circumstances and received little formal
education. Each remained unmarried and pursued
ambitious, public careers. In contradiction to their own
lives, however, they found it necessary to proscribe
similar paths for other women. In order to exercise
power, appear acceptable to their constituents, and
reconcile themselves to their own exceptionalism, they

defined womanhood in terms of marriage, home, and children. Although they based their own individual careers on an extension of the nurturing associated with that maternal role, they believed that they had sacrificed the concrete benefits of womanhood. Their public accomplishments granted Barnard, Robertson, and Johnson a life more celebrated than that of the traditional woman but denied each the fruits of the traditional woman's role—a loss that made each of them feel less than a woman. The substance of the lives of these three women confronted fundamental gender inequality during that progressive age and challenged an imbalance that refused to allow much freedom of movement for women between the public and private worlds.

These selected experiences of Oklahoma women indicate that women's understanding of themselves extended well beyond a limited rhetoric about separate sexual beings endowed with unique qualities. Oklahoma women understood their importance as individuals and as members of the family unit, and foremost in their minds was the desire to secure a better economic condition, if not affluence. Based on their abilities and efforts, they demanded respect, recognition, and basic equality from men. Women of all races crossed racial, economic, linguistic, and cultural barriers to interact with each other in private domestic concerns, but white women also adopted a progressive ethic. They attempted to homogenize the culture of Oklahoma into a cluster of middle-class values based on a shared understanding of attitudes about education, moral behavior, and social cohesion. They believed that these values promoted the welfare of all women. Indian women who conformed to these standards found easy integration into mainstream Oklahoma society. Those who did not suffered castigation.

Black-town women shaped their communities around similar ideals, but in this case the circumstance of race proved to be a stronger arbiter of acceptability than gender, background, or economic status.

The ambiguities and contradictions attendant to the relationships of women in Oklahoma as the state emerged from the settlement period are no less apparent in the history of the United States. Historian Angie Debo was correct in her observation that the facets of the American character are clearly revealed in the history of Oklahoma development. The founders of Oklahoma struggled to accommodate the differences among its population—differences that were evident from the beginning. That struggle engaged the efforts of both men and women. Their failures and triumphs could be seen in the death and destruction of the Tulsa race riot in 1921 and in the heroism of survival in the midst of dust and poverty during the Great Depression. Black, Indian, and white women and men formed partnerships on the land—partnerships that trespassed boundaries of gender, race, class, and culture to create a new state, another part of the mosaic of the American West.

Notes

Preface
1. Angie Debo, *Oklahoma, Footloose and Fancy-Free* (Norman: University of Oklahoma Press, 1949), vii; and Angie Debo, *Prairie City: The Story of an American Community* (Tulsa, Okla.: Council Oak Books, 1985), 23; Lucy Gage, "A Romance of Pioneering," *Chronicles of Oklahoma* 29 (Autumn 1951): 286.

Chapter 1. The Greatest Romance
1. Mrs. T. B. Ferguson, "The Truth About *Cimarron*," manuscript, n.d., p. 4, Mr. and Mrs. Walter Scott Ferguson Collection, Western History Collection, University of Oklahoma, Norman, Okla.
2. Anne Hodges Morgan maintained that Ferber's fictional portrayal of Sabra is more realistic than most historical accounts of pioneer women. See Anne Hodges Morgan and H. Wayne Morgan, eds., *Oklahoma: New Views of The Forty-Sixth State* (Norman: University of Oklahoma

Press, 1982), 178. Vicki Piekarski, however, believed that *Cimarron* was misunderstood as sentimental and escapist and that Ferber intended the story to be a "malevolent picture of what is known as American womanhood and American sentimentality." See Vicki Piekarski, *Westward the Women: An Anthology of Western Stories by Women* (Albuquerque: University of New Mexico Press, 1984), 8.

3. Edna Ferber, *Cimarron* (Garden City, N.Y.: Doubleday, Doran and Company, 1930), x; "Women as Journalists," *Sooner State Press* 23 (1 November 1930): 1–2; Mrs. Tom B. Ferguson, *They Carried the Torch* (Watonga, Okla.: Button Publishing Company, 1937; Reprint, Norman, Okla.: Levite of Apache, 1989), 47.

4. Frederick Jackson Turner, "The Significance of the Frontier in American History," in *The Turner Thesis: Concerning the Role of the Frontier in American History*, ed. George Rogers Taylor (Lexington, Mass.: D. C. Heath and Company, 1972), 3–4.

5. The "New West" historical construct is found in Patricia Limerick, *The Legacy of Conquest: The Unbroken Past of the American West* (New York: W. W. Norton & Company, 1987); Patricia Limerick, Clyde Milner, and Charles Rankin, eds., *Trails: Toward a New Western History* (Lawrence, Kans.: University Press of Kansas, 1991); and Richard White, *"It's Your Misfortune and None of My Own:" A New History of the American West* (Norman: University of Oklahoma Press, 1991). Turner's impact is discussed in Patricia Limerick's, "Turnerians All: The Dream of a Helpful History in an Intelligible World," *American Historical Review* 100 (June 1995): 697–716. While these writers have deplored the absence of women's presence in the historical writing of the West, none has specifically incorporated women in his or her work. David M. Potter, "American Women and American Character," in *History and American Society: Essays of David M. Potter*, ed. Don E. Fehrenbacher (New York: Oxford University Press, 1973): 303.

6. Edward Everett Dale, *Frontier Ways: Sketches of Life in the Old West* (Austin, Tex.: University of Texas Press, 1959): 79–88.

7. Sandra L. Myres, *Westering Women and the Frontier Experience, 1800–1915* (Albuquerque: University of New Mexico Press, 1987): 1–11. In a discussion of the nature of domestic ideology in the nineteenth-century American West, Robert L. Griswold has argued that the tenets of purity, piety, submissiveness, and domesticity were more a set of supple and elastic gender ideas that supplied a sense of stability than a rigid orthodoxy. See Robert L. Griswold, "Anglo Women and Domestic Ideology in the American West in the Nineteenth and Early Twentieth Centuries," in *Western Women: Their Land, Their Lives,* eds. Lillian Schlissel, Vicki L. Ruiz, and Janice Monk (Albuquerque: University of New Mexico Press), 15–33. See also Jacqueline S. Reinier, "Concepts of Domesticity on the Southern Plains Agricultural Frontier, 1870–1920," in *At Home on the Range: Essays on the History of Western Social and Domestic Life,* ed. John R. Wunder (Westport, Conn.: Greenwood Press, 1985), 57–70. John Mack Faragher has suggested the utility of exploring the multiplicity of female roles in his article, "History From the Inside-Out: Writing the History of Women in Rural America," *American Quarterly* 33 (Winter 1981): 537–57.

8. Julie Roy Jeffrey, *Frontier Women: The Trans-Mississippi West, 1840–1880* (New York: Hill and Wang, 1979), xiii.

9. LeRoy H. Fischer, "Oklahoma Territory, 1890–1907," *Chronicles of Oklahoma* 53 (Spring 1975): 3–8; Arrell M. Gibson, *Oklahoma: A History of Five Centuries* (Norman: University of Oklahoma Press, 1981), 173–90. Jerome O. Steffen has argued that Oklahoma history is not unique in that it evolved as a manifestation of national trends in "Stages of Development in Oklahoma History," in Morgan and Morgan, *Oklahoma: New Views,* 3–30.

Chapter 2. Going to God's Country

1. Ferguson, *They Carried the Torch,* 82.

2. Martha L. Smith, *Going To God's Country* (Boston: Christopher Publishing House, 1941), 41; John Womack, *Cleveland County, Oklahoma, Historical Highlights* (Noble,

Okla.: John Womack, 1983), 236–37; Dorcine Spignor-Littles, director, "Collective Visions: A Historical Overview of Black Women in Oklahoma from the Early 1800's–1920," Oklahoma Arts and Humanities Foundation, 1990, videotape.

3. Lonnie E. Underhill and Daniel F. Littlefield, Jr., "Women Homeseekers in Oklahoma Territory, 1889–1901," *Pacific Historian* 17, no. 3 (1973): 36–40; Kent Ruth, "Was 'Classy Lassie' Kentucky Daisey Oklahoma's First Liberated Woman?" *Daily Oklahoman*, 1 January and 22 January 1984.

4. Seignoria Russell Laune, *Sand in My Eyes* (Norman: University of Oklahoma Press, 1956), 160–64; Lawton Business and Professional Woman's Club, *'Neath August Sun, 1901: Dedicated to Those Who Came This Way in 1901* (Anadarko, Okla.: N. T. Plummer Printing Co., n.d.), 13–16. This book is a collection of first-hand reminiscences.

5. Lawton BPW Club, *'Neath August Sun*, 72–73.

6. Underhill and Littlefield, "Women Homeseekers," 42.; Henry Kilian Goetz, "Kate's Quarter Section: A Woman in the Cherokee Strip," *Chronicles of Oklahoma* 61 (Fall 1983): 246–67.

7. Goetz, "Kate's Quarter Section," 248.

8. Addie Bell Robertson Roedell in *Oklahoma: The First Hundred Years*, eds. William W. Zellner and Ruth L. Laird (Ada, Okla.: Galaxy Publications, 1989), 21. This book is a collection of pioneer family reminiscences. Billy M. Jones explores the failure of medical science to deal effectively with a number of nineteenth-century diseases and the subsequent search by large numbers of Americans for a curative climate in the Southwest. See *Health-Seekers in the Southwest, 1817–1900* (Norman: University of Oklahoma Press, 1967).

9. Isabella Walton Newby, letter, 7 October 1897, Bertha Newby Hutchins Collection, Kansas State Historical Society, Topeka, Kans.; Bertha Newby Hutchins, letter, 21 November 1897, Bertha Newby Hutchins Collection.

10. Max L. Lale, ed., "Letters from a Bride in Indian Territory, 1889," *Red River Valley Historical Review* 6

(Winter 1981): 16–18. Many of the documents that I have used in this book contain misspellings and awkward grammatical constructions. I have chosen to omit the use of the intrusive [*sic*] except in extreme cases so that the texture and sound of the prose are true to those of the authors.

11. Gage, "Romance of Pioneering," 286. Gage wrote the statutes establishing the first Oklahoma kindergarten education.

12. Maude Barnes Ross, "Retrospection of a Pioneer Doctor's Wife," typescript, p. 6, S. P. Ross Collection, Western History Collections, University of Oklahoma, Norman, Okla.

13. Ruth Yelton, "A Wagon Trip to Oklahoma: Passages from a Girl's Diary," *Chronicles of Oklahoma* 64 (Summer 1986): 99–100, 105–106.

14. Anna Gillespie, "Coxville, Nebraska to Fay, Oklahoma by Wagon (1899): The Journal of Anna Gillespie," *Nebraska History* 65, no. 3 (1984): 347; H. D. Ragland, ed., "The Diary of Mrs. Anna S. Wood: Trip to the Opening of the Cherokee Outlet in 1893," *Chronicles of Oklahoma* 50 (Autumn 1972): 309.

15. Gillespie, "Journal," 345–46, 348.

16. Ibid., 347; Ragland, ed., "Wood Diary," 320.

17. Yelton, "Wagon Trip," 103; Mary Bobbit Brown, Edna Hatfield Collection, Western History Collections, University of Oklahoma, Norman, Okla. This is an extensive collection of first-hand recollections of life in the Cherokee Outlet.

18. Smith, *Going To God's Country*, 54–55.

19. Catherine Ward Allen with Harry E. Chrisman, *Chariot of the Sun* (Denver, Colo.: Sage Books, 1964), 45.

20. "Nora Watson Cox's Story of Coming to Lawton 1901," in Lawton BPW Club, *'Neath August Sun*, 125–26; Smith, *Going To God's Country*, 47–48.

21. Smith, *Going to God's Country*, 49–50; The 89ers Association, *Oklahoma: The Beautiful Land* (Oklahoma City, Okla.: Times-Journal Publishing Company, 1943), 239. This book contains reminiscences from the original homesteaders of 1889. Glenda Riley outlines the European and

American influences shaping frontierswomen's fears of
Indians in *Women and Indians on the Frontier, 1825–1915*
(Albuquerque: University of New Mexico Press, 1984), 1–82.

    22. Candee, "Social Conditions," 432. For an alternative
and more positive contemporary description of women's lives
in Oklahoma see Marion Foster Washburne, "Women of the
Great West," *Harper's Bazaar* 40 (January and March 1906):
41–47, 210–16; Gloria Bish Hetherington, ed., *Diary of Mary
Henderson: Homesteading in Oklahoma Territory, November
12, 1901–December 31, 1906* (Sentinel, Okla.: Schoonmaker
Publishers, 1982), 23.

    23. Ross, "Pioneer Doctor's Wife," 59.

    24. Hetherington, ed., *Diary of Mary Henderson*, 74, 35,
279.

    25. Bertha Newby Hutchins, letter, 1 November 1897,
Bertha Newby Hutchins Collection, Kansas State Historical
Society, Topeka, Kans.

    26. Deborah J. Hoskins, "Brought, Bought, and Bor-
rowed: Material Culture on the Oklahoma Farming Frontier,
1889–1907," in Wunder, *At Home on the Range*, 121–36.

    27. Hetherington, ed., *Diary of Mary Henderson*, 84.

    28. Robert C. Lucas with Lucille Gilstrap, "Home-
steading the Strip," *Chronicles of Oklahoma* 51 (Fall 1973):
298–99. See also Green, *Our Foundation*, 96–97.

    29. Smith, *Going to God's Country*, 123–24.

    30. Ibid., 60–61; Allen, *Chariot of the Sun*, 230–32.

    31. Laune, *Sand in My Eyes*, 140.

    32. Bertha Newby Hutchins, letters, 27 April 1899 and
5 July 1899, Bertha Newby Hutchins Collection. Robert L.
Griswold has maintained that domestic ideology shaped
gender relations by providing the language of discourse for
women to check male prerogatives and demand respect
within marriage. Divorce evidence in California indicates
this debate. See Robert L. Griswold, *Family and Divorce in
California, 1850–1890: Victorian Illusions and Everyday
Realities* (Albany, N.Y.: State University of New York Press,
1982), 108–19, 120–41.

    33. Daniel F. Littlefield, Jr., and Lonnie E. Underhill,
"Divorce Seeker's Paradise, Oklahoma Territory, 1890–1897,"

Arizona and the West 17, no. 1 (1975): 21–34; "Early Day Scramble to Get Divorces Provided Some Gay Family Wars," *Daily Oklahoman*, 19 April 1925. See also Glenda Riley, "Torn Asunder: Divorce in Early Oklahoma Territory," *Chronicles of Oklahoma* 67, no. 4 (1989–90): 392–413.

34. Lola Clark Pearson, "The Drudge," *Oklahoma Farmer-Stockman* (15 July 1927): 10.

35. *Historical Statistics of the United States* (Washington, D.C.: United States Department of Commerce, Bureau of the Census, 1975), 33; Mary Horst Black, in *The Logan County History, Logan County, Oklahoma*, ed. Helen F. Holmes (Guthrie, Okla.: Logan County Extension Homemakers Council, 1978), 66.

36. Bertha Newby Hutchins, letters, 1897–99, Bertha Newby Hutchins Collection.

37. Ross, "Pioneer Doctor's Wife," 210–16.

38. Hetherington, ed., *Diary of Mary Henderson*, 258.

39. Zellner and Laird, eds., *First Hundred Years*, 161.

40. Hetherington, ed., *Diary of Mary Henderson*, 260.

41. Chloe Holt Glessner, *Far Above Rubies* (San Antonio, Tex.: Naylor Company, 1965), 90–91.

42. Smith, *Going to God's Country*, 163.

43. Letty Ward, *First Hundred Years*, 221.

Chapter 3. New Neighbors and Friends

1. Ferguson, *They Carried the Torch*, 22.

2. Mrs. J. M. Owen, "Plenty of Game," in 89ers Association, *Oklahoma: Beautiful Land*, 271. See also Allie B. Wallace, *Frontier Life in Oklahoma* (Washington, D.C.: Public Affairs Press, 1964), 25–30; Blanch Hunnicutt Dryden, in Zellner and Laird, *Oklahoma: First Hundred Years*, 43; Alice Lynn Boydstun, in Zellner and Laird, *Oklahoma: First Hundred Years*, 219.

3. Bernice Teeters Smith, in Zellner and Laird, *Oklahoma: First Hundred Years*, 130–31.

4. Edna Randolph Slaughter, in *Black History in Oklahoma*, ed. Kaye M. Teall (Oklahoma City: Oklahoma City Public Schools, 1971), 163; Donald J. Berthrong, "White Neighbors Come Among the Southern Cheyenne and

Arapaho," *Kansas Quarterly* 3 (Fall 1971): 113–15; Suzan Shown Harjo, "Western Women's History: A Challenge for the Future," in *The Women's West*, eds. Susan Armitage and Elizabeth Jameson (Norman: University of Oklahoma Press, 1987), 306.

  5. Millie M. Butler, Indian-Pioneer Collection, vol. 14, p. 133, Western History Collections, University of Oklahoma, Norman, Okla.

  6. Mrs. A. L. Welsh and Mrs. Netti K. Gates, "Beef Issue," in 89ers Association, *Oklahoma: The Beautiful Land*, 101.

  7. Gage, "Romance," 302–303; Hetherington, ed., *Diary of Mary Henderson*, 35. Lola M. Green remembered Indian dances as "good entertainment for the slack season," in *Firm, Our Foundation* (Montgomery, Ala.: Brown Printing Company, 1986), 95.

  8. U.S. Department of Commerce, Bureau of the Census, *Indian Population In The United States and Alaska, 1910*, 32, table 13; and 36, table 17; Mrs. Susie Grey letter, n.d., reproduced in V. A. Travis, "Life in the Cherokee Nation a Decade After the Civil War," *Chronicles of Oklahoma* 4 (March 1926): 28. Travis reported that numerous letters like this one were housed in the Cherokee Nation Collection at the Carnegie Library in Tahlequah, Oklahoma. See also mention of prominent white women married to Indian men in "Pioneer Women Had Romantic, Heroic, Sometimes Tragic Lives," *Daily Oklahoman*, 23 April 1939.

  9. Mayes, letters, 9 August 1893, 18 August 1893, and 12 January 1894, Jerry Whistler Snow Collection, Western History Collections, University of Oklahoma, Norman, Okla.

  10. Velma Taliaferro, *Memoirs of a Chickasaw Squaw* (Norman: Levite of Apache, 1987), 32–33.

  11. Gage, "Romance," 305–306. Glenda Riley argued that the domestic occupations of women provided the context for closer relationships among Euro-frontierswomen and Indian women than the public contacts between the men of both races in *Women and Indians on the Frontier*, 167–203; Mrs. John E. Hewitt in Lawton BPW Club, *'Neath August Sun*, 128.

12. Mrs. H. Ridgley, in Lawton BPW Club, *'Neath August Sun*, 117–18.

13. Leola Lehman, "Life in the Territories," *Chronicles of Oklahoma* 41 (Winter 1963–64): 373–74. Both smoking and chewing tobacco appeared to be common practices among rural Oklahoma women of all races.

14. Joyce Drew in Zellner and Laird, *Oklahoma: First Hundred Years*, 229–30; Ross, "Pioneer Doctor's Wife," 136.

15. Margaret Fullerton Frost, "Small Girl in a New Town," *Great Plains Journal* 19 (1980): 24; and Mrs. P. G. Fullerton in Lawton BPW Club, *'Neath August Sun*, 85. Frost's exceptional memoirs continue in volumes 20 and 21 of *Great Plains Journal*.

16. Frost, "Small Girl," 41–42, 49.

17. Ibid., 32.

18. Hattie Holladay, Mary Brown, Edward Teachman, Albert C. Davis, Edna Hatfield Collection, Western History Collections, University of Oklahoma, Norman, Oklahoma.

19. Arthur Baird, Hattie Holladay, Edna Hatfield Collection.

20. Green, *Our Foundation*, 138.

21. Margaret Jensen with Leila Williams, *Looking Back* (Denver, Colo.: Big Mountain Press, 1966), 12.

22. Teall, *Black History*, 163; "Negro Taken Away to Prevent Coup by Daltons," *Daily Oklahoman*, 19 April 1925.

23. Oreme Brown Bartel, *No Drums or Thunder* (San Antonio, Tex.: Naylor Company, 1970), 63.

24. Cassia Berry in *And Gladly Teach: Reminiscences of Teachers from Frontier Dugout to Modern Module*, ed. James Smallwood (Norman: University of Oklahoma Press, 1976), 59; Golda Slief in 89ers Association, *Oklahoma: Beautiful Land*, 301; Teall, *Black History*, 185–87.

25. Mrs. E. P. McMahon in Lawton BPW Club, *'Neath August Sun*, 87.

26. Helen C. Candee, "Social Conditions in Our Newest Territory," *Forum* 25 (June 1898): 437. Candee wrote one of the first novels about Oklahoma, *An Oklahoma Romance*, published in 1901; Helen C. Candee, "Oklahoma," *Atlantic Monthly* 86 (September 1900): 332. For a different point of

view about black contributions in Oklahoma see *New York Times* 9 April 1891, 12 April 1893, and 24 October 1898.

27. Wallace, *Frontier Life*, 102.

28. Frost, "Small Girl," 31–32.

29. Ibid., 32.

30. Ibid., 37.

31. Ibid., 38; See also Janice Holt Giles, *The Kinta Years: An Oklahoma Childhood* (Boston: Houghton Mifflin Company, 1973), 242. Many southern families refused to celebrate the Fourth of July and reserved fireworks for Christmas.

32. Giles, *Kinta Years*, 240. Giles published a number of historical novels about life in the rural West. For a further discussion of the impact of southern history see Danney Goble, "The Southern Influence on Oklahoma," in *"An Oklahoma I Had Never Seen Before": Alternative Views of Oklahoma History*, ed. Davis D. Joyce (Norman: University of Oklahoma Press, 1994), 280–301.

33. Giles, *Kinta Years*, 22.

34. Laressa Cox McBurney, *Dr. Charlie's Wife* (San Antonio, Tex.: Naylor Company, 1975), 1–17.

35. Tommy G. Lashley, "Oklahoma's Confederate Veterans Home," *Chronicles of Oklahoma* 55 (Spring 1977): 34–36. Lashley credits the UDC with making Oklahoma a leader among southern states in providing benefits to Confederate veterans.

36. Ora E. Reed, "Daughters of Confederacy," *Sturm's Magazine* 10 (June 1910): 37. See also Daryl Morrison, "Twin Territories: The Indian Magazine and Its Editor, Ora Eddleman Reed," *Chronicles of Oklahoma* 60 (Summer 1982): 136–66. For a discussion of the role of the southern woman after the Civil War see Anne Firor Scott, *The Southern Lady: From Pedestal to Politics, 1830–1930* (Chicago: University of Chicago Press, 1970).

37. Anna Lewis, "The Oklahoma College For Women," *Chronicles of Oklahoma* 27 (Summer 1949): 180–81.

38. Dixie Belcher, "A Democratic School for Democratic Women," *Chronicles of Oklahoma* 61 (Winter 1983–84), 414. For a description of college life for women at Oklahoma A

and M College (now Oklahoma State University) see John Cresswell and William Segall, "College Life in Oklahoma," in *Women in Oklahoma: A Century of Change*, ed. Malvena K. Thurman (Oklahoma City: Oklahoma Historical Society, 1982), 162–81.

Chapter 4. Educating the Cherokee Elite

1. Ferguson, *They Carried the Torch*, 9.

2. Journalists frequently employed the image of Oklahoma Territory as a cowboy and Indian Territory as an Indian princess in articles publicizing the Twin Territories. See Charles M. Harger, "Oklahoma and the Indian Territory As They Are Today," *American Review of Reviews* (February 1902): 178–81; Clinton O. Bunn and William C. Bunn, comp., *Constitution and Enabling Act of the State of Oklahoma, Annotated and Indexed* (Ardmore, Okla.: Bunn Brothers Publishers, 1907), 123.

3. Muriel H. Wright, "The Wedding of Oklahoma and Miss Indian Territory," *Chronicles of Oklahoma* 35 (Autumn 1957): 260, 255. Wright referred to Bennett as the "modern, beautiful Indian princess."

4. According to William W. Savage, Jr., "The cowboy is the predominant figure in American mythology." See William W. Savage, Jr., *Cowboy Life: Reconstructing an American Myth* (Norman: University of Oklahoma Press, 1975), 3. See also William W. Savage, Jr., *The Cowboy Hero: His Image in American History and Culture* (Norman: University of Oklahoma Press, 1979); and Joe B. Frantz and Ernest Choate, Jr., *The American Cowboy: The Myth and the Reality* (Norman: University of Oklahoma Press, 1955). L. G. Moses discusses the protest within the Bureau of Indian Affairs over the perceived exploitation of Indians in Wild West shows and the attendant negative publicity in "Wild West Shows, Reformers, and the Image of the American Indian, 1887–1914," *South Dakota History* 14 (1984): 193–221. James Welch discusses the special attraction of Buffalo Bill's Wild West show's staging of the Custer battle, with the image of American soldiers "slaughtered by savages," in *Killing Custer: The Battle of the Little Bighorn*

and the Fate of the Plains Indians (New York: W. W. Norton and Company, 1995), 281–83. Rayna Green defines the difficulty in subscribing to the princess versus squaw duality applied to Indian women in American culture in "The Pocahontas Perplex: the Image of Indian Women in American Culture," *Massachusetts Review* 16, no. 4 (1975): 698–714. This work addresses the acculturative opportunities in the Cherokee Nation. It does not include those Cherokees who remained alienated from these experiences.

5. Murial H. Wright, *A Guide to the Indian Tribes of Oklahoma* (Norman: University of Oklahoma Press, 1951), 57. For a general history of the Cherokees see Wright, *Guide*, 56–76; Grant Foreman, *The Five Civilized Tribes* (Norman: University of Oklahoma Press, 1934), 281–426; Morris L. Wardell, *A Political History of the Cherokee Nation* (Norman: University of Oklahoma Press, 1938); and David H. Corkran, *The Cherokee Frontier: Conflict and Survival, 1740–62* (Norman: University of Oklahoma Press, 1962). See also Henry Thompson Malone, *Cherokees of the Old South: A People in Transition* (Athens: The University of Georgia Press, 1956), 12–31. Malone described the transformation of the Cherokee culture into a "red-white amalgam" in the early nineteenth century that produced "Southern red men." See Malone, *Cherokees*, xii, 183.

6. Quoted in Mary E. Young, "Women, Civilization, and the Indian Question," in *Clio Was a Woman: Studies in the History of American Women*, eds. Mabel E. Deutrich and Virginia S. Purdy (Washington, D.C.: Howard University Press, 1980), 100.

7. Jeremiah Evarts quoted in Young, "Women," 107; Wright, *Guide*, 62–63. Margaret Connell Szasz explores the failure of externally imposed education on Indian girls in early American history in " 'Poor Richard' Meets the Native American: Schooling for Young Indian Women in Eighteenth Century Connecticut," *Pacific Historical Review* 59 (May 1980): 215–35. Szasz identified three factors contributing to failure as: the persistence of Native culture, the artificial school environment, and racial prejudice. In an extensive study of Presbyterian missionaries, Michael Coleman has

maintained that the missionaries judged Indian life from a near-absolute ethnocentricism that demanded a complete rejection of tribal culture, but that they "did not succumb to the rising racism of their age" in their dealings with individuals. See Michael C. Coleman, *Presbyterian Missionary Attitudes Toward American Indians, 1837–1893* (Jackson: University Press of Mississippi, 1985), 5–6.

8. Wright, *Guide*, 64–65. Factions of the Cherokee Nation had already emigrated first to land in Arkansas, then to northeastern Oklahoma before the final removal treaty was signed. See also Grant Foreman, *Indian Removal: The Emmigration of the Five Civilized Tribes of Indians* (Norman: University of Oklahoma Press, 1934), 229–312.

9. Wright estimated four thousand deaths on the overland trip in *Guide*, 65. Michael F. Doran used reports by army investigator Ethan Allen Hitchcock to support his position in "Population Statistics of Nineteenth Century Indian Territory," *Chronicles of Oklahoma* 53 (Winter 1975–76): 491–515. See U.S. Department of Commerce, Bureau of Census, *Indian Population in the United States and Alaska, 1910*, 33, table 14.

10. Doran, "Population Statistics," 499–500, 507; Wright, *Guide*, 67. For a history of the importance of Dwight Mission see O. B. Campbell, *Mission to the Cherokees* (Oklahoma City: Metro Press, 1973). See also Tom Holm, "Cherokee Colonization in Oklahoma," in *America's Exiles: Indian Colonization in Oklahoma*, ed. Arrell M. Gibson (Oklahoma City: Oklahoma Historical Society, 1976), 60–76. The history of the full-blood Cherokee is still cloaked in mystery, but Jack F. and Anna G. Kilpatrick have attempted to capture some of their history in *The Shadow of Sequoyah: Social Documents of the Cherokees, 1862–1964* (Norman: University of Oklahoma Press, 1965) and *Run Toward the Nightland: Magic of the Oklahoma Cherokees* (Dallas: Southern Methodist University Press, 1967).

11. Wright, *Guide*, 67; Grant Foreman, *Five Civilized Tribes*, 401. Biographical sketches of Delia Vann, Joseph Vann, Oliver Hazard Perry Brewer, *père* and *fils*, appear in C. W. West, *Among the Cherokees: A Biographical History of*

the Cherokees Since the Removals (Muskogee, Okla.: Muscogee Publishing Company, 1981), 80–85, 57–58. For extensive research completed by Emmet Starr in 1921 on Cherokee genealogy and history, see *Starr's History of the Cherokee Indians*, eds. Jack Gregory and Rennard Strickland (Fayetteville, Ark.: Indian Heritage Association, 1967). Delia Vann is listed as an alumnus of the Cherokee Female Seminary, opened in 1851 at Park Hill, and she is mentioned in the historical remarks made by Mrs. R. L. Fite in "An Illustrated Souvenir Catalog of the Cherokee National Female Seminary, Tahlequah, Indian Territory, 1850 to 1906," *Journal of Cherokee Studies* 10 (Spring 1985): 120, 174. She does not appear on Emmet Starr's list of graduates (Gregory and Strickland, *Starr's History*, 232–33), nor does Vann's son mention her graduation specifically in his sketch of her in West, *Among The Cherokees*, 81. Delia's sister, Mary, was an 1856 graduate.

12. Pierce M. Butler quoted in Grant Foreman, *Five Civilized Tribes*, 390; Grant Foreman, *Five Civilized Tribes*, 376–77, 390.

13. Ibid., 388–89; *Cherokee Advocate*, 21 August 1845, cited in Grant Foreman, *Five Civilized Tribes*, 376. See also Richard Sattler, "Women's Status Among the Muskogee and Cherokee," in Laura Klein and Lillian Ackerman, *Women and Power in Native North America* (Norman: University of Oklahoma Press, 1995), 214–29.

14. Information about the earliest period of the Male and Female Seminaries is scanty due to the fires that destroyed both of the original structures and most of their contents. The most complete information about the Female Seminary is contained in Devon A. Mihesuah, *Cultivating the Rosebuds: The Education of Women at the Cherokee Female Seminary, 1851–1909* (Urbana: University of Illinois Press, 1993); two other excellent sources are Carolyn Foreman, *Park Hill* (Muskogee, Okla.: Star Printery Press, 1948); and Althea Bass, *A Cherokee Daughter of Mount Holyoke* (Muscatine, Iowa: Prairie Press, 1937). See also Gregory and Strickland, *Starr's History*, 225–46; Brad Agnew, "A Legacy of Education: The History of the Cherokee

Seminaries," *Chronicles of Oklahoma* 63 (Summer 1985): 128–47; and Hugh T. Cunningham, "A History of the Cherokee Indians," *Chronicles of Oklahoma* 8 (December 1930): 418–20.

15. Whitmore letter quoted in Agnew, "Legacy," 132; Gregory and Strickland, *Starr's History*, 232–33.

16. Hannah Worcester Hitchcock quoted in Grace Steele Woodward, *The Cherokees* (Norman: University of Oklahoma Press, 1963), 244; Narcissa Owen, *Memoirs of Narcissa Owen, 1831–1907* (n.p., 1908), 120–25.

17. Kate Pearson Burwell, "Indian Territory Federation of Women's Clubs," *Sturm's Statehood Magazine* 11 (May 1906): 3.

18. Carolyn Thomas Foreman, *Oklahoma Imprints, 1835–1907, A History of Printing in Oklahoma Before Statehood* (Norman: University of Oklahoma Press, 1936), 244; Gregory and Strickland, *Starr's History*, 233.

19. West, *Among the Cherokees*, 59–60, 81; "Illustrated Souvenir Catalog," 122.

20. A discussion of the cultural interchange between Cane Hill, Arkansas and Tahlequah, Indian Territory, appears in T. L. Ballenger, "The Cultural Relations Between Two Pioneer Communities," *Chronicles of Oklahoma* 34 (Autumn 1956): 286–95; Lieutenant J. M. Lynch letter quoted in Ballenger, "Cultural Relations," 293; "Illustrated Souvenir Catalog," 120.

21. Ballenger, "Cultural Relations," 289–90; Devon Abbott, "Ann Florence Wilson, Matriarch of the Cherokee Female Seminary," *Chronicles of Oklahoma* 67 (Winter 1989–90): 426–37; Carolyn Thomas Foreman, "A Cherokee Pioneer, Ella Flora Coodey Robinson," *Chronicles of Oklahoma* 7 (December 1929): 364–74.

22. Lola Garrett Bowers and Katheleen Garrett, *A. Florence Wilson, Friend and Teacher* (Tahlequah, Okla.: Rockett's Printers and Publishers, 1951), 15, 22, 4. This publication represents a collection of reminiscences about Wilson from members of every seminary class during her tenure.

23. See Abbott, "Ann Florence Wilson," 426–37; R. H. Halliburton, Jr., "Northeastern's Seminary Hall," *Chronicles*

of Oklahoma 51 (Winter 1973–74): 391–98; and Agnew, "Legacy," 128–47.

24. Sarah Worcester quoted in Devon Abbott, "'Commendable Progress': Acculturation at the Cherokee Female Seminary," *American Indian Quarterly* 14 (Summer 1987): 189. For an account of music instruction at the seminary and in the Cherokee Nation see Kathleen Garrett, "Music on the Indian Territory Frontier," *Chronicles of Oklahoma* 33 (Autumn 1955): 339–49; "Illustrated Souvenir Catalog," 153.

25. Abbott, "Ann Florence Wilson," 426–37; Agnew, "Legacy," 128–47; and Halliburton, "Seminary Hall," 391–98. For discussion of diseases and health care at the seminary, see Devon Irene Abbott, "Medicine for the Rosebuds: Health Care at the Cherokee Female Seminary, 1876–1909," *American Indian Culture and Research Journal* 12, no. 1 (1988): 59–71.

26. Bowers and Garrett, *Friend and Teacher*, 17.

27. Halliburton, "Seminary Hall," p. 395.

28. Bowers and Garrett, *Friend and Teacher*, 13.

29. Ibid., 18, 21, 5.

30. "Illustrated Souvenir Catalog," 162; U.S. Department of the Interior, Office of Indian Affairs, *Annual Reports of the Department of the Interior, 1906*, 769. The new building had an ample water supply from a nearby spring, steam heat, and inside bathroom facilities. Superintendent Spencer Stephens purchased linen tablecloths and napkins and silver dishes, knives, and forks for the dining room. When challenged about the cost, he explained that "young ladies of the best families demanded the best"; see Theda Perdue, *Nations Remembered: An Oral History of the Five Civilized Tribes, 1865–1907* (Westport, Conn.: Greenwood Press, 1980), 135.

31. "Illustrated Souvenir Catalog," 158, 154; U.S. Department of Interior, *Annual Report, 1906*, 770–76.

32. Garrett, "Music," 344; Ida Wetzel Tinnin, "Educational and Cultural Influences of the Cherokee Seminaries," *Chronicles of Oklahoma* 37 (Spring 1959): 64–66.

33. Owen, "Memoirs," 116.

34. "Illustrated Souvenir Catalog," 172, 183. Marriages among Male and Female Seminary graduates are listed in Gregory and Strickland, *Starr's History*, 232–43.

35. A biographical profile of Eliza Bushyhead Alberty appears in Carolyn Thomas Foreman, "Aunt Eliza of Tahlequah," *Chronicles of Oklahoma* 9 (March 1931): 43–55; and in West, *Among the Cherokees*, 152–54.

36. Carolyn Foreman, "Aunt Eliza," 5; Nannie Daniel Fite quoted in Carolyn Foreman, "Aunt Eliza," 55.

37. See Murial H. Wright, "Rachel Caroline Eaton," *Chronicles of Oklahoma* 6 (December 1938): 509–10.

38. *Bartlesville Daily Enterprise*, 14 November 1944, quoted in Lillian Delly, "Ellen Howard Miller," *Chronicles of Oklahoma* 26 (Summer 1948): 174–77.

39. See Thomas H. Harrison, "Carlotta Archer," *Chronicles of Oklahoma* 25 (Summer 1947): 159–60.

40. Carolyn Thomas Foreman, "Mrs. Anna C. Trainor Matheson," *Chronicles of Oklahoma* 18 (March 1940): 101–102. See also Wright, "The Wedding," 260.

Chapter 5. Christianity for the Kiowas

1. Ferguson, *They Carried the Torch*, 38–39.

2. Mildred P. Mayhall in *The Kiowas* (Norman: University of Oklahoma Press, 1962), 134–35, describes Kiowa women as menials and drudges. Alice Mariott took a slightly more positive attitude toward the position of women in *Kiowa Years, A Study in Culture Impact* (New York: Macmillan Company, 1968), 15–22; and in her book for children, *Indians On Horseback* (New York: Thomas Y. Crowell Company, 1948), 22–42, 74–83.

3. Mayhall, *Kiowas*, 92–99; N. Scott Momaday, *The Way to Rainy Mountain* (New York: Ballantine Books, 1969), 17–18; Wright, *Guide*, 169–77; U.S. Department of the Interior, *The Kiowa* (Anadarko, Okla.: Southern Plains Indian Museum and Craft Center, n.d.). The most extensive study of Kiowa Indians was made in the 1890s by James Mooney and was published as *Calendar History of the Kiowa Indians*, extract from the Seventeenth Annual Report of the Bureau of American Ethnology (Washington, D.C.: Govern-

ment Printing Office, 1898). See also Bernard Miskin, *Rank and Warfare Among the Plains Indians* (Seattle: University of Washington Press, 1940); E. Buford Morgan, *The Wichita Mountains: Ancient Oasis of the Prairies* (Waco, Tex.: E. Buford Morgan, 1973); and Blue Clark, *Lone Wolf v. Hitchcock: Treaty Rights and Indian Law at the End of the Nineteenth Century* (Lincoln: University of Nebraska Press, 1994).

4. Momaday, *Rainy Mountain*, 79. Both John Treat Irving and Edwin Thompson Denig described Plains tribes women as ugly, filthy, immoral, and thieving. See John Treat Irving, Jr., *Indian Sketches: Taken During An Expedition to the Pawnee Tribes, 1833*, ed. John Frances McDermott (Norman: University of Oklahoma Press, 1961), 152–53. Thomas C. Battey, a Quaker teacher on the reservation, wrote that daughters were welcome additions to a family only in the prospect of "servile assistance in the household" in *The Life And Adventures of A Quaker Among the Indians* (Boston: Lee and Shepard Publishers, 1875; reprint, Norman: University of Oklahoma Press, 1968), 330. Mayhall, *Kiowas*, 122–23; Momaday, *Rainy Mountain*, 78.

5. Mayhall, *Kiowas*, 100–105; Battey, *Life and Adventures*, 319–33.

6. Mayhall, *Kiowas*, 110–13; Marriott, *Kiowa Years*, 15–22.

7. Mayhall, *Kiowas*, 125–26, 135; Alice Marriott, *The Ten Grandmothers* (Norman: University of Oklahoma Press, 1945), ix–x. Margaret Connell Szasz provides an excellent overview of childhood treatment and early education within Native American cultures in "Native American Children," in *American Childhood: A Research Guide and Historical Handbook*, eds. Joseph M. Hawes and N. Ray Hiner (Westport, Conn.: Greenwood Press, 1985), 311–42.

8. A collection of essays that suggests a number of innovative and interdisciplinary methods for reconstructing Plains Indians culture is *The Hidden Half: Studies of Plains Indian Women*, eds. Patricia Albers and Beatrice Medicine (Lanham, Md.: University Press of America, 1983). The first three essays in *The Hidden Half* attempt to refute the

distortion of early observers, historians, and anthropologists, especially Katherine Weist in her essay "Beasts of Burden and Menial Slaves: Nineteenth Century Observations of Northern Plains Indian Women" (pp. 29–52). Valerie Shirer Mathes reinforces this position in "A New Look at the Role of Women in Indian Society," *American Indian Quarterly* 2 (Summer 1975): 131–39. She maintains that daily routines were not very different from those of white women. Susan Hartmann goes a step farther and argues that late-nineteenth-century warfare altered Indian social organization by creating a disadvantaged position for women from which they were forced to surrender once-powerful economic and social contributions. See Susan Hartmann, "Women's Work Among the Plains Indians," *Gateway Heritage* 3, no. 4 (1983): 2–9.

9. Mayhall, *Kiowas*, 183–254; Arrell Morgan Gibson, *Oklahoma: A History of Five Centuries*, 2nd ed. (Norman: University of Oklahoma Press, 1965), 143–56; Wilbur Sturtevant Nye, *Bad Medicine and Good: Tales of the Kiowas* (Norman: University of Oklahoma Press, 1962), vii–xxii.

10. Mayhall, *Kiowas*, 265–66; N. Scott Momaday poignantly wrote that his grandmother witnessed the last attempt at the Sun Dance and that "Without bitterness, and for as long as she lived, she bore a vision of deicide." See Momaday, *Rainy Mountain*, 10–11.

11. Mooney, *Calendar History*, 234; William T. Hagan, *United States–Comanche Relations: The Reservation Years* (New Haven, Conn.: Yale University Press, 1976), 198. Newspaper clipping quoted in Hugh D. Corwin, *The Kiowa Indians, Their History and Life Stories* (Lawton, Okla.: Hugh D. Corwin, 1958), 116.

12. U.S. Department of the Interior, Office of Indian Affairs, *Sixtieth Annual Report of the Commissioner of Indian Affairs to the Secretary of the Interior, 1891*, part 2, *Statistics*, 82–83; U.S. Department of the Interior, Office of Indian Affairs, *Sixtieth Annual Report of the Commissioner of Indian Affairs to the Secretary of the Interior, 1891*, part 1, 351.

13. William T. Hagan, *American Indians* (Chicago: University of Chicago Press, 1961), 125. Hagan provides an

account of the reservation problems and of the Kiowa School difficulties in particular in *United States–Comanche Relations*, 161–65, 194–200.

14. James Louis Avant manuscript, Floy Avant Duncum Collection, Western History Collections, University of Oklahoma, Norman, Okla. For a description of education available on the reservation see George Posey Wild, "History of Education of the Plains Indians of Southwestern Oklahoma since the Civil War" (Ph.D. diss., University of Oklahoma, 1941); and Ila Cleo Moore, "Schools and Education Among the Kiowa and Comanche Indians, 1870–1940" (master's thesis, University of Oklahoma, 1940).

15. James Louis Avant, Duncum Collection. See Margaret Connell Szasz, "Native American Children," in Hawes and Hiner, *American Childhood*, 320.

16. Marriott, *Ten Grandmothers*, 194–95; U.S. Department of the Interior, *Sixtieth Annual Report*, 351; William S. Nye, *Carbine and Lance: The Story of Old Fort Sill* (Norman: University of Oklahoma Press, 1937), 274–75.

17. Quoted in Sally J. McBeth, *Ethnic Identity and the Boarding School Experience of West-Central Oklahoma American Indians* (Washington, D.C.: University Press of America, 1983), 118; Myrtle Paudlety Ware, interview, Jacquelyn Patchin interviewer, Doris Duke American Indian Oral History Collection, Western History Collections, University of Oklahoma, Norman, Okla. For a discussion of the possibilities and limitations of the historical use of these interviews collected in the late 1960s, see Julia A. Jordan, "Oklahoma's Oral History Collection: New Source for Indian History," *Chronicles of Oklahoma* 49 (Summer 1971): 150–72.

18. U.S. Department of the Interior, Office of Indian Affairs, *Annual Reports of the Department of the Interior for the Fiscal Year Ended June 30, 1900*, 335.

19. Annie Sumty Bigman, interview, David Jones interviewer, Duke Collection. Both Ware and Bigman returned to Rainy Mountain School and served as assistant matrons there. Quoted in McBeth, *Ethnic Identity*, 105. Corporal punishment at the schools is outlined in McBeth, *Ethnic*

Identity, 105–108. Michael C. Coleman reviews the responses of Indian children to mission schools as adaptability, ambivalence, acceptance, active manipulation of the school, resistance, and rejection in "The Responses of American Indian Children to Presbyterian Schooling in the Nineteenth Century: An Analysis Through Missionary Sources," *History of Education Quarterly* 27 (Winter 1987): 473–97.

20. U.S. Department of the Interior, Office of Indian Affairs, *Annual Reports of the Department of the Interior for the Fiscal Year Ended June 30, 1905*, part 1, 303. Reasons for attending boarding schools are discussed in McBeth, *Ethnic Identity*, 108–11. For a discussion of the problems in female Indian education see Robert A. Trennert, "Educating Indian Girls at Nonreservation Boarding Schools, 1878–1920," *Western Historical Quarterly* 13 (July 1982): 271–90. For a more positive interpretation of the reservation school experience as a location of Kiowa identity see Clyde Ellis, " 'A Remedy for Barbarism': Indian Schools, the Civilizing Program, and the Kiowa-Comanche-Apache Reservation, 1871–1915," *American Indian Culture and Research Journal* 18, no. 3 (1994): 85–120.

21. Gage, "Romance of Pioneering," 303. Isabel Crawford had the same reaction to the dance at Saddle Mountain. See Salvatore Mondello, "Isabel Crawford and The Kiowa Indians," *Foundations* 22, no. 1 (1979): 35. For more information on the measles epidemic see Hagan, *United States–Comanche Relations*, 198; and for the Kiowa reaction, see Hugh D. Corwin, "Saddle Mountain Mission and Church," *Chronicles of Oklahoma* 36 (Summer 1958): 121. See also Weston LaBarre, *The Peyote Cult* (New York: Schocken Books, 1969), 43, 87, 98, 113; Hazel W. Hertzberg, *The Search for an American Indian Identity: Modern Pan-Indian Movements* (New York: Syracuse University Press, 1971), 150, 239, 241, 252, 255, 273; and Omer C. Stewart, *Peyote Religion: A History* (Norman: University of Oklahoma Press, 1987), 68–127.

22. Lone Wolf quoted in Corwin, "Saddle Mountain Mission," 119.

23. For a discussion of women on the Kiowa-Comanche Reservation see Rebecca Jane Herring, "Failed Assimilation:

Anglo Women on the Kiowa-Comanche Reservation, 1867–1906" (Master's thesis, Texas Tech University, 1983).

24. See Nye, *Bad Medicine and Good*, 267–75. Lauretta Ballew accepted the position of field matron for the United States government to teach Indian women domestic skills. See Rebecca Herring, "Their Work Was Never Done, Women Missionaries on the Kiowa-Comanche Reservation," *Chronicles of Oklahoma* 44 (Spring 1986): 69–83.

25. Barbara Welter outlines the entrance of women into the missionary field in the nineteenth century and the advantages and limitations they had in working intimately with other cultures. See "She Hath Done What She Could: Protestant Women's Missionary Careers in Nineteenth-Century America," *American Quarterly* 30 (Winter 1978): 624–38. See also Peggy Pascoe, *Relations of Rescue: The Search for Female Moral Authority in the American West, 1874–1939* (New York: Oxford University Press, 1990) for a discussion of the implications that the search for female moral authority had in cross-cultural relations between female missionaries and Native American women.

26. Isabel Crawford, *Joyful Journey, Highlights on the High Way* (Philadelphia: Judson Press, 1951), 1–40. Salvatore Mondello, "Isabel Crawford, The Making of a Missionary," *Foundations* 21, no. 4 (1978): 322–26.

27. Isabel Crawford, *Kiowa: The History of a Blanket Indian Mission* (New York: Fleming H. Revell Company, 1915), 8; Crawford, *Joyful Journey*, 42.

28. Crawford, *Joyful Journey*, 41; see also Mondello, "Making of a Missionary," 326–31; Crawford, *Joyful Journey*, 54–55.

29. Crawford quoted in Mondello, "Making of a Missionary," 337. See also Mondello, "Crawford and the Kiowa Indians," 28–34; and Corwin, "Saddle Mountain Mission," 118–22; Crawford, *Joyful Journey*, 63; Ernestine Kauahguo Kauley, interview, Robert L. Miller interviewer, April 8, 1967, Duke Collection, T-43, p. 13.

30. Isabel Crawford and Mary G. Burdette eds., *Young Women Among Blanket Indians, The Heroine of Saddle Mountain* (Chicago: R. R. Donnelly and Sons Company,

1903), 26; Mondello, "Crawford and the Kiowa Indians," 30. The citations to Burdette, Mondello, and Corwin reflect works that reproduced large segments of the journals that Crawford kept while she was in the mission field; Crawford quoted in Corwin, "Saddle Mountain Mission," 123.

31. Quoted in Isabel Crawford and Mary G. Burdette, eds., *From Tent to Chapel at Saddle Mountain* (Chicago: Women's Baptist Home Mission Society, n.d.), 16; Mondello, "Crawford and the Kiowa Indians," 32.

32. Crawford quoted in Mondello, "Crawford and the Kiowa Indians," 30; Crawford and Burdette, eds., *Young Women*, 28. The failure to turn Kiowa men into farmers is outlined in William D. Pennington, "Government Agricultural Policy on the Kiowa Reservation, 1869–1901," *Indian Historian* 11, no. 1 (1978): 11–16.

33. Mondello, "Crawford and the Kiowa Indians," 37; Crawford, *Joyful Journey*, 64; Crawford and Burdette, eds., *From Tent to Chapel*, 3.

34. Crawford, *Joyful Journey*, 67; also Corwin, *The Kiowas*, 118–21.

35. Corwin, *The Kiowas*, 127; Murial Wright, "Notes on Saddle Mountain Mission Church and Miss Isabel Crawford, Missionary," *Chronicles of Oklahoma* 36 (Autumn 1958): 318; and Marriott, *Ten Grandmothers*, 216–21.

36. Crawford and Burdette, eds., *From Tent to Chapel*, 5; Crawford, *Joyful Journey*, 75.

37. Pope-bah quoted in Corwin, "Saddle Mountain Mission," 126; Crawford, *Joyful Journey*, 82.

38. Crawford, *Joyful Journey*, 81. See also Mondello, "Crawford and the Kiowa Indians," 37.

39. Domot quoted in Corwin, *The Kiowas*, 129; Corwin, *The Kiowas*, 127–31.

40. Mondello, "Crawford and the Kiowa Indians," 40–42; Corwin, *The Kiowas*, 134–40.

41. Mondello, "Crawford and the Kiowa Indians," 40–42.

42. Tully Morrison, "Isabel Crawford: Missionary to the Kiowa Indians," *Chronicles of Oklahoma* 40 (Summer 1962): 76–78; Wright, "Notes," 318–19.

43. Lone Wolf, quoted in Hertzberg, *Search for Indian Identity*, 150; U.S. Department of Commerce, Bureau of the Census, *Indian Population in the United States and Alaska, 1910*, 17–18, table 9; 32, table 14; 165, table 66; 220, table 92; 238–39, table 99; 253, table 103. Jerrold E. Levy maintained that changes in Kiowa culture were incorporated on the basis of pragmatic evaluation consistent with the inner logic of their conceptual system in "After Custer: Kiowa Political and Social Organization from the Reservation Period to the Present" (Ph.D. diss., University of Chicago, 1959), 125–34.

Chapter 6. Lifting as We Climb

1. Riley, *Female Frontier*, 1–13. Research on American black women has increased in the last decade, producing some exceptional studies such as Jacqueline Jones, *Labor of Love, Labor of Sorrow: Black Women, Work, and the Family from Slavery to the Present* (New York: William Morrow and Company, 1984). To date there has not been a comprehensive study of black women in the American West. The premier article on this subject continues to be Lawrence B. deGraaf, "Race, Sex, and Region: Black Women in the American West, 1850–1920," *Pacific Historical Review* 49 (Summer 1980): 285–313, although Glenda Riley suggests a number of research avenues in "American Daughters: Black Women in the West," *Montana, The Magazine of Western History* 38 (Spring 1988): 14–27. In national studies of race relations, Oklahoma is generally analyzed as a southern state. See, for example, Joel Williamson, *The Crucible of Race: Black-White Relations in the American South Since Emancipation* (New York: Oxford University Press, 1984), 241–43. Some material in chapter 6 of this book was published originally in Linda W. Reese, "'Working in the Vinyard': African Women in All-Black Communities," *Kansas Quarterly* 25, no. 2 (1994): 7–16.

2. George P. Rawick, gen. ed., *The American Slave: A Composite Autobiography*, 31 vols. Supplement, series 1, vol. 12, *Oklahoma Narratives* (Westport, Conn.: Greenwood Press, 1977): 1–3. The WPA interviews must be used with

care. Such is the case with the interviews of this aged woman, whose statements of fact, such as her birthdate, sometimes contradicted reality. The interviews were conducted by inexperienced whites who attempted to capture the dialect of their subjects. In spite of the problems inherent in these "translations," I have reproduced the source as it was published; any of this information that is used in *Women in Oklahoma 1890–1920* corresponds to other primary sources.

3. William Loren Katz, gen. ed., *The American Negro, His History and Literature. Negro Population in the United States, 1790–1915* (New York: Arno Press and The New York Times, 1968), 43, table 13; 51, table 5; 150, table 5; 252, table 18; 827, table 3. For push/pull factors of westward migration see George R. Woolfolk, "Turner's Safety-Valve and Free Negro Westward Migration," *Journal of Negro History* 50 (July 1965): 185–97; Darlene Clark Hine presents an interesting discussion of the importance of black women's need to claim control over themselves as sexual beings and control over their children as a motive for female migration in "Rape and the Inner Lives of Black Women in the Middle West," *Signs* 14, no. 4 (1989): 912–20. See also Lori Bogle, "On Our Way to the Promised Land: Black Migration from Arkansas to Oklahoma, 1889–1893," *Chronicles of Oklahoma* 72 (Summer 1994): 160–77.

4. Norman L. Crockett presents a comprehensive study of Oklahoma black towns in relation to other prominent American all-black communities in *The Black Towns* (Lawrence, Kans.: Regents Press, 1979); see also Arthur L. Tolson, *The Black Oklahomans: A History, 1541–1972* (New Orleans: Edwards Printing Company, 1974); Jimmie Lewis Franklin, *Journey Toward Hope: A History of Blacks in Oklahoma* (Norman: University of Oklahoma Press, 1982); and Kenneth M. Hamilton, *Black Towns and Profit: Promotion and Development in the Trans-Appalachian West, 1877–1915* (Urbana: University of Illinois Press, 1991). Because some of the all-black communities were temporary colonies, the number is uncertain. Tolson lists twenty-seven.

5. *Boley Progress*, 20 July 1905; 10 May and 17 May 1906. The official name of the school was the Colored Agri-

cultural and Normal University, but Oklahoma blacks always called it Langston University. In 1941 the name was officially changed to Langston University.

6. *Langston City Herald,* 17 November 1892, 20 October 1894; Mrs. Willis Monroe, quoted in Tolson, *Black Oklahomans,* 50–51; Zella J. Black Patterson, *Langston University: A History* (Norman: University of Oklahoma Press, 1979), 3–12; Kenneth M. Hamilton, "The Origin and Early Developments of Langston, Oklahoma," *Journal of Negro History* 62 (March 1977): 270–87.

7. Chaney McNair, narrative, quoted in Rawick, *American Slave,* vol. 12, 217–19; Alice Douglass, narrative, quoted in Rawick, *American Slave,* vol. 7, 74. Bettina Aptheker presents a convincing Marxist-feminist argument in evaluating the productive nature of domestic labor (i.e., producing surplus value) and in defining domestic labor as an independent political issue in *Woman's Legacy: Essays on Race, Sex, and Class in American History* (Amherst: University of Massachusetts Press, 1982), 111–27.

8. *Boley Informer,* 19 May 1911; Mrs. George Busby, interview, Indian-Pioneer Collection, vol. 4, p. 12; *Langston City Herald,* 20 October 1894.

9. Alafair Carter Adams, quoted in Thomas W. Pew, Jr., "Boley, Oklahoma, Trial in American Apartheid," *American West* 17 (July 1980): 17; William E. Bittle and Gilbert Geis, *The Longest Way Home: Chief Alfred C. Sam's Back-to-Africa Movement* (Detroit: Wayne State University Press, 1964), 19–39; Polly Colbert, narrative, in Rawick, *American Slave,* vol. 7, 33. For relations between Indians and freedmen see Donald A. Grinde, Jr., and Quintard Taylor, "Red vs. Black: Conflict and Accommodation in the Post Civil War Indian Territory, 1865–1907," *American Indian Quarterly* 8 (Summer 1984): 211–29; Daniel F. Littlefield, Jr., *The Cherokee Freedmen: From Emancipation to American Citizenship* (Westport, Conn.: Greenwood Press, 1978); and Daniel F. Littlefield, Jr., *The Chickasaw Freedmen: A People Without a Country* (Westport, Conn.: Greenwood Press, 1980); Alafair Carter Adams, quoted in Pew, "Boley, Oklahoma," 17.

10. *Boley Progress, Boley Informer, Clearview Tribune, Clearview Patriarch,* 1905–15, passim; Mrs. Essie B. Williams, letter to author, 13 November 1987.

11. Katz, *American Negro,* 512, table 15; *Boley Progress, Boley Informer, Clearview Tribune, Clearview Patriarch,* 1905–15, passim; Williams to Reese, *op. cit.;* M. C. [Metella Clement], "What Shall I Do for a Livelihood," *Langston City Herald,* 7 September 1895.

12. *Boley Informer,* 10 May 1911. Bonnie Thornton Dill argues in "Our Mothers' Grief: Racial Ethnic Women and the Maintenance of Families," research paper 4, Center for Research on Women, Memphis, Tenn., 1986) that racial-ethnic women worked both in the public (productive) and private (reproductive) spheres in order to sustain and stabilize their families and that the contradiction between the prevailing domestic ideology and the reality of their lives created conflicts and stereotypes. In the all-black Oklahoma communities this duality strengthened and nurtured self-esteem and worth, as men and women were committed to a higher communal goal of economic independence and racial example.

13. Katz, *American Negro,* 515, table 16. Susan Archer Mann maintains that the position of freed women improved subjectively and objectively in the transition from slavery to sharecropping in "Social Change and Sexual Inequality: The Impact of the Transition from Slavery to Sharecropping on Black Women," Working paper 3, Center for Research on Women, Memphis, Tenn., 1986. In her excellent study, *Labor of Love, Labor of Sorrow,* Jacqueline Jones argues that at a time when industrialization was creating a male-female division of the labor system, black sharecropping families struggled to create a pattern of joint, complementary work in spite of economic adversity and without the institutional supports that were given to white farm families (pp. 79–109). In the Oklahoma black towns the institutional reinforcement was there, but economic handicaps haunted their efforts. See also Minnie Miller Brown, "Black Women in American Agriculture," *Agricultural History* 50 (January 1976): 202–12; Williams to Reese, *op. cit.*

14. *Boley Progress*, 29 December 1908.

15. *Boley Beacon*, 20 February 1908; *Oklahoma Guide* (Guthrie), 24 July 1902.

16. Mabel Irene Bridgewater, "Insanity Among the Women of Oklahoma" (Bachelor's thesis, University of Oklahoma, 1911), 17, 11. See also Jennings J. Rhyne, *Social and Community Problems of Oklahoma* (Guthrie, Okla.: Cooperative Publishing Company, 1929). Neither Bridgewater nor Rhyne separated mental cases by race, but Rhyne indicated that in criminal cases blacks were arrested three times more often than whites.

17. *Boley Progress*, 23 March 1905; Eugene S. Richards, "Trends of Negro Life in Oklahoma As Reflected by Census Reports," *Journal of Negro History* 33 (January 1948): 48–51.

18. Patterson, *Langston University*, 15–20, 75–76.

19. Ibid., 80–98, 125–26.

20. "Opening of the Public School," *Boley Progress*, 14 September 1905; Katz, *American Negro*, 386, diagram 4; 387, table 15; 415, table 19; Patterson, *Langston University*, 111.

21. *Clearview Patriarch*, 21 September 1911; *Clearview Patriarch*, 1911–14, passim. In Boley, Miss Herrieze Perry's accomplishments and activities dominated the news.

22. *Clearview Patriarch*, 2 March 1911; Patterson, *Langston University*, 206–208.

23. Donald Spivey, "Crisis on a Black Campus: Langston University and Its Struggle for Survival," *Chronicles of Oklahoma* 59 (Winter 1981–82): 430–47; Patterson, *Langston University*, 26–34.

24. Ralph Ellison, *Going to the Territory* (New York: Random House, 1986), 134–37; Patterson, *Langston University*, 238–39; Teall, *Black History in Oklahoma*, 200–201. For a lively discussion of the development of popular music in Oklahoma see William W. Savage, Jr., *Singing Cowboys and All That Jazz* (Norman: University of Oklahoma Press, 1983).

25. Ellison, *Going to the Territory*, 137.

26. "The Damnation of Women," in *W. E. B. Dubois, Writings*, ed. Nathan Huggins (New York: Literary Classics of the U.S., 1986), 953, 967.

27. Tolson, *Black Oklahomans*, 150.

28. "A Brutal Outrage," *Oklahoma Guide*, 17 April 1902; "Makes Wife Pray Then Shoots Her," *Western Age* (Langston, Okla.), 10 July 1908; *Oklahoma Guide*, 24 December 1903. Joyce Carol Thomas poignantly develops the theme of the strength of black women in adversity in her novel *Marked by Fire* (New York: Avon Books, 1982). The heroine, growing up near Ponca City, Oklahoma, is abandoned by her father and raped by a local farmer. Through the love and nurture of her mother and friends, she is able to overcome the assault and seek a better future.

29. "A Prayer for all Mothers," *Boley Beacon*, 24 November 1910; "The Ideal Home," *Boley Progress*, 20 July 1905.

30. Carrie Lynwood, "Negro Man's Ideal of Womanhood," *Oklahoma Guide*, 7 January 1904; Nick Comfort, "Boley," *Oklahoma Journal of Religion* 1 (July 1944): 8–11; Crockett, *Black Towns*, 71.

31. Lynwood, "Negro Man's Ideal," *Oklahoma Guide*, 7 January 1904. For a discussion of role prescription within the black press, see Bess Beatty, "Black Perspectives of American Women: The View from Black Newspapers, 1865–1900," *Maryland Historian* 9 (Fall 1978): 39–50. Sociologist Mozell Hill wrote a dissertation and several articles on the Oklahoma all-black communities. Hill has maintained that black-town residents have a higher regard for their own race than other blacks and that the older generation held firm to the idea of racial separation out of fear of racial friction. See Mozell Hill, "The All-Negro Society in Oklahoma" (Ph.D. diss., University of Chicago, 1946); "A Comparative Study of Race Attitudes in the All-Negro Community in Oklahoma," *Phylon* 7 (Third Quarter 1946): 260–68; "Basic Racial Attitudes Toward Whites in the Oklahoma All-Negro Community," *American Journal of Sociology* 49 (May 1944): 519–23.

32. *Western Age*, 23 February 1906; Ada Upshaw, "The Position of the Colored Girl in Society," *Western Age*, 23 February 1906.

33. Ibid.

34. *Langston City Herald*, 27 July 1895.

35. *Langston City Herald*, 30 March 1895; Nettie Carlisle, "Cleanliness," *Langston City Herald*, 2 November 1895.

36. *The Langston City Herald*, 27 July and 10 August 1895.

37. The founding of the black women's club movement is discussed in Paula Giddings, *'When and Where I Enter': The Impact of Black Women on Race and Sex in America* (New York: William Morrow and Company, 1984), 75–117. The importance of the direction of Mary Church Terrell, who served as first NACW president, is outlined in Beverly W. Jones, "Mary Church Terrell and The National Association of Colored Women, 1896 to 1901," *Journal of Negro History* 67 (Spring 1982): 20–33. Rosalyn Terborg-Penn addresses the discrimination against black women in "Discrimination Against Afro-American Women in the Women's Movement, 1830–1920," *The Afro-American Woman: Struggles and Images* eds. Sharon Harley and Rosalyn Terborg-Penn (Port Washington, N.Y.: Kennikat Press, National University Publications, 1978) 17–27. An excellent analysis of the manipulation of the "True Womanhood" concept and of the racist sympathies of white suffrage leaders is developed by Barbara Hilkert Andolsen in *'Daughters of Jefferson, Daughters of Bootblacks': Racism and American Feminism* (Macon, Ga.: Mercer University Press, 1986).

38. "National Federation of Afro-American Women," *Langston City Herald*, 26 October 1895; Fannie Barrier Williams, "Woman's Sphere," *Langston City Herald*, 11 January 1896.

39. *Boley Progress*, 10 December 1908; "Mothers Club for Boley City School," *Boley Progress*, 24 November 1910. The historical invisibility of these organizations as well as the central role they played in the creation of the black community are discussed in Anne Firor Scott, "Most Invisible of All: Black Women's Voluntary Associations," *Journal of Southern History* 56 (February 1990): 3–22.

40. *Clearview Patriarch*, 1 August 1912.

41. *Clearview Patriarch,* 23 March 1911; "Timely Suggestions by a Woman of the Race," *Oklahoma Guide* (Guthrie), 23 July 1903.

42. Harriet Price Jacobson, quoted in Willa Allegra Strong, "The Origin, Development, and Current Status of the Oklahoma Federation of Colored Women's Clubs" (Ph.D. diss., University of Oklahoma, 1957), 61.

43. *Bookertee Searchlight,* 21 February 1919.

44. Strong, "Colored Women's Clubs," 76, 87–88, 166–68.

45. One of the best discussions of the political and social harassment of Oklahoma blacks is in Robert Bruce Shepard, "Black Migration As a Response to Repression: The Background Factors and Migration Of Oklahoma Blacks to Western Canada 1905–1912, As a Case Study" (Masters thesis, University of Saskatchewan, 1976). Bittle and Geis discuss the pressure on the black-town area, primarily in Okfuskee County, in *The Longest Way Home,* 19–67. See also Philip Mellinger, "Discrimination and Statehood in Oklahoma," *Chronicles of Oklahoma* 49 (Autumn 1971): 340–78; and Orben J. Casey, "Governor Lee Cruce, White Supremacy and Capital Punishment, 1911–1915," *Chronicles of Oklahoma* 52 (Winter 1974–75): 456–75; and Jimmie L. Franklin, "Black Oklahomans and Sense of Place," in Joyce, *Oklahoma: Alternative Views,* 265–79.

46. Bittle and Geis, *Longest Way Home,* 34, 55–56; *The Crisis,* July 1911, in *Black Women in White America, A Documentary History* ed. Gerda Lerner (New York: Vintage Books, 1973), 161–62.

47. Crockett, *Black Towns,* xiv, 155–87.

48. Steward Grow, "The Blacks of Amber Valley: Negro Pioneering in Northern Alberta," *Canadian Ethnic Studies* 6 (1974): 17–38; Shepard, "Black Migration," 83–87.

49. Martha Murphy Edwards, quoted in Grow, "Blacks of Amber Valley," 29, 33.

50. Harold Martin Troper discusses the actions Canadian officials took to limit the movement of blacks into Canada in "The Creek-Negroes of Oklahoma and Canadian

Immigration, 1909–1911," *Canadian Historical Review* 53 (1972): 272–88. Troper maintains that the majority of the emigrants were Creek-Negroes dissatisfied with their declining status. R. Bruce Shepard ably refutes this position by documenting the family history of movement out of the South to Oklahoma and then to Canada for most of the emigrants, in "North to the Promised Land, Black Migration to the Canadian Plains," *Chronicles of Oklahoma* 66 (Fall 1988): 306–27. Shepard also documents the discrimination against the black settlers in Canada, in "The Little 'White' Schoolhouse: Racism in a Saskatchewan Rural School," *Saskatchewan History* 39 (March 1986): 81–93. See also Robin W. Winks, *The Blacks in Canada: A History* (New Haven, Conn.: Yale University Press, 1971). For push/pull factors of migration see George R. Woolfolk, "Turner's Safety-Valve and Free Negro Westward Migration," *Journal of Negro History* 50 (July 1965): 185–97.

51. Shepard, "Black Migration," 133.

52. Unknown woman quoted in Bittle and Geis, *Longest Way Home*, 8–9; Maggie-Marie MacMullen, quoted in Pew, "Boley, Oklahoma," 55; Alafair Carter Adams, quoted in Pew, "Boley, Oklahoma," 55.

Chapter 7. In Love with an Ideal

1. *Oklahoma State Capitol*, 10 December 1901; Ferguson, *They Carried the Torch*, 70–73.

2. Ferguson, *They Carried the Torch*, 80.

3. Carl N. Degler, *At Odds: Women and the Family in America from the Revolution to the Present* (New York: Oxford University Press, 1980), 298–327; William O'Neill, *Everyone Was Brave: The Decline and Fall of Feminism in America* (Chicago: Quadrangle Books, 1969), 142–43; Jill Conway, "Women Reformers and American Culture, 1870–1930," *Journal of Social History* 5 (Winter 1971–72): 164–77. Although the essay is now dated, David Potter identified the dilemma of the modern woman in attempting to reconcile the principle of equality with the practice of wifehood and motherhood in "American Women and the American Character," in *History and American Society: Essays of David M.*

Potter (pp. 299–300). For a recent treatment see Nancy F. Cott, "What's in a Name? The Limits of 'Social Feminisim'; or, Expanding the Vocabulary of Women's History," *Journal of American History* 76, no. 3 (December 1989): 809–29. Robyn Muncy maintains in *Creating a Female Dominion in American Reform, 1890–1935* (New York: Oxford University Press, 1991) that an interlocking set of organizations and agencies staffed by professionalized, reform-minded women provided a bridge between the Progressive Era and the New Deal.

4. Kate Barnard, "Reference of Her Life Work," typescript, p. 75, Fayette and Edith Copeland Collection, Western History Collections, University of Oklahoma, Norman, Okla. In any quotation I have reproduced from this typescript, I have retained the punctuation and capitalization used in the typescript. The most complete examination of Kate Barnard is Julia A. Short, "Kate Barnard: Liberated Woman" (Master's thesis, University of Oklahoma, 1972).

5. Joseph B. Thoburn, *A Standard History of Oklahoma*, 5 vols. (Chicago: American Historical Society, 1916), vol. 3, 1329–33; and Danney Goble, *Progressive Oklahoma: The Making of a New Kind of State* (Norman: University of Oklahoma Press, 1980), 183–86. Only Angie Debo separates the legend and the woman in stating that Barnard traded on her femininity and engaged in political tricks. See Angie Debo, *And Still the Waters Run: The Betrayal of the Five Civilized Tribes* (New Jersey: Princeton University Press, 1940; reprint, Norman: University of Oklahoma Press, 1984), 184.

6. Quoted in Thoburn, *Standard History*, vol. 3, 1332. Biographical sketches of Kate Barnard appear in J. H. McKiddy, "Kate Barnard—Unsung Heroine," *Daily Oklahoman*, 23 February 1941; and Glenn Shirley, "Oklahoma Kate—Woman of Destiny," *The West* 8 (March 1968): 18–21, 56–58. See also Edward T. Janes, ed., *Notable American Women: A Biographical Dictionary*, 3 vols. (Cambridge, Mass.: Belknap Press of Harvard University Press, 1971), vol. 1, 90–92; and *The National Cyclopedia of American Biography* (New York: James T. White and Company, 1916),

vol. 15, 110–11. There is much confusion as to Barnard's birth year among these sources, ranging from 1874 to 1879. This book uses the date documented by Short, "Kate Barnard," 3. Rachel Shiell Barnard had two sons by a previous marriage. These two and the son born in John Barnard's second marriage were Kate's nearest relatives.

7. Short, "Kate Barnard," 8; and Junetta Davis, "Woman Influences Constitution," *Daily Oklahoman*," 11 December 1983.

8. Albert McRill, *And Satan Came Also* (Oklahoma City: Albert McRill, 1955), 114–15. McRill cites his source as a society editor who was intimately acquainted with Barnard. This was probably Edith C. Johnson of the *Daily Oklahoman*.

9. Kate Barnard, "Through the Windows of Destiny: How I Visualized My Life Work," *Good Housekeeping* 55 (November 1912): 600; McRill, *Satan Came Also*; *National Cyclopedia*, 110.

10. Kate Barnard, "Oklahoma's Child Labor Laws," *Sturm's Magazine* 5 (February 1908): 42.

11. "'Miss Kate', Livest Wire in Prison Reform, Visits Us," *New York Times*, 8 December 1912.

12. Barnard, "Through the Windows," 600–601. Barnard does not give the name of the city for this speech, but it most likely concerned the disaster at Witteville in 1906. See Philip A. Kalish, "Ordeal of the Oklahoma Coal Miners: Coal Mine Disasters in the Sooner State, 1886–1945," *Chronicles of Oklahoma* 48 (Fall 1970): 331–40; "'Miss Kate'," *New York Times, op.cit.*

13. Kate Barnard, "Human Ideals in Government," *Survey* 23 (2 October 1909): 20.

14. McRill, *Satan Came Also*, 115–16; Keith L. Bryant, Jr., "Kate Barnard, Organized Labor, and Social Justice in Oklahoma During the Progressive Era," *Journal of Southern History* 35 (May 1969): 148–51; Janes, *Notable American Women*, 90.

15. Short, "Kate Barnard," 19–24; Bryant, "Progressive Era," 149–52.

16. Ivie, Mattie Louise, "Woman Suffrage in Oklahoma, 1890–1918" (Master's thesis, Oklahoma State University, 1971), 7–24.

17. Charles Zueblin quoted in Short, "Kate Barnard," 134–35; Janes, *Notable American Women*, 91.

18. Kate Pearson Burwell, "Oklahoma and Indian Territory Federation of Women's Clubs," *Sturm's Statehood Magazine* 11 (April 1906): 4.

19. Susan L. Allen, "Progressive Spirit: The Oklahoma and Indian Territory Federation of Women's Clubs," *Chronicles of Oklahoma* 66 (Spring 1988): 12–16.

20. Charles N. Haskell quoted in Louise Boyd James, "The Woman Suffrage Issue in the Oklahoma Constitutional Convention," *Chronicles of Oklahoma* 56 (Winter 1978): 389; see also James R. Wright, Jr., "The Assiduous Wedge: Woman Suffrage and the Oklahoma Constitutional Convention," *Chronicles of Oklahoma* 51 (Winter 1973): 421–43; Irvin Hurst, *The 46th Star* (Oklahoma City: Semco Color Press, 1957), 14–15; Ivie, "Woman Suffrage," 23–31. Barnard's name was often misspelled as Bernard.

21. Kate Barnard, speech, National Conference of Charities and Corrections, quoted in Short, "Kate Barnard," 71–72.

22. Short, "Kate Barnard," 43, 57; Thoburn, *Standard History*, vol. 3, 1331; see also Clinton O. Bunn and William C. Bunn, comp., *Constitution and Enabling Act of the State of Oklahoma, Annotated and Indexed* (Ardmore, Okla.: Bunn Brothers Publishers, 1907), 41–42.

23. Barnard, "Life Work," 47–48.

24. Barnard, "Child Labor Laws," 42; Barnard, "Human Ideals," 20; *Daily Oklahoman*, 23 February 1908; Keith L. Bryant, Jr., *Alfalfa Bill Murray* (Norman: University of Oklahoma Press, 1968), 80–81; James R. Scales and Danney Goble, *Oklahoma Politics: A History* (Norman: University of Oklahoma Press, 1982), 42–43.

25. *South McAlester Daily News*, 15 August 1908, cited in Short, "Kate Barnard," 84–85; William H. Murray, *Memoirs of Governor Murray and True History of Oklahoma,*

3 vols. (Boston: Meador Publishing Company, 1945), vol. 1, 42; "Fake Brand Put on Murray Story," *Daily Oklahoman*, 1 August 1910. See also Suzanne J. Crawford and Lynn R. Musslewhite, "Progressive Reform and Oklahoma Democrats: Kate Barnard versus Bill Murray," *The Historian* 53, no. 3 (1991), 473–88; and Suzanne Crawford and Lynn Musslewhite, "Kate Barnard, Progressivism, and the West," in Joyce, *Oklahoma: Alternative Views*, 62–77.

26. Harvey R. Hougen, "Kate Barnard and the Kansas Penitentiary Scandal, 1908–1909," *Journal of the West* 17, no. 1 (1978): 9–18; Hurst, *46th Star*, 97–104; McRill, *Satan Came Also*, 114–18; and Short, "Kate Barnard," 90–99.

27. Charles N. Haskell, letter, 12 September 1908, quoted in Hougen, "The Kansas Scandal," 11; *Topeka Daily Capitol*, 12 December 1908, cited in Hougen, "The Kansas Scandal," 11; Haskell quoted in Hurst, *46th Star*, 101.

28. Charles N. Haskell letter, 22 December 1908, quoted in Hougen, "Kansas Penitentiary Scandal," 11–12; George W. P. Hunt, "An Appreciation of Miss Barnard," *Good Housekeeping* 55 (November 1912): 606–607; *New York Times*, 8 December 1912.

29. Barnard, "Life Work," 30; Kate Barnard, "America the Beautiful," *Daily Oklahoman*, 27 November 1910; *Cherokee Republican*, 15 July 1910, cited in Short, "Kate Barnard," 162–63, 167; see also Ivie, "Woman Suffrage," 33–37.

30. Kate Barnard, "For the Orphans of Oklahoma, Children of the Disinherited," *Survey* 33 (7 November 1914): 154–61; Short, "Kate Barnard," 170–77.

31. "An Official Champion of the Weak," *Outlook* 102 (3 August 1923): 751; Alexander Johnson, "The Commissioner of Charities in Oklahoma," *Survey* 30 (26 April 1913): 138–39; Debo, *And Still the Waters Run*, 184–92.

32. "Politicians Seek to Wreck Office, Says Miss Kate," *Daily Oklahoman*, 8 May 1913; Short, "Kate Barnard," 194–208.

33. *Report of the Thirty-Second Annual Lake Mohonk Conference of the Friends of the Indians and Other Dependent Peoples* (Mohonk Lake, N.Y.: Thirty-Second

Annual Lake Mohonk Conference, 1914), 23; see Barnard, "For the Orphans," 154–64; "Woman Sees Plot to Rob Indians," *New York Times*, 14 November 1914; "Working to Stop Robbery of Indians, Indian Commissioner Defends Steps Taken Against Land Thieves in Oklahoma," *New York Times*, 15 November 1914; Barnard, "Life Work," 75.

34. Barnard, "Life Work," 13, 77. These memoirs document an extensive list of doctors, hospitals, and medicines Barnard tried in order to cure this mysterious illness. She insisted that doctors attributed her symptoms to a microscopic "animal parasite," but her description seems to resemble closely the disease known today as shingles. Barnard also had heart trouble. "Death Claims Kate Barnard in City Hotel," *Daily Oklahoman*, 25 February 1930; "Edith Johnson's Column," *Daily Oklahoman*, 25 February 1930; Hurst, *46th Star*, 171; Barnard quoted in Thoburn, *Standard History*, vol. 3, 1332.

Chapter 8. Public Pioneering

1. Ferguson, *They Carried the Torch*, 81, 79.

2. Janes, *Notable American Women*, vol. 3, 177–78; and Robert McHenry, ed., *Liberty's Women* (Springfield, Mass.: G. and C. Merriam Company, Publishers, 1980), 350.

3. The most complete and perceptive biography of Alice Robertson is Joe Powell Spaulding, "The Life of Alice Mary Robertson" (Ph.D. diss., University of Oklahoma, 1959). Spaulding made extensive use of the more than 2,500 documents in the Alice Robertson Collection at the McFarlin Library at the University of Tulsa. See Guy Logsden, "Indian Studies Resources at the University of Tulsa," *Chronicles of Oklahoma* 55 (Spring 1977): 64–77. See also Edith C. Johnson, "'My Election Was An Answer to Prayer,' Second Woman Congresswoman Says," *Daily Oklahoman*, 6 November 1920; and Marguerite Mooers Marshall, "Woman's Place in Politics," *Woman's Home Companion* 48 (October 1921), 15. For a history of the Robertson family work at the Tullahassee Mission see Althea Bass, *The Story of Tullahassee* (Oklahoma City: Semco Color Press, 1960); and Althea Bass, "The Inheritance of Alice Robertson,"

manuscript, 1955, Althea Bass Collection, Western History Collections, University of Oklahoma, Norman, Okla.

4. Robertson essay, quoted in Spaulding, "Alice Robertson," 44.

5. Ruth Moore Stanley, "Alice M. Robertson, Oklahoma's First Congresswoman," *Chronicles of Oklahoma* 45 (Autumn 1967): 276–78; Spaulding, "Alice Robertson," 45–52.

6. Robertson quoted in Rella Montice Looney, "Miss Alice Left Her Mark on Oklahoma," in *Twin Territory Times: The Way It Was in Old Oklahoma*, ed. Edward A. Shaw (Oklahoma City: Indian Territory Posse of Oklahoma Westerners, 1982), 148. Looney knew Alice Robertson and worked with her at the Red Cross during World War I.

7. Samuel J. Barrows, ed., *Proceedings of the Sixth Annual Meeting of the Lake Mohonk Conference of Friends of the Indian* (Mohonk Lake, N.Y.: Sixth Annual Lake Mohonk Conference, 1889), 120; Susan Tiger, quoted in Spaulding, "Alice Robertson," 56; *Proceedings of Sixth Annual Lake Mohonk Conference*, 120.

8. Joe C. Jackson, "Church School Education in the Creek Nation, 1898 to 1907," *Chronicles of Oklahoma* 46 (Autumn 1968): 312–29; Spaulding, "Alice Robertson," 57–61; Grant Foreman, "The Hon. Alice M. Robertson," *Chronicles of Oklahoma* 10 (March 1932): 13–17; Theodore Roosevelt, *The Rough-Riders* (New York: Charles Scribner's Sons, 1899), 227–29, 235–36.

9. *Sixth Annual Lake Mohonk Conference*, 120.

10. Robertson quoted in Joe C. Jackson, "Summer Normals in Indian Territory After 1898," *Chronicles of Oklahoma* 37 (Autumn 1959): 312; Spaulding, "Alice Robertson," 61–64. Robertson was co-founder of the Indian Territory Teachers Association in 1884 and was elected vice-president of the National Education Association in 1905.

11. Robertson quoted in Louise B. James, "Alice Mary Robertson—Anti-Feminist Congresswoman," *Chronicles of Oklahoma* 5 (Winter 1977): 456, 457; Spaulding, "Alice Robertson," 65–73.

12. Spaulding, "Alice Robertson," 82; Edith Johnson, "My Election Was an Answer,"; Robertson quoted in

Spaulding, "Alice Robertson," 79. See also Maitreyi
Mazumdar, "Alice's Restaurant: Expanding a Woman's
Sphere," *Chronicles of Oklahoma* 70, no. 3 (1992), 302–25.

13. Spaulding, "Alice Robertson," 85; "Death Comes to
Miss Alice, State Leader," *Daily Oklahoman*, 2 July 1931;
Grant Foreman, "The Lady from Oklahoma," *Independent*
105 (March 1921): 311, 326.

14. Scales and Goble, *Oklahoma Politics*, 97–117; Edith
Johnson, "My Election Was an Answer."

15. Ivie, "Woman Suffrage," 39–68; Louise Boyd James,
"Woman's Suffrage, Oklahoma Style, 1890–1918," in
Thurman, *Women in Oklahoma*, 182–97.

16. Edith Johnson, "My Election Was an Answer,";
Marshall, "Woman's Place," 15.

17. Stanley, "Alice M. Robertson," 263, 261; "A Woman
Who Got into Congress Through the Want-Ad Column,"
Literary Digest 67 (4 December 1920): 56.

18. Edith Johnson, "My Election Was an Answer," For
discussion of the deteriorating conditions in Oklahoma see
Donald E. Green, ed., *Rural Oklahoma* (Oklahoma City:
Oklahoma Historical Society, 1977); and John Thompson,
*Closing the Frontier: Radical Response in Oklahoma,
1889–1923* (Norman: University of Oklahoma Press, 1986).

19. Marshall, "Woman's Place," 15; Edith C. Johnson,
"Will Alice Robertson Succeed Where Jeannette Rankin
Failed?" *Daily Oklahoman*, 10 January 1921; "Woman Who
Got into Congress," 58.

20. Letter from Mary C. Thaw to Alice Robertson, 26
November 1920, quoted in Spaulding, "Alice Robertson,"
127; Bernice Norman Crockett, "'No Job for a Lady,'"
Chronicles of Oklahoma 61 (Summer 1983): 148–67.

21. Edith Johnson, "Will Robertson Succeed?";
Robertson letter to Mary Thaw, 2 December 1922, quoted in
Spaulding, "Alice Robertson," 127; Edith Johnson, "Will
Robertson Succeed?"; Edith Johnson, "My Election Was an
Answer"; Edith Johnson, "Will Robertson Succeed?"

22. Alice Robertson, letters to Ann Augusta Moore,
quoted in Stanley, "Alice M. Robertson," 273; "'Miss Alice' to
be Meek In Congress," *New York Times*, 26 February 1921.

23. Alice Robertson, letter to Ann Augusta Moore, 1 March 1921, quoted in Spaulding, "Alice Robertson," 122.

24. Letter from Alice Robertson to Frank Craig, President, Oklahoma Americanization Society, 1922, quoted in Stanley, "Alice M. Robertson," 268; and Spaulding, "Alice Robertson," 138.

25. Stanley, "Alice M. Robertson," 269–70; Spaulding, "Alice Robertson," 134–37.

26. "Opposes Woman Voters' League," *New York Times*, 25 February 1921; Stanley, "Alice M. Robertson," 264–65; Spaulding, "Alice Robertson," 132; "Women Urge Woman Delegate," *New York Times*, 18 August 1921; "Congress-woman Doubts Woman Envoy," *Daily Oklahoman*, 17 August 1921.

27. Marshall, "Woman's Place," 15; James, "Anti-Feminist Congresswoman," 458.

28. Marshall, "Woman's Place," 15; "Woman Assails Maternity Bill," *New York Times*, 11 August 1921; Spaulding, "Alice Robertson," 129–33; Mrs. Chester H. Peoples, *Wagoner Record-Democrat*, 4 May 1922, cited in Spaulding, "Alice Robertson," 129–33.

29. "Cheated, Says Miss Robertson," *New York Times*, 9 November 1922; and "Miss Robertson Angry, Would Quit Muskogee," *New York Times*, 12 November 1922.

30. Edith C. Johnson, "Miss Alice," *Daily Oklahoman*, 2 July 1931; "Death Comes to Miss Alice, State Leader," *Daily Oklahoman*, 2 July 1931; Spaulding, "Alice Robertson," 79.

Chapter 9. Grand Work in Newspaper Fields

1. Ferguson, *They Carried the Torch*, 81. Some material in this chapter was published originally in Linda W. Reese, "'Dear Oklahoma Lady': Women Journalists Speak Out," *Chronicles of Oklahoma* 67 (Fall 1989): 264–95.

2. *Watonga Republican*, 31 July 1919 and c. January 1920.

3. "Illusions and Disillusions," *Watonga Republican*, 25 November 1920; Ferguson, *They Carried the Torch*, 12–13.

4. "How It Seems to Be a Citizen," *Watonga Republican*, c. January 1920.

5. "Women in Politics," *Watonga Republican*, c. May 1920.

6. Clyde Richard King, "The T. B. Ferguson Family in Oklahoma Journalism," (Master's thesis, University of Oklahoma, 1949); "Women as Journalists," 2.

7. Ferguson, *They Carried the Torch*, 130–31.

8. "Woman with a Gift," and "Woman's Column," *Watonga Republican*, 19 July 1919.

9. Mrs. Walter Ferguson, "Shameful Tyranny," *Watonga Republican*, c. January 1920.

10. Mrs. Walter Ferguson, "Women and the National Conscience," *Watonga Republican*, 13 January 1921.

11. King, "Ferguson Family," 108–19.

12. *Ibid.*, 111; Hope Holway, "Lucia Loomis Ferguson," *Chronicles of Oklahoma* 41 (Winter 1963–64), 365–69; Barbara Elaine Bungardt, "A Biography of Mrs. Walter Scott Ferguson," paper, in files of H. H. Herbert School of Journalism, University of Oklahoma, Norman, Okla.

13. Cited in King, "Ferguson Family," 117.

14. Bungardt, "Biography of Mrs. Ferguson," 12.

15. Mrs. Walter Ferguson, "Turn About," *Watonga Republican*, 20 January 1921.

16. Mrs. Walter Ferguson, "Give the Girl a Chance," *Watonga Republican*, 14 September 1922.

17. Mrs. Walter Ferguson, "Circumstances Alter Cases," *Watonga Republican*, 7 September 1922.

18. Mrs. Walter Ferguson, "Good Times," *Watonga Republican*, 2 December 1920.

19. Mrs. Walter Ferguson, "The Unfortunates," *Watonga Republican*, 21 August 1922; Mrs. Walter Ferguson, "Insidious Propaganda," *Watonga Republican*, 14 September 1922.

20. Mrs. Walter Ferguson, "What Women Must Learn," *Watonga Republican*, 28 July 1921.

21. Mrs. Walter Ferguson, "No Need for Worry," *Watonga Republican*, 2 March 1922; Mrs. Walter Ferguson, "Hints for Husbands," *Watonga Republican*, 3 March 1921.

22. Conway, "Women Reformers," 164.

23. Edith Johnson, *The Story of My Life* (Oklahoma City: Oklahoma Publishing Company, 1940), 9.

24. Edith Johnson, "If I Were Not a Newspaper Writer," *University of Oklahoma Magazine* 7 (March 1918): 6; Naomi Taylor Casey, "Miss Edith Johnson, Pioneer Newspaper Woman," *Chronicles of Oklahoma* 60 (Spring 1982): 66–73.

25. Johnson, "If I Were Not a Writer," 6.

26. Edith C. Johnson Collection, correspondence file, Western History Collections, University of Oklahoma, Norman, Okla.

27. Edith Johnson, "We Women—What the New Year Holds for Us," *Daily Oklahoman*, 1 January 1916; Edith Johnson, "Let American Women Not Meddle with Armistice," *Daily Oklahoman*, 16 November 1918; Edith Johnson, "Women's Clubs and the Spirit of Democracy," *Daily Oklahoman*, 19 May 1916; Lauretta Rainey, *History of Oklahoma State Federation of Women's Clubs* (Guthrie, Okla.: Co-Operative Publishing Company, 1939), 48.

28. Edith Johnson, "'Votes for Women' in Chicago," *Daily Oklahoman*, 10 June 1916.

29. Edith Johnson, "Women's Privileges and Men's Rights," *Daily Oklahoman*, 9 January 1917.

30. Edith Johnson, "Humanism Sums Up in a Word Meaning of Term Feminism," *Daily Oklahoman*, 29 April 1917.

31. Edith Johnson, "How Much Will You Save This Year?" *Daily Oklahoman*, 6 January 1916; Edith Johnson, "The Housewives' League Militant," *Daily Oklahoman*, 7 December 1916; Edith Johnson, "Let Us Have Scientific Municipal Housekeeping," *Daily Oklahoman*, 22 October 1918; "Why Not a Community Kitchen for Oklahoma?" *Daily Oklahoman*, 30 October 1918; and "What Shall We Do with the Poor and Unclean?" *Daily Oklahoman*, 1 November 1918.

32. Edith Johnson, "Our Women and This War," *Daily Oklahoman*, 25 June 1916; Edith Johnson, "The Self-Made Woman," *Daily Oklahoman*, 27 November 1916; Edith Johnson, "Miss Rankin Act vs. Woman's Cause," *Daily Oklahoman*, 10 April 1917.

33. Edith Johnson, "Mrs. Pankhurst's After-War Program," *Daily Oklahoman*, 9 October 1918; "What Women

Can Do for Bread Supply," 20 April 1917; "Making the Apron Symbol of Thrift," 3 May 1917; "Women Should Serve Country in Capacity Best Suited to Them," 15 April 1917.

34. Edith Johnson, "Slackers in War Same in Marriage," *Daily Oklahoman*, 12 April 1917; Edith Johnson, "Don't Whine to the Man in Camp," *Daily Oklahoman*, 14 October 1918.

35. Edith Johnson, "Eleventh Hour in the Liberty Loan," *Daily Oklahoman*, 12 October 1918; Edith Johnson, "A Critical Hour, This, Are You Going to Fail?" *Daily Oklahoman*, 12 November 1918; Edith Johnson, "Let American Women Not Meddle with Armistice," *Daily Oklahoman*, 16 November 1918; Johnson, *Story of My Life*, 21.

36. Johnson, *Story of My Life*, 2.

37. Edith Johnson, "Will Women Be Drafted for the Next Big War?" *Daily Oklahoman*, 15 April 1921.

38. Edith Johnson, "Women On Juries," *Daily Oklahoman*, 14 November 1924.

39. Edith Johnson, "Assets of Modern Wife," *Daily Oklahoman*, 11 October 1924; Edith Johnson, "Women's Power in Politics," *Daily Oklahoman*, 7 November 1924.

40. Edith Johnson, "Women and Fame," *Daily Oklahoman*, 28 May 1927.

41. Johnson, "Women's Power in Politics."

42. Edith Johnson, "Woman Lives for a King, Man for a Kingdom," *Daily Oklahoman*, 12 April 1921; Edith Johnson, "Women and the Cigaret," *Daily Oklahoman*, 5 November 1924.

43. Edith Johnson, "Back to Home Movement Is What America Needs," *Daily Oklahoman*, 16 April 1921; Edith Johnson, *Illusions and Disillusions* (Oklahoma City: Edith C. Johnson, 1920), 29, 66; Edith Johnson, "Give Absolute Divorce Only to the Guiltless," *Daily Oklahoman*, 17 May 1921.

44. Edith Johnson, *To Women of the Business World* (Philadelphia: J. B. Lippincott Company, 1923), x, 18–19.

45. Edith Johnson, *To Women*, 45, 39–48, 130–31; see also Edith Johnson, "A Mother's Best Gift to Daughter or Son," *Daily Oklahoman*, 10 July 1927.

46. Edith Johnson, *To Women*, 176–85; Edith Johnson, "Enemies of the Home," *Daily Oklahoman*, 27 June 1927.

47. "State's Twenty-Four Women Leaders Selected," *Daily Oklahoman*, 17 September 1930; see also Reese, "'Dear Oklahoma Lady'," 264–95.

Bibliography

Primary Sources
Unpublished Materials
Manuscript Collections
Kansas State Historical Society, Topeka, Kansas
    Hutchins, Bertha Newby
McFarlin Library, Department of Special Collections, University of Tulsa, Tulsa, Oklahoma
    Robertson, Alice
Western History Collections, University of Oklahoma, Norman, Oklahoma
    Bass, Althea
    Copeland, Fayette and Edith
    Doris Duke American Indian Oral History
    Duncum, Floy Avant
    Ferguson, Mr. and Mrs. Walter Scott
    Hatfield, Edna
    Indian-Pioneer

Johnson, Edith C.
Ross, S. P.
Snow, Jerry Whistler

Theses and Dissertations

Bridgewater, Mabel Irene. "Insanity Among the Women of Oklahoma." Bachelor's thesis, University of Oklahoma, 1911.

Herring, Rebecca Jane. "Failed Assimilation: Anglo Women on the Kiowa-Comanche Reservation, 1867–1906." Master's thesis, Texas Tech University, 1983.

Hill, Mozell. "The All-Negro Society in Oklahoma." Ph.D. diss., University of Chicago, 1946.

Ivie, Mattie Louise. "Woman Suffrage in Oklahoma, 1890–1918." Master's thesis, Oklahoma State University, 1971.

King, Clyde Richard. "The T. B. Ferguson Family in Oklahoma Journalism." Master's thesis, University of Oklahoma, 1949.

Levy, Jerrold E. "After Custer: Kiowa Political and Social Organization From the Reservation Period to the Present." Ph.D. diss., University of Chicago, 1959.

Moore, Ila Cleo. "Schools and Education Among the Kiowa and Comanche Indians, 1870–1940." Master's thesis, University of Oklahoma, 1940.

Shepard, Robert Bruce. "Black Migration As a Response to Repression: The Background Factors and Migration of Oklahoma Blacks to Western Canada, 1905–1912, As a Case Study." Master's thesis, University of Saskatchewan, 1976.

Short, Julia A. "Kate Barnard: Liberated Woman." Master's thesis, University of Oklahoma, 1972.

Spaulding, Joe Powell. "The Life of Alice Mary Robertson." Ph.D. diss., University of Oklahoma, 1959.

Strong, Willa Allegra. "The Origin, Development, and Current Status of the Oklahoma Federation of Colored Women's Clubs." Ph.D. diss., University of Oklahoma, 1957.

Wild, George Posey. "History of Education of the Plains
    Indians of Southwestern Oklahoma Since the Civil
    War." Ph.D. diss., University of Oklahoma, 1941.

Published Materials
Books

Allen, Catherine Ward, and Harry E. Chrisman *Chariot of
    the Sun.* Denver: Sage Books, 1964.
Barrows, Samuel J., ed. *Proceedings of the Sixth Annual
    Meeting of the Lake Mohonk Conference of Friends of
    the Indian.* New York: Lake Mohonk Conference, 1889.
Bartel, Irene Brown. *No Drums Or Thunder.* San Antonio,
    Tex.: Naylor Company, 1970.
Battey, Thomas C. *The Life and Adventures of a Quaker
    Among the Indians.* Boston: Lee and Shepard Pub-
    lishers, 1875. Reprint, Norman: University of Okla-
    homa Press, 1968.
Bowers, Lola Garrett, and Kathleen Garrett *A. Florence
    Wilson, Friend and Teacher.* Tahlequah, Okla.:
    Rockett's Printers and Publishers, 1951.
Bunn, Clinton O., and William C. Bunn, comp. *Constitution
    and Enabling Act of the State of Oklahoma,
    Annotated and Indexed.* Ardmore, Okla.: Bunn
    Brothers Publishers, 1907.
Crawford, Isabel. *Joyful Journey, Highlights on the High
    Way.* Philadelphia: Judson Press, 1951.
———. *Kiowa: The History of a Blanket Indian Mission.* New
    York: Fleming H. Revell Company, 1915.
———, and Mary G. Burdette. *From Tent to Chapel at
    Saddle Mountain.* Chicago: Woman's Baptist Home
    Missions Society, n.d.
———. *Young Women Among Blanket Indians, The Heroine
    of Saddle Mountain.* Chicago: R. R. Donnelly and
    Sons Company, 1903.
Denig, Edwin Thompson. *Five Tribes of the Upper Missouri:
    Sioux, Arickaras, Assiniboines, Crees, Crows.* Edited
    by John C. Ewers. Norman: University of Oklahoma
    Press, 1961.

89ers Association. *Oklahoma, The Beautiful Land.* Oklahoma City: Times-Journal Publishing Company, 1943.

Ferguson, Mrs. Tom B. *They Carried the Torch: The Story of Oklahoma's Pioneer Newspapers.* Kansas City, Mo.: Burton Publishing Company, 1937. Reprint, Norman, Okla.: Levite of Apache, 1989.

Giles, Janice Holt. *The Kinta Years: An Oklahoma Childhood.* Boston: Houghton Mifflin Co., 1973.

Glessner, Chloe Holt. *Far Above Rubies.* San Antonio, Tex.: Naylor Company, 1965.

Green, Lola M. *Firm, Our Foundation.* Montgomery, Ala.: Brown Printing Company, 1986.

Hetherington, Gloria Bish, ed. *Diary of Mary Henderson: Homesteading in Oklahoma Territory, November 12, 1901–December 31, 1906.* Sentinel, Okla.: Schoonmaker Publishers, 1982.

Huggins, Nathan, ed. *W. E. B. Dubois, Writings.* New York: Literary Classics of the United States, 1986.

Irving, John Treat, Jr. *Indian Sketches: Taken During An Expedition to the Pawnee Tribes* (1833). Edited by John Francis McDermott. Norman: University of Oklahoma Press, 1955.

Jensen, Margaret, and Leila Williams. *Looking Back.* Denver, Colo.: Big Mountain Press, 1966.

Johnson, Edith. *Illusions and Disillusions.* Oklahoma City: Edith C. Johnson, 1920.

———. *The Story of My Life.* Oklahoma City: Oklahoma Publishing Company, 1940.

———. *To Women of the Business World.* Philadelphia: J. B. Lippincott Company, 1923.

Katz, William Loren, gen. ed. *The American Negro, His History and Literature. Negro Population in the United States, 1790–1915.* New York: Arno Press and *New York Times,* 1968.

Kilpatrick, Jack F., and Anna G. Kilpatrick. *Run Toward The Nightland: Magic of the Oklahoma Cherokees.* Dallas: Southern Methodist University Press, 1967.

————. *The Shadow of Sequoyah: Social Documents of the Cherokees, 1862–1964.* Norman: University of Oklahoma Press, 1965.

Laune, Seigniora Russell. *Sand In My Eyes.* Norman: University of Oklahoma Press, 1956.

Lawton Business and Professional Woman's Club. *'Neath August Sun, 1901: Dedicated to Those who Came This Way in 1901.* Plummer Printing Co., n.d.

Lerner, Gerda, ed. *Black Women in White America: A Documentary History.* New York: Vintage Books, 1973.

McBurney, Laressa Cox. *Dr. Charlie's Wife.* San Antonio, Tex.: Naylor Company, 1975.

Mooney, James. *Calendar History of the Kiowa Indians.* Extract from the Seventeenth Annual Report of the Bureau of American Ethnology. Washington, D.C.: Government Printing Office, 1898.

Murray, William H. *Memoirs of Governor Murray and True History of Oklahoma.* 3 vols. Boston: Meador Publishing Company, 1945.

Owen, Narcissa. *Memoirs of Narcissa Owen, 1831–1907.* N.p., 1908.

Perdue, Theda. *Nations Remembered: An Oral History of the Five Civilized Tribes, 1865–1907.* Westport, Conn.: Greenwood Press, 1980.

Rawick, George P., gen. ed. *The American Slave: A Composite Autobiography.* Vol. 7, *Oklahoma and Mississippi Narratives.* Westport, Conn.: Greenwood Press, 1977.

————. *The American Slave: A Composite Autobiography.* Vol. 12, *Oklahoma Narratives.* Westport, Conn.: Greenwood Press, 1977.

Report of the Thirty-Second Annual Lake Mohonk Conference of the Friends of the Indians and Other Dependent Peoples. New York: Lake Mohonk Conference, 1914.

Roosevelt, Theodore. *The Rough-Riders.* New York: Charles Scribner's Sons, 1899.

Smallwood, James, ed. *And Gladly Teach: Reminiscences of Teachers from Frontier Dugout to Modern Module.* Norman: University of Oklahoma Press, 1976.

Smith, Martha L. *Going To God's Country.* Boston: Christopher Publishing House, 1941.

Taliaferro, Velma. *Memoirs of a Chickasaw Squaw.* Norman, Okla.: Levite of Apache, 1987.

Teall, Kaye M., ed. *Black History of Oklahoma: A Resource Book.* Oklahoma City: Oklahoma City Public Schools, 1971.

Thoburn, Joseph B. *A Standard History of Oklahoma.* 5 vols. Chicago: American Historical Society, 1916.

Wallace, Allie B. *Frontier Life in Oklahoma.* Washington, D.C.: Public Affairs Press, 1964.

Zellner, William W., and Ruth L. Laird, eds. *Oklahoma, The First Hundred Years.* Ada, Okla.: Galaxy Publications, 1989.

Articles

Barnard, Kate. "For the Orphans of Oklahoma, Children of the Disinherited." *Survey* 33 (7 November 1914): 154–55, 161–64.

———. "Human Ideals in Government." *Survey* 23 (2 October 1909): 17–20.

———. "Oklahoma's Child Labor Laws." *Sturm's Magazine* 5 (February 1908): 42–44.

———. "Through the Windows of Destiny: How I Visualized my Life Work." *Good Housekeeping* 55 (November 1912): 600–606.

Burwell, Kate Pearson. "Indian Territory Federation of Women's Clubs." *Sturm's Statehood Magazine* 11 (April 1906): 3–7.

———. "Oklahoma and Indian Territory Federation of Women's Clubs." *Sturm's Statehood Magazine* 11 (April 1906): 3–5.

Candee, Helen C. "Oklahoma." *Atlantic Monthly* 86 (September 1900): 328–36.

———. "Social Conditions In Our Newest Territory." *Forum* 25 (June 1898): 426–37.

Foreman, Grant. "The Hon. Alice M. Robertson." *Chronicles of Oklahoma* 10 (March 1932): 13–17.

————. "The Lady From Oklahoma." *Independent* 105 (March 1921): 311, 326.

Frost, Margaret Fullerton. "Small Girl in a New Town." *Great Plains Journal* 19 (1980): 2–73.

Gage, Lucy. "A Romance of Pioneering." *Chronicles of Oklahoma* 29 (Autumn 1951): 284–313.

Gillepsie, Anna. "Coxville, Nebraska to Fay, Oklahoma by Wagon (1899): The Journal of Anna Gillespie." *Nebraska History* 65, no. 3 (1984): 344–65.

Harger, Charles M. "Oklahoma and The Indian Territory As They Are Today." *American Review of Reviews* 25 (February 1902): 178–81.

Hunt, George W. P. "An Appreciation of Miss Barnard." *Good Housekeeping* 55 (November 1912): 606–607.

"An Illustrated Souvenir Catalog of The Cherokee Female Seminary, Tahlequah, Indian Territory, 1850 to 1906." *Journal of Cherokee Studies* 10 (Spring 1985): 115–85.

Johnson, Alexander. "The Commissioner of Charities in Oklahoma." *Survey* 30 (26 April 1913): 138–39.

Johnson, Edith. "If I Were Not a Newspaper Writer." *University of Oklahoma Magazine* 7 (March 1918): 6.

Lale, Max L. "Letters From a Bride in Indian Territory, 1889." *Red River Valley Historical Review* 6 (Winter 1981): 12–24.

Lehman, Leola. "Life In The Territories." *Chronicles of Oklahoma* 41 (Winter 1963–64): 370–81.

Lucas, Robert C., and Lucille Gilstrap. "Homesteading The Strip." *Chronicles of Oklahoma* 51 (Fall 1973): 285–304.

Marshall, Marguerite Mooers. "Woman's Place in Politics." *Women's Home Companion* 48 (October 1921): 15.

"An Official Champion of the Weak." *Outlook* 102 (3 August 1912): 751.

Pearson, Lola Clark. "The Drudge." *The Oklahoma Farmer-Stockman* (July 15, 1927): 10.

Ragland, H. D., ed. "The Diary of Mrs. Anna S. Wood: Trip to the Opening of the Cherokee Outlet in 1893." *Chronicles of Oklahoma* 50 (Autumn 1972): 307–27.

Reed, Ora E. "Daughters of Confederacy." *Sturm's Magazine*
        10 (June 1910): 37–40.
Tinnin, Ida Wetzel. "Educational and Cultural Influences of
        The Cherokee Seminaries." *Chronicles of Oklahoma*
        37 (Spring 1959): 59–67.
Washburne, Marion Foster. "Women of The Great West."
        Harper's Bazaar 40 (January and March 1906):
        41–47, 210–16.
"Which Is Your Choice For The Pioneer Woman?" *Oklahoma
        Farmer-Stockman* (1 December 1927): 7.
"A Woman Who Got Into Congress Through the Want-Ad
        Column." *Literary Digest* 67 (4 December 1920):
        56–57.
Yelton, Ruth. "A Wagon Trip to Oklahoma: Passages From a
        Girl's Diary." *Chronicles of Oklahoma* 64 (Summer
        1986): 95–106.

Newspapers

Boley (Okla.) Beacon
Boley (Okla.) Informer
Boley (Okla.) Progress
Bookertee (Okla.) Searchlight
Clearview (Okla.) Tribune
Daily Oklahoman
Langston City (Okla.) Herald
New York Times
Oklahoma Guide (Guthrie)
Oklahoma State Capital
Watonga (Okla.) Republican
Western Age (Langston, Okla.)

Government Documents

U.S. Department of Commerce. Bureau of the Census.
        *Historical Statistics of the United States, Colonial
        Times to 1970.* Washington, D.C.: U.S. Department of
        Commerce, 1975.
U.S. Department of Commerce. Bureau of the Census. *Indian
        Population In The United States and Alaska, 1910.*
        Washington, D.C.: Government Printing Office, 1915.

U.S. Department of the Interior. Office of Indian Affairs. *Annual Report of the Department of the Interior for the Fiscal Year Ended June 30, 1900.*

U.S. Department of the Interior. Office of Indian Affairs. *Annual Reports of the Department of the Interior for the Fiscal Year Ended June 30, 1905.*

U.S. Department of the Interior. Office of Indian Affairs. *Annual Reports of the Department of the Interior, 1906.*

U.S. Department of the Interior. *The Kiowa.* Anadarko, Okla.: Southern Plains Indian Museum and Craft Center, n.d.

U.S. Department of the Interior. Office of Indian Affairs. *Sixtieth Annual Report of the Commissioner of Indian Affairs to the Secretary of the Interior, 1891.*

Seconday Sources
Books

Albers, Patricia, and Beatrice Medicine, eds. *The Hidden Half: Studies of Plains Indian Women.* Lanham, Md.: University Press of America, 1983.

Andolsen, Barbara Hilkert. *'Daughters of Jefferson, Daughters of Bootblacks': Racism and American Feminism.* Macon, Ga.: Mercer University Press, 1986.

Aptheker, Bettina. *Women's Legacy: Essays on Race, Sex, and Class in American History.* Amherst: University of Massachusetts Press, 1982).

Armitage, Susan, and Elizabeth Jameson, eds. *The Women's West.* Norman: University of Oklahoma Press, 1987.

Bass, Althea. *A Cherokee Daughter of Mount Holyoke.* Muscatine, Iowa: Prairie Press, 1937.

―――. *The Story of Tullahassee.* Oklahoma City: Semco Color Press, 1960.

Bittle, William E., and Gilbert Geis. *The Longest Way Home: Chief Alfred C. Sam's Back-to-Africa Movement.* Detroit, Mich.: Wayne State University Press, 1964.

Brown, Dee. *The Gentle Tamers: Women of The Old West.* New York: Putnam, 1958. Reprint, Lincoln, Nebr.: University of Nebraska Press, 1968.

Bryant, Keith L., Jr. *Alfalfa Bill Murray.* Norman: University of Oklahoma Press, 1968.

Campbell, O. B. *Mission to the Cherokees.* Oklahoma City: Metro Press, 1973.

Carter, L. Edward. *The Story of Oklahoma Newspapers, 1844–1984.* Muskogee, Okla.: Western Heritage Books, 1984.

Clark, Blue. *Lone Wolf v. Hitchcock: Treaty Rights and Indian Law at the End of the Nineteenth Century.* Lincoln: University of Nebraska Press, 1994.

Coleman, Michael C. *Presbyterian Missionary Attitudes Toward American Indians, 1837–1893.* Jackson: University Press of Mississippi, 1985.

Corkran, David H. *The Cherokee Frontier: Conflict and Survival, 1740–1762.* Norman: University of Oklahoma Press, 1962.

Corwin, Hugh D. *The Kiowa Indians, Their History and Life Stories.* Lawton, Okla.: Hugh D. Corwin, 1958.

Crockett, Norman L. *The Black Towns.* Lawrence, Kans.: Regents Press, 1979.

Dale, Edward Everett. *Frontier Ways; Sketches of Life in the Old West.* Austin: University of Texas Press, 1959.

Debo, Angie. *And Still The Waters Run: The Betrayal of the Five Civilized Tribes.* New Jersey: Princeton University Press, 1940. Reprint, Norman: University of Oklahoma Press, 1984.

———. *Oklahoma, Footloose and Fancy-Free.* Norman: University of Oklahoma Press, 1949.

———. *Prairie City: The Story of an American Community.* Tulsa, Okla.: Council Oak Books, 1985.

Degler, Carl N. *At Odds: Women and the Family in America from the Revolution to the Present.* New York: Oxford University Press, 1980.

Ellison, Ralph. *Going to the Territory.* New York: Random House, 1986.

Ferber, Edna. *Cimarron.* Garden City, N.Y.: Doubleday, Doran and Company, 1930.

Foreman, Carolyn Thomas. *Oklahoma Imprints, 1835–1907: A History of Printing in Oklahoma Before Statehood.* Norman: University of Oklahoma Press, 1936.

————. *Park Hill.* Muskogee, Okla.: Star Printery Press, 1948.

Foreman, Grant. *Indian Removal: The Emigration of the Five Civilized Tribes of Indians.* Norman: University of Oklahoma Press, 1934.

————. *The Five Civilized Tribes.* Norman: University of Oklahoma Press, 1934.

Franklin, Jimmie Lewis. *Journey Toward Hope: A History of Blacks in Oklahoma.* Norman: University of Oklahoma Press, 1982.

Frantz, Joe B., and Ernest Choate, Jr. *The American Cowboy: The Myth and the Reality.* Norman: University of Oklahoma Press, 1955.

Gibson, Arrell M. *America's Exiles: Indian Colonization in Oklahoma.* Oklahoma: Oklahoma Historical Society, 1976.

————. *Oklahoma: A History of Five Centuries.* 2nd ed. Norman: University of Oklahoma Press, 1981.

Giddings, Paula. *'When and Where I Enter': The Impact of Black Women on Race and Sex in America.* New York: William Morrow and Company, 1984.

Goble, Danney. *Progressive Oklahoma: The Making of a New Kind of State.* Norman: University of Oklahoma Press, 1980.

Green, Donald E., ed. *Rural Oklahoma.* Oklahoma City: Oklahoma Historical Society, 1977.

Gregory, Jack, and Rennard Strickland, eds. *Starr's History of the Cherokee Indians.* Fayetteville, Ark.: Indian Heritage Association, 1967.

Griswold, Robert L. *Family and Divorce in California, 1850-1890: Victorian Illusions and Everyday Realities.* Albany: State University of New York Press, 1982.

Hagan, William T. *American Indians.* Chicago: University of Chicago Press, 1961.

————. *United States–Comanche Relations: The Reservation Years.* New Haven, Conn.: Yale University Press, 1976. Reprint, Norman: University of Oklahoma Press, 1990.

Hamilton, Kenneth M. *Black Towns and Profit: Promotion and Development in the Trans-Appalachian West, 1877–1915.* Urbana: University of Illinois Press, 1991.

Harley, Sharon, and Rosalyn Terborg-Penn, eds. *The Afro-American Woman: Struggles and Images.* Port Washington, N.Y.: National University Publications, 1978.

Hertzberg, Hazel W. *The Search for an American Indian Identity, Modern Pan-Indian Movements.* New York: Syracuse University Press, 1971.

Holmes, Helen F., ed. *The Logan County History, Logan County, Oklahoma.* Guthrie, Okla.: Logan County Extension Homemakers Council, 1978.

Hurst, Irwin. *The 46th Star.* Oklahoma City: Semco Color Press, 1957.

Jeffrey, Julie Roy. *Frontier Women: The Trans-Mississippi West, 1840–1880.* New York: Hill and Wang, 1979.

Jensen, Joan M., and Darlis A. Miller, eds. *New Mexico Women: Intercultural Perspectives.* Albuquerque: University of New Mexico Press, 1986.

Janes, Edward T., ed. *Notable American Women: A Biographical Dictionary.* 3 vols. Cambridge, Mass.: Belknap Press of Harvard University Press, 1971.

Jones, Billy M. *Health-Seekers in the Southwest, 1817–1900.* Norman: University of Oklahoma Press, 1967.

Jones, Jacqueline. *Labor of Love, Labor of Sorrow: Black Women, Work, and the Family from Slavery to the Present.* New York: Basic Books, 1985.

Joyce, Davis D. *"An Oklahoma I Had Never Seen Before": Alternative Views of Oklahoma History.* Norman: University of Oklahoma Press, 1994.

Klein, Laura, and Lillian Ackerman. *Women and Power in Native North America.* Norman: University of Oklahoma Press, 1995.

La Barre, Weston. *The Peyote Cult*. New York: Schocken Books, 1969.

Limerick, Patricia. *The Legacy of Conquest*. New York: W. W. Norton and Company, 1987.

Limerick, Patricia, Clyde Milner, and Charles Rankin. *Trails: Toward a New Western History*. Lawrence: University Press of Kansas, 1991.

Littlefield, Daniel F., Jr. *The Cherokee Freedmen: From Emancipation to American Citizenship*. Westport, Conn.: Greenwood Press, 1978.

————. *The Chickasaw Freedmen: A People Without a Country*. Westport, Conn.: Greenwood Press, 1980.

McBeth, Sally J. *Ethnic Identity and the Boarding School Experience of West-Central Oklahoma American Indians*. Washington, D.C.: University Press of America, 1983.

McHenry, Robert, ed. *Liberty's Women*. Springfield, Mass.: G. and C. Merriam Company, Publishers, 1980.

McRill, Albert. *And Satan Came Also*. Oklahoma City: Albert McRill, 1955.

Malone, Henry Thompson. *Cherokees of the Old South: A People in Transition*. Athens: The University of Georgia Press, 1956.

Marable, Mary Hays, and Elaine Boylan, eds. *A Handbook of Oklahoma Writers*. Norman: University of Oklahoma Press, 1939.

Marriott, Alice. *Indians On Horseback*. New York: Thomas Y. Crowell Company, 1948.

————. *Kiowa Years, A Study in Culture Impact*. New York: Macmillan Company, 1968.

————. *The Ten Grandmothers*. Norman: University of Oklahoma Press, 1945.

Mayhall, Mildred P. *The Kiowas*. Norman: University of Oklahoma Press, 1963.

Mihesuah, Devon A. *Cultivating the Rosebuds: The Education of Women at the Cherokee Female Seminary, 1851–1909*. Urbana: University of Illinois Press, 1993.

Miskin, Bernard. *Rank and Warfare Among the Plains Indians*. Seattle: University of Washington Press, 1940.

Momaday, N. Scott. *The Way to Rainy Mountain*. New York: Ballantine Books, 1969.

Morgan, Anne Hodges, and Rennard Strickland, eds. *Oklahoma Memories*. Norman: University of Oklahoma Press, 1981.

Morgan, Anne Hodges, and Wayne H. Morgan, eds. *Oklahoma: New Views of the Forty-Sixth State*. Norman: University of Oklahoma Press, 1982.

Morgan, E. Buford. *The Wichita Mountains: Ancient Oasis of the Prairies*. Waco, Tex.: E. Buford Morgan, 1973.

The National Cyclopedia of American Biography. New York: James T. White and Company, 1916.

Nye, Wilbur Sturtevant. *Bad Medicine and Good: Tales of the Kiowas*. Norman: University of Oklahoma Press, 1962.

———. *Carbine and Lance: The Story of Old Fort Sill*. Norman: University of Oklahoma Press, 1937.

O'Neill, William. *Everyone Was Brave: The Decline and Fall of Feminism in America*. Chicago: Quadrangle Books, 1969.

Pascoe, Peggy. *Relations of Rescue: The Search for Female Moral Authority in the American West, 1874–1939*. New York: Oxford University Press, 1990.

Patterson, Zella J. Black. *Langston University: A History*. Norman: University of Oklahoma Press, 1979.

Piekarski, Vicki. *Westward the Women: An Anthology of Western Stories by Women*. Albuquerque: University of New Mexico Pres, 1984.

Potter, David M. "American Women and the American Character." In *History and American Society: Essays of David M. Potter*. Edited by Don E. Fehrenbacher, 177–303. New York: Oxford University Press, 1973.

Rainey, Luretta. *History of Oklahoma State Federation of Women's Clubs*. Guthrie, Okla.: Co-operative Publishing company, 1939.

Rhyne, Jennings J. *Social and Community Problems of Oklahoma*. Guthrie, Okla.: Co-operative Publishing Company, 1929.

Riley, Glenda. *The Female Frontier: A Comparative View of Women on the Prairie and Plains*. Lawrence: University Press of Kansas, 1988.

———. *Women and Indians on the Frontier, 1825–1915*. Albuquerque: University of New Mexico Press, 1984.

Savage, William W., Jr. *The Cowboy Hero: His Image in American History and Culture*. Norman: University of Oklahoma Press, 1979.

———. *Cowboy Life: Reconstructing an American Myth*. Norman: University of Oklahoma Press, 1975.

———. *Singing Cowboys and All That Jazz: A Short History of Popular Music in Oklahoma*. Norman: University of Oklahoma Press, 1982.

Scales, James R., and Danney Goble. *Oklahoma Politics: A History*. Norman: University of Oklahoma Press, 1982.

Schlissel, Lillian, Vicki L. Ruiz, and Janice Monk, eds. *Western Women: Their Land, Their Lives*. Albuquerque: University of New Mexico Press, 1988.

Scott, Anne Firor. *The Southern Lady: From Pedestal to Politics, 1830–1930*. Chicago: University of Chicago Press, 1970.

Shaw, Edward A., ed. *Twin Territory Times: The Way It Was in Old Oklahoma*. Oklahoma City: Indian Territory Posse of Oklahoma Westerners, 1982.

Stewart, Omer C. *Peyote Religion: A History*. Norman: University of Oklahoma Press, 1987.

Szasz, Margaret Connell. "Native American Children." In *American Childhood: A Research Guide and Historical Handbook*. Edited by Joseph M. Hawes and N. Ray Hines, 311–42. Westport, Conn.: Greenwood Press, 1985.

Taylor, George Rogers, ed. *The Turner Thesis: Concerning the Role of the Frontier in American History*. 3d ed. Lexington, Mass.: D. C. Heath and Company, 1972.

Thomas, Joyce Carol. *Marked by Fire.* New York: Avon Books, 1982.

Thompson, John. *Closing the Frontier: Radical Response in Oklahoma, 1889–1923.* Norman: University of Oklahoma Press, 1986.

Thurman, Malvena K., ed. *Women in Oklahoma: A Century of Change.* Oklahoma City: Oklahoma Historical Society, 1982.

Tolson, Arthur L. *The Black Oklahomans: A History, 1541–1972.* New Orleans: Edwards Printing Company, 1974.

Wardell, Morris L. *A Political History of the Cherokee Nation.* Norman: University of Oklahoma Press, 1938.

Welch, James, with Stekler, Paul. *Killing Custer: The Battle of the Little Bighorn and the Fate of the Plains Indians.* New York: W.W. Norton and Company, 1995.

West, C. W. *Among the Cherokees: A Biographical History of the Cherokees Since the Removals.* Muskogee, Okla.: Muscogee Publishing Company, 1981.

White, Richard. *"It's Your Misfortune and None of My Own:" A New History of the American West.* Norman: University of Oklahoma Press, 1991.

Williamson, Joel. *The Crucible of Race: Black-White Relations in the American South Since Emancipation.* New York: Oxford University Press, 1984.

Winks, Robin W. *The Blacks in Canada.* New Haven, Conn.: Yale University Press, 1971.

Womack, John. *Cleveland County, Oklahoma, Historical Highlights.* Noble, Okla.: John Womack, 1983.

Woodward, Grace Steele. *The Cherokees.* Norman: University of Oklahoma Press, 1963.

Wright, Murial H. *A Guide to the Indian Tribes of Oklahoma.* Norman: University of Oklahoma Press, 1951.

Wunder, John R., ed. *At Home on the Range: Essays on the History of Western Social and Domestic Life.* Westport, Conn.: Greenwood Press, 1985.

Young, Mary E. "Women, Civilization, and the Indian Question." In *Clio Was a Woman: Studies in the*

History of American Women. Edited by Mabel E. Deutrich and Virginia S. Purdy, 98–110. Washington, D.C.: Howard University Press, 1980.

Articles

Abbott, Devon. "Ann Florence Wilson, Matriarch of the Cherokee Female Seminary." *Chronicles of Oklahoma* 67 (Winter 1989–90): 426–37.

———. "'Commendable Progress': Acculturation at the Cherokee Female Seminary." *American Indian Quarterly* 14 (Summer 1987): 187–201.

———. "Medicine for the Rosebuds: Health Care at the Cherokee Female Seminary, 1876–1909." *American Indian Culture and Research Journal* 12, no. 1 (1988): 59–71.

Agnew, Brad. "A Legacy of Education: The History of the Cherokee Seminaries." *Chronicles of Oklahoma* 63 (Summer 1985): 128–47.

Allen, Susan L. "Progressive Spirit: The Oklahoma and Indian Territory Federation of Women's Clubs." *Chronicles of Oklahoma* 66 (Spring 1988): 4–21.

Bailyn, Bernard. "The Challenge of Modern Historiography." *American Historical Review* 87 (February 1982): 1–24.

Ballenger, T. L. "The Cultural Relations Between Two Pioneer Communities." *Chronicles of Oklahoma* 34 (Autumn 1956): 286–95.

Beatty, Bess. "Black Perspectives of American Women: The View from Black Newspapers, 1865–1900." *Maryland Historian* 9 (Fall 1978): 39–50.

Belcher, Dixie. "A Democratic School For Democratic Women." *Chronicles of Oklahoma* 61 (Winter 1983–84): 414–21.

Berthrong, Donald J. "White Neighbors Come Among the Southern Cheyenne and Araphao." *Kansas Quarterly* 3 (Fall 1971): 105–15.

Bogle, Lori. "On Our Way to the Promised Land: Black Migration from Arkansas to Oklahoma, 1889–1893," *Chronicles of Oklahoma* (Summer 1994): 160–77.

Brown, Minnie Miller. "Black Women in American Agriculture." *Agricultural History* 50 (January 1976): 202–12.

Bryant, Keith L., Jr. "Kate Barnard, Organized Labor, and Social Justice in Oklahoma During the Progressive Era." *Journal of Southern History* 35 (May 1969): 145–64.

Casey, Naomi Taylor. "Miss Edith Johnson, Pioneer Newspaper Woman." *Chronicles of Oklahoma* 60 (Spring 1982): 66–73.

Casey, Orben J. "Governor Lee Cruce, White Supremacy and Capital Punishment, 1911–1915." *Chronicles of Oklahoma* 52 (Winter 1974–75): 456–75.

Coleman, Michael C. "The Responses of American Indian Children to Presbyterian Schooling in the Nineteenth Century: An Analysis Through Missionary Sources." *History of Education Quarterly* 27 (Winter 1987): 473–97.

Comfort, Nick. "Boley." *Oklahoma Journal of Religion* 1 (July 1944): 8–11.

Conway, Jill. "Women Reformers and American Culture, 1870–1930." *Journal of Social History* 5 (Winter 1971–72): 164–77.

Corwin, Hugh D. "Saddle Mountain Mission and Church." *Chronicles of Oklahoma* 36 (Summer 1958): 118–29.

Crawford, Suzanne, and Lynn Musslewhite. "Progressive Reform and Oklahoma Democrats: Kate Barnard Versus Bill Murray." *The Historian* 53, no. 3 (1991): 473–88.

Crockett, Bernice Norman. "'No Job For a Woman'." *Chronicles of Oklahoma* 61 (Summer 1983): 148–67.

deGraaf, Lawrence B. "Race, Sex, and Region: Black Women in the American West, 1850–1920." *Pacific Historical Review* 49 (Summer 1980): 285–313.

Delly, Lillian. "Ellen Howard Miller." The Chronicles of Oklahoma 26 (Summer 1948): 174–77.

Doran, Michael F. "Population Statistics of Nineteenth Century Indian Territory." *Chronicles of Oklahoma* 53 (Winter 1975–76): 491–515.

Ellis, Clyde. "'A Remedy for Barbarism': Indian Schools, the Civilizing Program, and the Kiowa-Comanche-Apache Reservation, 1871–1915." *American Indian Culture and Research Journal* 18, no. 3 (1994): 85–120.

Etulain, Richard W. "Revisioning the Feminine Frontier." *American Quarterly* 39 (Summer 1987): 301–305.

Faragher, John Mack. "History from the Inside-Out: Writing the History of Women in Rural America." *American Quarterly* 33 (Winter 1981): 537–57.

Fischer, LeRoy H. "Oklahoma Territory, 1890–1907." *Chronicles of Oklahoma* 53 (Spring 1975): 3–8.

Foreman, Carolyn Thomas. "A Cherokee Pioneer, Ella Flora Coodey Robinson." *Chronicles of Oklahoma* 7 (December 1929): 364–74.

———. "Aunt Eliza of Tahlequah." *Chronicles of Oklahoma* 9 (March 1931): 43–55.

———. "Mrs. Anna C. Trainor Matheson." *Chronicles of Oklahoma* 18 (March 1940): 101–102.

Garrett, Kathleen. "Music on the Indian Territory Frontier." *Chronicles of Oklahoma* 33 (Autumn 1955): 339–49.

Goetz, Henry Kilian. "Kate's Quarter Section: A Woman in The Cherokee Strip." *Chronicles of Oklahoma* 61 (Fall 1983): 246–67.

Green, Rayna. "The Pocahontas Perplex: The Image of Indian Women in American Culture." *The Massachusetts Review* 16, no. 4 (1975): 698–714.

Grinde, Donald A., Jr., and Quintard Taylor. "Red vs. Black: Conflict and Accommodation in the Post Civil War Indian Territory, 1865–1907." *American Indian Quarterly* 8 (Summer 1984): 211–29.

Grow, Stewart. "The Blacks of Amber Valley: Negro Pioneering in Northern Alberta." *Canadian Ethnic Studies* 6 (1974): 17–38.

Halliburton, R. H., Jr., "Northeastern's Seminary Hall." *Chronicles of Oklahoma* 51 (Winter 1973–74): 391–98.

Hamilton, Kenneth M. "The Origin and Early Developments of Langston, Oklahoma." *Journal of Negro History* 62 (March 1977): 270–87.

Harrison, Thomas H. "Carlotta Archer." *Chronicles of Oklahoma* 25 (Summer 1947): 159–60.

Hartmann, Susan. "Women's Work Among the Plains Indians." *Gateway Heritage* 3, no. 4 (1983): 2–9.

Herring, Rebecca Jane. "Their Work Was Never Done: Women Missionaries on the Kiowa-Comanche Reservation." *Chronicles of Oklahoma* 44 (Spring 1986): 69–83.

Hill, Mozell. "A Comparative Study of Race Attitudes in the All-Negro Community in Oklahoma." *Phylon* 7 (Third Quarter 1946): 260–68.

———. "Basic Racial Attitudes Toward Whites in the Oklahoma All-Negro Community." *American Journal of Sociology* 49 (May 1944): 519–23.

Hine, Darlene Clark. "Rape and the Inner Lives of Black Women in the Middle West." *Signs* 14, no. 4 (1989): 912–20.

Holway, Hope. "Lucia Loomis Ferguson." *Chronicles of Oklahoma* 41 (Winter 1963–64): 365–69.

Hougen, Harvey R. "Kate Barnard and the Kansas Penitentiary Scandal, 1908–1909." *Journal of the West* 17, no. 1 (1978): 9–18.

Jackson, Joe C. "Church School Education in the Creek Nation, 1898 to 1907." *Chronicles of Oklahoma* 46 (Autumn 1968): 312–29.

———. "Summer Normals in Indian Territory After 1898." *Chronicles of Oklahoma* 37 (Autumn 1959): 307–29.

James, Louise B. "Alice Mary Robertson—Anti-Feminist Congresswoman." *Chronicles of Oklahoma* 55 (Winter 1977): 454–61.

———. "The Woman Suffrage Issue in the Oklahoma Constitutional Convention." *Chronicles of Oklahoma* 56 (Winter 1978): 379–92.

Jameson, Elizabeth. "Toward a Multicultural History of Women in the Western United States." *Signs* 13 (Summer 1988): 761–91.

———. "Women as Workers, Women as Civilizers: True Womanhood in the American West." *Frontiers* 7, no. 3 (1984): 1–8.

Jensen, Joan M., and Darlis A. Miller. "The Gentle Tamers Revisited: New Approaches to the History of Women in the American West." *Pacific Historical Review* 49 (May 1980): 173–213.

Jones, Beverly W. "Mary Church Terrell and the National Association of Colored Women, 1896 to 1901." *Journal of Negro History* 67 (Spring 1982): 20–33.

Jordan, Julia A. "Oklahoma's Oral History Collection: New Source For Indian History." *Chronicles of Oklahoma* 49 (Fall 1970): 331–40.

Kalisch, Philip A. "Ordeal of the Coal Miners: Coal Mine Disasters in the Sooner State, 1886–1945." *Chronicles of Oklahoma* 48 (Fall 1970): 331–40.

Lashley, Tommy G. "Oklahoma's Confederate Veterans Home." *Chronicles of Oklahoma* 55 (Spring 1977): 34–45.

Limerick, Patricia. "Turnerians All: The Dream of a Helpful History in an Intelligible World." *American Historical Review* 100 (June 1995): 697–716.

Lewis, Anna. "The Oklahoma College for Women." *Chronicles of Oklahoma* 27 (Summer 1949): 179–86.

Littlefield, Daniel, F., Jr., and Lonnie E. Underhill. "Divorce Seeker's Paradise, Oklahoma Territory, 1890–1897." *Arizona and the West* 17, no. 1 (1975): 21–34.

Logsden, Guy. "Indian Studies Resources at the University of Tulsa." *Chronicles of Oklahoma* 55 (Spring 1977): 64–77.

Mathes, Valerie Shirer. "A New Look at the Role of Women in Indian Society." *American Quarterly* 2 (Summer 1975): 131–39.

Mazumdar, Maitreyi. "Alice's Restaurant: Expanding a Woman's Sphere." *Chronicles of Oklahoma* 70, no. 3 (1992): 302–25.

Mellinger, Phillip. "Discrimination and Statehood in Oklahoma." *Chronicles of Oklahoma* 49 (Autumn 1971): 340–78.

Mondello, Salvatore. "Isabel Crawford and The Kiowa Indians." *Foundations* 22, no. 1 (1979): 28–42.

———. "Isabel Crawford: The Making of a Missionary." *Foundations* 21, no. 4 (1978): 322–39.

Morrison, Daryl. "Twin Territories: The Indian Magazine
    and Its Editor, Ora Eddleman Reed." *Chronicles of
    Oklahoma* 60 (Summer 1982): 136–66.
Moses, L. G. "Wild West Shows, Reformers, and the Image of
    the American Indian, 1887–1914." *South Dakota
    History* 14 (1984): 193–221.
Pennington, William D. "Government Agricultural Policy on
    the Kiowa Reservation, 1869–1901." *Indian Histor-
    ian* 11, no. 1 (1978): 11–16.
Pew, Thomas W., Jr. "Boley, Oklahoma: Trial in American
    Apartheid." *American West* 17 (July 1980): 14–21,
    54–56, 63.
Reese, Linda W. "'Dear Oklahoma Lady': Women Journal-
    ists Speak Out." *Chronicles of Oklahoma* 67 (Fall
    1989): 264–95.
———. "'Working in the Vinyard': African American
    Women in All-Black Communities." *Kansas Quar-
    terly* 25, no. 2 (1994): 7–16.
Richards, Eugene S. "Trends of Negro Life in Oklahoma As
    Reflected by Census Reports." *Journal of Negro
    History* 33 (January 1948): 38–52.
Riley, Glenda. "American Daughters: Black Women in the
    West." *Montana, The Magazine of Western History* 38
    (Spring 1988): 14–27.
———. "Torn Asunder: Divorce in Early Oklahoma Terri-
    tory." *Chronicles of Oklahoma* 67, no. 4 (1989–90):
    392–413.
Scott, Anne Firor. "Most Invisible of All: Black Women's
    Voluntary Associations." *Journal of Southern History*
    56 (February 1990): 3–22.
Shepard, R. Bruce. "North to the Promised Land, Black
    Migration to the Canadian Plains." *Chronicles of
    Oklahoma* 66 (Fall 1988): 306–27.
———. "The Little 'White' Schoolhouse: Racism in a Sas-
    katchewan Rural School." *Saskatchewan History* 39
    !March 1986): 81–93.
Shirley, Glenn. "Oklahoma Kate—Woman of Destiny." *The
    West* 9 (March 1968): 18–21, 56–58.

Spivey, Donald. "Crisis on a Black Campus: Langston University and Its Struggle for Survival." *Chronicles of Oklahoma* 59 (Winter 1981–82): 430–47.

Stanley, Ruth Moore. "Alice M. Robertson, Oklahoma's First Congresswoman." *Chronicles of Oklahoma* 45 (Autumn 1967): 259–89.

Szasz, Margaret Connell. "'Poor Richard' Meets the Native American: Schooling for Young Indian Women in Eighteenth Century Connecticut." *Pacific Historical Review* 59 (March 1926): 16–30.

Travis, V. A. "Life in the Cherokee Nation a Decade After the Civil War." *Chronicles of Oklahoma* 4 (March 1926): 16–30.

Trennert, Robert A. "Educating Indian Girls at Nonreservation Boarding Schools, 1878–1920." *Western Historical Quarterly* 13 (July 1982): 271–90.

Troper, Harold Martin. "The Creek-Negroes of Oklahoma and Canadian Immigration, 1909–1911." *Canadian Historical Review* 53 (1972): 272–88.

Underhill, Lonnie E., and Daniel F. Littlefield, Jr. "Women Homeseekers in Oklahoma Territory, 1889–1901." *Pacific Historian* 17, no. 3 (1973): 36–47.

Welter, Barbara. "She Hath Done What She Could: Protestant Women's Missionary Careers in Nineteenth-Century America." *American Quarterly* 30 (Winter 1978): 624–38.

"Women As Journalists." *Sooner State Press* 23 (1 November 1930): 1–2.

Woolfolk, George R. "Turner's Safety-Valve and Free Negro Westward Migration." *Journal of Negro History* 50 (July 1965): 185–97.

Wright, James R., Jr. "The Assiduous Wedge: Woman Suffrage and the Oklahoma Constitutional Convention." *Chronicles of Oklahoma* 51 (Winter 1973): 421–43.

Wright, Murial. "Rachel Caroline Eaton." *Chronicles of Oklahoma* 6 (December 1938): 509–10.

———. "The Wedding of Oklahoma and Miss Indian Territory." *Chronicles of Oklahoma* 35 (Autumn 1957): 255–61.

Miscellaneous

Bungardt, Barbara Elaine. A Biography of Mrs. Walter Scott
    Ferguson. Unpublished paper, H. H. Herbert School
    of Journalism, University of Oklahoma, Norman,
    n.d.
Dill, Bonnie Thornton. "Our Mothers' Grief: Racial Ethnic
    Women and the Maintenance of Families." Research
    paper 4, Center for Research on Women, Memphis,
    Tenn., 1986.
Littles, Dorscine Spignor. *Collective Visions: A Historical
    Overview of Black Women in Oklahoma from the
    Early 1800s–1920*. Oklahoma City: Oklahoma Arts
    and Humanities Foundation, 1990. Videotape.
Mann, Susan Archer. "Social Change and Sexual Inequality:
    The Impact of the Transition from Slavery to
    Sharecropping on Black Women." Working paper 3,
    Center for Research on Women, Memphis, Tenn.
    1986.

Index

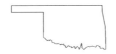